SPARKNOTES™

SAT Math Workbook

2004 Edition

Editorial Director Justin Kestler

Executive Editor Ben Florman

Director of Technology Tammy Hepps

Series Editor John Crowther

Managing Editor Vincent Janoski

Contributing Editors Matt Blanchard, Jennifer Chu

This edition published by Spark Publishing.

Spark Publishing
A Division of SparkNotes LLC
120 Fifth Avenue, 8th Floor
New York, NY 10011

03 04 05 06 07 SN 9 8 7 6 5 4 3 2 1

Please submit all comments and questions or report errors to www.sparknotes.com/errors

Library of Congress information available upon request

Printed and bound in Canada

ISBN 1-58663-956-0

SAT and PSAT are registered trademarks of the College Entrance Examination Board, which was not involved with the production of and does not endorse this product.

SparkNotes is neither affiliated with nor endorsed by Harvard University.

Orientation

SAT Math Review

SAT Geometry 155

Special SAT Math: Charts, Logic, Symbols. 231

Practice Tests

General SAT Strategies

T HE MATH PORTION OF THE SAT IS A multiple-choice test, with three timed sections. Two of the math sections contain only multiple-choice questions, while the third is made up of quantitative comparison questions and grid-in questions. In general, questions increase in difficulty as you progress through a group of same-type questions. All questions are worth the same number of points, and for all questions except grid-ins, there are penalties for wrong answers. In this chapter, we will show you that the structure of the math SAT is very important to your success.

Imagine two children playing tag in the forest. Who will win—the girl who never stumbles because she knows the placement of every tree and all the twists, turns, and hiding spots, or the kid who keeps falling down and tripping over roots because he does not pay any attention to the landscape? The answer is obvious. Even if the other kid is faster and more athletic, the girl will still win because she knows how to navigate the landscape and use it to her advantage.

This example of tag in the forest is extreme, but it illustrates the point. The structure of the SAT is the forest. Taking the test is the game of tag.

Basic Rules

You should observe the following rules in every section of the SAT. Essentially, they are just common sense guidelines, but if you follow them, you will save time and cut down on careless errors.

Know the instructions for each section. The math SAT is timed, and you will definitely need every second. Don't waste time reading the instructions. Make sure you know the instructions so that you don't even have to glance at them on test day.

Use your test booklet as scratch paper. Some students feel as though they must keep their test booklets clean and pretty. There's no truth to that. When you finish with your test booklet, it just gets thrown away. Plus, writing on your test booklet can benefit you. If you need to write down an equation to help you think through a problem, why not do it right next to the question? If you come to a question you want to skip and come back to later, mark it. (Do not make unnecessary marks on your answer sheet—it is definitely not scratch paper!)

Answer easy questions before hard questions. All questions are worth the same number of points regardless of difficulty, so it makes sense to answer the questions you find easy and less time-consuming first and the more difficult questions later. This way you'll be sure to accumulate more points. The structure of the test helps you to identify easy and difficult questions, as is explained in the "Order of Difficulty" section. And remember, you can skip around within a timed section. If you wanted to, you could answer all the easy sentence completions in a 30-minute verbal section, then skip over to the easy analogies, then go back to the moderate sentence completions, and so on.

Don't get bogged down. While taking seven minutes to solve a particularly difficult question may feel like a moral victory, it's quite possible that you could have used that same time to answer three other questions. Do not be scared to skip a question if it's giving you a lot of trouble—you can come back to it if you have time at the end.

Know when to guess. We will cover the specific strategies for guessing later.

Avoid carelessness. There are two types of carelessness, and both will cost you points. The first type of carelessness results from moving too fast. In speeding through the test, you make yourself vulnerable to misinterpreting the question, failing to see that the question contains some subtlety or extra nuance, overlooking one of the answer choices, or simply making a mathematical or logical mistake. So don't speed through the test. Make sure that you are moving quickly, but not so quickly that you become reckless.

The second type of carelessness results from lack of confidence. Do not simply assume out of frustration that you will not be able to answer a question without even looking at it. You should at least glance at every question to see if it's something you can answer. Skipping a question you could have answered is almost as bad as answering incorrectly a question you should have gotten right.

Be careful gridding in your answers. The scoring computer is unintelligent and unmerciful. If you answered a question correctly, but somehow made a mistake in marking your answer grid, the computer will mark that question wrong. If, somehow, you skipped question 5, but put the answer to question 6 in row 5, and the answer to question 7 in row 6, and so on, thereby throwing off your answers for an entire section . . . well, that would not be good.

Be very careful when filling out your answer grid. Many people will tell you many different ways that are the "best" way to fill out the sheet. We don't care how you do it as long as you're careful. We will give one piece of advice: talk to yourself. As you fill in the answer sheet, say to yourself: "number 23, B; number 24, E; number 25, A." Seriously. Talking to yourself will force you to look at the details and will increase your accuracy.

Answering SAT Multiple-Choice Questions

By now, you know that the SAT is a multiple-choice test. What you may not know is how the multiple-choice structure should affect your approach to answering the questions. Lucky for you, we're going to explain how.

Only the Answer Matters

A machine, not a person, will score your SAT. The scoring machine does not care how you came to your answers; it cares only whether your answers are correct and readable in little oval form. The test booklet in which you worked out your answers gets thrown in the garbage, or, if your proctor is conscientious, into a recycling bin.

The SAT has no partial credit, and no one looks at your work. If you get a question right, it doesn't matter if you did pristine work. In fact, it doesn't even matter whether you knew the answer or guessed. The multiple-choice structure of the test is a message to you from ETS: *we only care about your answers.* Remember, the SAT is your tool to get into college, so treat it as a tool. It wants right answers. Give it right answers, as many as possible, using whatever strategies you can.

Multiple-Choice and Scratch Work

Because the SAT is a timed test, and since your work doesn't matter, there's no reason to do more work than necessary to solve a problem. Speed matters on the SAT, so don't try to impress the test with excellent work. Do only what you have to do to ensure that you get the right answer and aren't working carelessly.

Multiple-Choice: You've Already Got the Answers

Even though this book covers the verbal SAT, here's an example of a simple multiple-choice math problem:

$$2 + 2 = ?$$

(A)   1
(B)   8
(C)   22
(D)   154
(E)   8006

It's immediately obvious that this is a bad question: all of the answers are wrong. You will never see a question like this on the SAT. Every SAT multiple-choice question will have exactly one correct answer. Again, obvious, but let's look at the implications of this fact.

When you look at any SAT multiple-choice question, the answer is already right there in front of you. Of course, ETS doesn't just give you the correct answer; they hide it among a bunch of incorrect answer choices. Your job on each question is to find the right answer. The important thing to realize is that a multiple-choice question is vulnerable to two separate methods :

- Find the **right answer**.

- Look at the answer choices and **eliminate wrong answers** until there's only one answer left—in other words, work backward.

Both methods have their advantages: you are better off using one in some situations. In a perfect scenario, when you are sure how to answer a question, the first method is clearly better than the second. Coming to a conclusion about a problem and then picking the single correct choice is a much simpler process than going through every answer choice and discarding the four that are wrong. However, when you are unsure how to solve the problem, the second method becomes more attractive: you should focus on eliminating the incorrect answer choices rather than trying to pick out the right answer.

You might be able to use the answer choices to lead you in the right direction, or to solve the problem through trial and error. You also might be able to eliminate answer choices through a variety of strategies (these strategies vary by question type; we'll cover them in the chapters dedicated to each specific type of question). In some cases, you might be able to eliminate all the wrong answers. In others, you might only be able to eliminate one, which will still improve your odds when you attempt to guess.

Part of your task in preparing for the SAT will be to get some sense of when to use the correct strategy. Using the right strategy can increase your speed without affecting your accuracy, giving you more time to work on and answer as many questions as possible.

Guessing on the SAT

Should you guess on the SAT? We'll begin to answer this question by posing another SAT question:

> Ben is holding five cards, numbered 1–5. Without telling you, he has selected one of the numbers as the "correct" card. If you pick a single card, what is the probability that you will choose the "correct" one?

Okay, this isn't really an SAT question, and the answer choices aren't that important, though the answer is $\frac{1}{5}$. But the question does precisely describe the situation you're in when you guess blindly on any SAT question with five answer choices. If you were to guess on five multiple-choice questions with five answer choices, you would probably get one question right for every five guesses you made.

ETS took these probabilities into account when devising its system to calculate raw scores. As described in the introduction, for every right answer on the SAT, you get one point added to your raw score. For each answer left blank, you get zero points. For each incorrect multiple-choice answer you lose a fraction of a point:

- $\frac{1}{4}$ for incorrect five-choice questions
- $\frac{1}{3}$ for incorrect four-choice questions (quantitative comparisons)
- 0 points for incorrectly answering a grid-in question.

It's easy to figure out why ETS chose the wrong-answer penalties that it did. Let's look at each type of question and examine what its penalty value means.

Five-choice. If you guess blindly on a math question, probability dictates that you will get one question right for every four wrong. Since you get 1 point for your right answer and lose $\frac{1}{4}$ point for each wrong answer, you're left with $1 - 4 \times \frac{1}{4} = 0$ points. Guessing blindly for five-choice questions is a waste of time.

Quantitative comparisons. If you guess blindly on math questions, probability says that you will get one question right for every three wrong. Since you get 1 point for your right answer, and lose $\frac{1}{3}$ point for each wrong answer, you're left with $1 - 3 \times \frac{1}{3} = 0$ points. Guessing blindly for four-choice questions is, once again, a waste of time.

Grid-ins. These are not multiple-choice questions. There are so many possible answers that guessing the answer is immensely improbable. If you have even a vague idea of what the answer might be, you might as well guess, though, since there's no penalty.

Intelligent Guessing

The numbers above show that the wrong-answer penalty renders any sort of blind guessing pointless. But what if your guessing isn't blind? Let's say you're answering the following sentence completion question:

In Greek mythology, Hades, the realm of the dead, is guarded by ---- dog.

(A)   an anthropomorphic
(B)   a protean
(C)   a sesquipedalian
(D)   a delicious
(E)   a sanguinary

It seems likely that you don't know the meanings of the words **anthropomorphic, protean, sesquipedalian,** or **sanguinary** since we purposely chose words that were more obscure than the vocabulary that appears on the SAT. But you probably do know the meaning of **delicious,** and can tell immediately that it does not fit correctly into the sentence (a delicious dog?). Once you've eliminated delicious as a possible answer, you only have to guess between four rather than five choices. Is it now worth it to guess? If you guess among four choices, you will get one question right for every three you get wrong. For that one correct answer you'll get 1 point, and for the three incorrect answers you'll lose a total of a total of 3⁄4 of a point. $1 - \frac{3}{4} = \frac{1}{4}$, meaning that if you can eliminate one answer, then the odds of guessing turn in your favor: you become more likely to gain points than lose points.

The rule for guessing, therefore, is simple: if you can eliminate even one answer choice on a question, you should definitely guess. The only time you should ever leave a question blank is if you cannot eliminate any of the answer choices.

Guessing as Partial Credit

Some students feel that guessing correctly should not be rewarded with full credit. But instead of looking at guessing as an attempt to gain undeserved points, you should look at it as a form of partial credit. Let's use the example of the sentence completion about the dog guarding Hades. Most people taking the test will only know the word delicious, and will only be able to throw out that word as a possible answer, leaving them with a 1 in 4 chance of guessing correctly. But let's say that you knew that protean means "able to change shape," and that the dog guarding Hades was not protean. When you look at this question, you can throw out both "delicious" and "protean" as answer choices, leaving you with a 1 in 3 chance of getting the question right if you guess. Your extra knowledge gives you better odds of getting this question right.

Order of Difficulty

SAT questions are divided into groups. For example, in one of the 30 minute verbal sections, the 10 sentence completions are grouped together as questions 1–10, the 13 analogies are listed together as questions 11–23, and the 12 reading comprehension questions make up questions 24–35. Math questions are similarly organized by groups: regular multiple choice, quantitative comparisons, and grid-ins are all listed separately from each other. All of these groups of questions are arranged by difficulty, from easiest to most difficult.

Making Decisions Based on the Order of Difficulty

Imagine that you are taking a test that consists of two questions. After your teacher hands out the test, and before you set to work, a helpful little gnome whispers to you from the corner, "The first problem is very simple, the second is much harder." Would the gnome's statement affect the way you approach the two problems? The answer, of course, is yes. For a "very simple" question, it seems likely that you should be able to answer it quickly and without much, or any, agonized second-guessing. On a "much harder" question, you will probably have to spend much more time, both to come up with an answer and to check your work to make sure you didn't make an error somewhere along the way.

And what about all the other students who didn't hear the gnome? They might labor over the first easy question, exhaustively checking their work and wasting time that they'll need for the tricky second problem. Then, when those other students do get to the second problem, they might not check their work or be wary of traps, since they have no idea that the problem is so difficult.

Because SAT questions are ordered by difficulty, it's as if you have that helpful little gnome sitting next to you for the entire test. The simple knowledge of question difficulty can help you in a variety of ways.

Knowing Where to Spend Your Time

As discussed earlier, you should try to avoid getting bogged down, and you don't have to answer questions in numerical order. In fact, in some situations it can be a good idea to skip an occasional question. Think about it: every question on the SAT is worth the same number of raw points, so what matters most on the test is answering as many questions correctly as possible. If skipping a question that's giving you trouble allows you the time to answer three other questions, then it's a good bargain.

How many questions you should skip depends entirely on your target math score. If you have a target score of 700 or higher, you need to answer every question, so there isn't much of a reason to skip around. But if, for example, your target score is a 550, you can afford to skip 2–3 questions in every group. In this case, if you encounter a sentence completion you just can't answer, don't spend a ton of time trying to figure it out. Skip it and move on to the next. If the sentence completions you find difficult happen to be the last one or two in the group, don't worry about leaving them behind, and move on to the analogies.

Please note that we are *not* suggesting that you skip all the questions in a group as soon as you hit one that you find difficult. Don't just assume that all questions appearing after a question that you find hard will be too hard for you. Sometimes, for whatever reason, a question will be hard for you even if the question after it is easy. The location of a question is a clue about its difficulty, but you shouldn't let the test dictate what you can and cannot answer simply based on its location. If you have a sense of how difficult a question probably is, and a similar sense of how many questions you can afford to skip, you should be able to make an informed decision about whether to skip a question or not. But make sure that your decision is informed: at least try to glance at every question in a group to see if you might be able to answer it.

Knowing When to Be Wary

Most students answer the easy SAT questions correctly. Only some students get moderately difficult questions right. Very few students get difficult questions right. What does this mean to you? It means that when you are going through the test, you can often trust your first instincts on an easy question. With difficult questions, however, you should be much more cautious. There is a reason most people get these questions wrong: not only are they more difficult, containing more sophisticated vocabulary or mathematical concepts, they are also often tricky, full of enticing wrong answers that seem as if they must be correct. But because the SAT orders its questions by difficulty, the test tips you off about when to take a few extra seconds to make sure you haven't been fooled by an answer that only *seems* right.

Pacing

The SAT presents you with a lot of questions and not that much time to answer them. As you take the test, you will probably feel some pressure to answer quickly. As we've already discussed, getting bogged down on a single question is not a good thing. But rushing too quickly isn't any good either. In the end, there's no real difference between answering very few questions and answering lots of questions incorrectly: both will lead to low scores. What you have to do is find a happy medium, a groove, a speed at which you can be both accurate and efficient and get the score you want.

Setting a Target Score

The previous paragraph sure makes it sound easy. But how do you actually go about finding a good speed? First, before anything else, you should recognize that you absolutely do not have to answer every question on the test. Remember, the SAT is your tool to help you get into one of the schools of your choice, and it probably won't take a perfect score to get you there. You should set a target score, and your efforts should be directed toward gaining that score.

In setting a target score, the first rule is always this: be honest and realistic. Base your target score on the schools you want to go to and have a realistic chance of getting into. Talking to a college counselor can help you gauge how reasonable your choices are. You can also gauge your expectations by your first practice test. If you score a 450 on the first math practice test, it's foolish to set your target score at 750. Instead, your target should be about 50–100 points higher on each section than your score on your first practice test. That's a total of 100–200 points higher for the whole test.

If you reach your target score during preparation, give yourself a cookie or some other treat and take a break from working. But just because you hit your target score doesn't mean you should stop working altogether. In fact, you should view reaching your target score as a clue that you can do better than that score: set a new target 50–100 points above your original, pick up your pace a little bit, and skip fewer questions. By working to improve in manageable increments, you can slowly work up to your top speed, integrating your new knowledge of how to take the test and the subjects the test covers without overwhelming yourself by trying to take on too much too soon. If you can handle working just a little faster without becoming careless and losing points, your score will certainly go up. If you meet your new target score again, repeat the process.

Your Target Score Determines Your Overall Strategy

Your target score can, and should, deeply affect your strategy. If you want to get a 500 on the math section of the SAT, your strategy will differ significantly from that of someone aiming for a 700. A person who wants a 700 must work fast and try to answer almost every question. He or she must be able to work very quickly without carelessness. A person looking to score a 600 does not have to answer every question. In fact, that person probably shouldn't try to answer every question. So, what's the moral? Adjust your pacing to the score you want. The chart below shows the approximate raw scores necessary to achieve certain scaled target scores on each section of the SAT.

If your target score is a 500 on math, you need a raw score of 34. Think about what this means. There are a total of 78 possible raw points on the verbal SAT. To get a 500, you need to get a little less than half of those points. In other words, you need to answer a little less than half of the questions cor

Math

Target Score	Raw Score
800	60
750	56
700	53
650	49
600	43
550	35
500	29
450	22
400	15

rectly (assuming you don't answer any questions wrong). If we take into account that you probably will answer at least a few questions incorrectly, then you know that you need to get a few more than half of the questions right. Even so, a little over half only constitutes the easy and moderate questions on the test. You could probably get a 500 without answering a single difficult question—this realization should help you pace yourself accordingly. Instead of rushing to answer as many questions as possible, spend the time you need to avoid errors and make sure you'll hit your target.

Knowing the Clock

When you take both your practice tests and the real SAT, you should be aware of the clock. You should not become obsessed with the clock and lose time by constantly glancing at those terrible ticking seconds, but you should have a sense of the time to keep yourself on proper pace.

We recommend that you always take practice tests with the clock. Since your proctor will enforce the time on the real SAT strictly, you should do the same on your practice tests. By using the clock on practice tests, you will learn to manage your time and become more familiar with taking the test as the clock ticks down to zero.

Luck

If you have lucky clothes, or any other lucky items, you might as well wear them, carry them, twirl them over your head and dance beneath them: do whatever works. A little luck never hurt anyone.

The Math SAT

THE MATH HALF OF THE SAT SPANS THREE timed sections, three different question types, and a total of 60 questions. The three types of math questions are quite different from each other. For now, we will just name them, but we will cover each type in more detail later. On the test, you will find:

- 35 multiple-choice questions (MC)
- 15 quantitative comparisons (QC)
- 10 grid-ins (GI)

These three question types are always divided into the following sections.

- A 30-minute section containing 25 MCs
- A 30-minute section containing 15 QCs and 10 GIs
- A 15-minute section containing 10 MCs

The questions in these timed sections are ordered by difficulty. The first third of the questions will generally be easy, the second third moderate, and the last third difficult.

Knowing Math Fundamentals

Many test prep companies state that the SAT only tests your ability to take the SAT and doesn't actually test any real learning or knowledge. This statement is misleading, especially in reference to the Math SAT. Someone who has studied and understands the math topics on this test will do better than someone who only studied the SAT tricks. Knowing the tricks can be helpful, of course, but it will only augment your math knowledge. We'll state it again, just because we are so annoyed at the test prep companies who self-servingly deny this fact: if you understand math, you will do better on the Math SAT than someone who knows little math, no matter which of you knows more tricks.

This does not mean you should study *all* of high-school math, and neither does it mean you should *avoid* learning the strategies and tricks. It means you should study the right topics in math—the math covered on the SAT, all of which is covered in the following chapters. It also means that you should learn and think about strategic ways to approach questions as a way to enhance your skill, speed, and accuracy, not as a replacement.

General Math Strategies

Knowing math is the most important ingredient to doing well on the Math SAT. Knowing how to approach math questions strategically can make your math skill shine. This section discusses math strategy, explaining how you can maximize your time and give yourself the opportunity to earn the most points you possibly can.

Know What's in the Reference Area

Each math section comes with a reference area that provides you with basic geometric formulas and information.

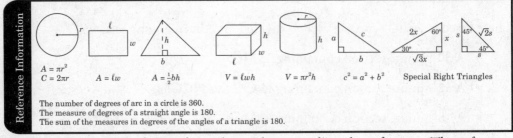

You should know all of these formulas without needing the reference. The reference area should only be used as a last resort. If you can avoid flipping through your test book to remember formulas, you will save time.

Move through the Sections Strategically

We mentioned this strategy in the verbal section: know where you are in the order of difficulty, and use that knowledge to help you strategize for particular problems as well as the entire section. For instance, in the 30-minute section with QCs and GIs, each group of questions is ordered by difficulty: first the QCs will progress from easiest to hardest, then the GIs will do the same. Remember to use the order of difficulty to your advantage: there is no sense struggling with a difficult QC when a number of easy GIs are ripe for the plucking.

Don't get bogged down on a hard question if there are easier questions left to answer. When a question seems like it's too difficult, either mark it as something to return to, or eliminate whatever answers you can and guess.

Write All Over Your Test Booklet

Draw diagrams or write out equations to help you think. Mark up graphs or charts as necessary. Cross out answers that can't be right. Basically, the test booklet is yours to write on, and writing can often help clarify things so that you can work more quickly with fewer mistakes.

Remember that the SAT Rewards Answers, Not Work

Now that we've told you to write in your test book, we're going to qualify that advice. Doing math scratchwork can definitely help you avoid careless errors, but doing pristine work, or more work than necessary, can be worthlessly consuming. You must find a balance between speed and accuracy. You need to be able to follow and understand your work, but other people don't. Nobody will look at or reward your work, so don't write it out as if you're being judged.

Avoid Carelessness

Carelessness is the worst, leading to lost points and lost dreams. Here are two ways to avoid being careless on the math section of the test.

Don't get tricked by the test. Do not look at the answer choices immediately after reading a question. Instead, you should first take a second to process the question, making sure you understand what the question is asking and what method you think you should use to solve it. Then come up with your own answer. Only then should you look at answers. This way, you won't get bamboozled by tricks in the question or distractor answers.

Don't get tricked by yourself. After you come to an answer, quickly plug the answer back into the question. Take a few seconds to make sure you haven't made a careless mistake.

Know When to Guess

Guessing on the math section is a little different from guessing on the verbal. For the regular MC and QC questions, you should guess if you can eliminate one possible answer choice. But be careful: just because QC questions have only four possible answer choices, don't assume you should automatically guess. The guessing penalty for QC questions is slightly higher than it is for the MCs, so you still have to eliminate an answer to make guessing beneficial. There is no guessing penalty for GIs, but that's because it's incredibly unlikely that you will be able to guess correctly. There's no real point to blind guessing on GIs, but since there's no penalty, if you come up with an answer, *any* answer, you should grid it in.

Calculators and the SAT

You are allowed to use calculators during the SAT, and statistics show that those who use calculators often do a little better on the math section than those who do not. If you are careful entering data, calculators can help you avoid careless computational errors.

Here are the rules for calculators on the SAT. The actual rules are those that you'll see in the test instructions. The practical rules are the common-sense rules that the actual rules don't tell you.

Actual

- If you want to use your calculator, you must provide your own calculator.

- Your calculator can be a normal, everyday calculator, a scientific calculator, or a graphing calculator.

- Your calculator cannot be a pocket organizer, a minicomputer, anything that has a typewriter-style keypad, anything that uses paper or a printer, anything that makes noise, or anything that needs to connect to a wall outlet.

Practical

- Know your calculator before the test. Be comfortable and familiar with it so you don't waste time searching for buttons during the test, or—heaven forbid!—make a mistake by hitting the wrong button.

- Don't assume a calculator will allow you to breeze through the math. A calculator is a tool; it can't answer anything for you if you have no idea what direction to go in.

- Don't automatically reach for your calculator. A calculator can increase your speed, but there will be math questions on the SAT that you might be able to answer more quickly *without* the calculator. Also, if using a calculator replaces scratchwork, it can be harder to check your computations .

- Make sure your batteries are in good shape. We understand that giving this advice makes us sound like your mother, but who wants to be the fool whose batteries run out in the middle of the test?

SAT Math Trickiness

ETS is a pretty big company, but it can also be a tricky little sucker. In the math sections, the test writers attempt to separate the elite math students from the average ones by using enticing wrong answers to lure the unwary.

Difficult SAT math questions are made more difficult by the inclusion of possible answer choices that *seem* like the right answers because they are answers you would get if you were to make a mistake while working on the problem. For example, let's say you're flying through the test and have to multiply $6 \times 8 \times 3$. So you quickly multiply 6 and 8 to get 42 and then multiply 42 by 3 to get 126. You look down at the answers and there's 126! That's the answer you came to, and there it is among the answer choices like a little stamp of approval, so you mark it down as your answer. Of course, you'd be wrong ($6 \times 8 = 48$ not 42, making the correct answer 144).

Just because the answer you got is among the answer choices *does not* mean you definitely have it right. The SAT is designed to punish those who make careless errors. Don't be one of them. After you get an answer, quickly plug the answer back into the question.

Math Questions and Time

There are often several ways to answer an SAT math question: you can use trial and error; you can set up and solve an equation: for some questions, you might be able to answer the question quickly, intuitively, and elegantly, if you can just spot how. These different approaches to answering questions vary in the amount of time they take. Trial and error generally takes the longest, while the elegant method of relying on an intuitive understanding of conceptual knowledge takes the least amount of time.

Take, for example, the following problem:

> Which has a greater area, a square with sides measuring 4 cm or a circle with a radius of the same length?

The most obvious way to solve this problem is by plugging 4 into the formula for the area of a square and then the area of a circle. Let's do it. Area of a square $= s^2$, so the area of this square $= 4^2 = 16$. Area of a circle $= \pi r^2$, so the area of this circle must be $\pi 4^2 = 16\pi$. 16π is obviously bigger than 16, so the circle must have a larger area than the square. But a faster approach would have been to draw a quick to-scale diagram with the square and circle superimposed.

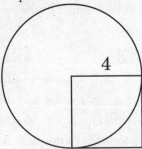

An even quicker way would have been to understand the area equations for squares and circles so well that it was just *obvious* that the circle was bigger, since the equation for the circle will square the 4 and multiply it by π, whereas the equation for the square will square only the 4.

While you may not be able to become a math whiz and just *know* the answer, you can learn to look for a quicker route, such as choosing to draw a diagram instead of working out the equation. As with the example above, a quicker route is not necessarily a less accurate one. Making such choices comes down to practice, an awareness that other routes are out there, and basic mathematical ability.

The value of time-saving strategies is obvious: less time spent on some questions allows you to devote more time to difficult problems. It is this issue of time that separates the students who score high on the math section from those who merely do well. Whether or not the ability to find accurate shortcuts is an actual measure of mathematical prowess is not for us to say (though we can think of arguments on either side), but the ability to find those shortcuts absolutely matters on this test.

Shortcuts Are Really Math Intuition

To some extent, through practice, you can teach yourself to recognize when a question might contain a shortcut. For example, from the problem above, you know that there will probably be a shortcut for all those questions that give you the dimensions of two shapes and ask you to compare them: you can just draw a diagram. A smart test-taker would see the information given and then seize on the simplest route and work out the equations.

You shouldn't go into every question searching for a shortcut. In some questions, a shorcut may not exist. In others, for whatever reason, you may not find one that does exist. If you have to search and search for a shortcut, it might end up taking *longer* than the first route to solving the problem that came into your mind. Rather than searching for shortcuts, you should be aware of them. Just knowing shortcuts exist can help you find them; don't get so focused and frantic about getting a question right that you miss the possibility that a shortcut exists.

Finally, the fact that we advocate using shortcuts doesn't mean you shouldn't focus on learning how to work a problem out. In fact, we can guarantee that you're not going to find a shortcut for a problem *unless* you know how to work it out the "long" way. After all, a shortcut is just using your knowledge to see a faster way to answer the question. To put it another way, while we've been using the term *math shortcut,* we could just as easily have used the term *math intuition.* If you don't have that knowledge base to work from, you're not going to have anything on which to base your intuition. In contrast, you might be able to figure out an answer by trial and error, even if you don't see exactly how to answer the problem.

Strategy = Target Score

Your strategy in the math section, and particularly the extent of your efforts to find shortcuts, should be based on your target score. If you're looking to get a 550 or lower on the Math SAT, there simply is no need to go looking for shortcuts. You can get a 550, or even a 600, without answering quite a number of questions, so there's no need to race through the test. You should focus on getting questions right. Of course, you should remain aware that shortcuts exist and use them when you see them, but don't get upset or worried if you're not unearthing a shortcut in every other question.

Students looking to score a 650 or above on the Math SAT, though, should not be working out every question. Finding quicker ways to answer questions *must* be part of your strategy, because it is only through these faster methods that you will give yourself the time to answer the last few difficult questions in the math section that can make all the difference. On these last few questions, even the best students might have to guess their way through using trial and error, which takes a bit of time. So you must give yourself time by moving quickly through the earlier stages of the test.

Be wary: this advice does *not* imply that you should simply work faster. It recommends that you look for the shorter but *just as accurate* route to the answer. Do not sacrifice accuracy to speed. If you can find the short but accurate route, great. Otherwise, it's better to make sure you answer the question correctly, not that you find the wrong answer super-fast.

Types of Questions on the Math SAT

A S YOU KNOW BY NOW, THERE ARE THREE types of math questions on the SAT: 35 regular multiple-choice, 15 quantitative comparisons, and 10 grid-ins. This section looks in detail at all three question types, explaining strategies specific to each one.

General Math Instructions

Before looking at each particular type of math question, it's a good idea to look at SAT math questions in general. All three types of math questions come with a standard core of directions. For the regular MCs, these core instructions are the only directions you'll need. QCs and GIs come with additional instructions that we'll cover later. Now, without further ado, here are the general math instructions:

> In this section solve each problem, using any available space on the page for scratchwork. Then decide which is the best of the choices given and fill in the corresponding oval on the answer sheet.
>
> Notes:
>
> 1. The use of a calculator is permitted. All numbers are real numbers.
> 2. Figures that accompany problems in this test are intended to provide information useful in solving the problems. They are drawn as accurately as possible EXCEPT when it is stated in a specific problem that the figure is not drawn to scale. All figures lie in a plane unless otherwise indicated.

The first note tells you the reassuring news that you will only have to deal with real numbers. If you've done some high school math, you should know that real numbers constitute all integers and all the fractions that exist between those integers.

The second note tells you two things. First, for all normal diagrams, if one angle looks bigger than another, it truly will be bigger: you can trust the diagrams and use them to help you. Second, this statement warns you to check if a diagram is marked "This figure is not drawn to scale." If a diagram is marked in that way , you know to be careful and to trust your knowledge of geometry rather than the given figure. You also might want to draw your own figure that *is* to scale.

Approaching Multiple-Choice Questions

MC questions are the most common type of math question on the test. These problems involve a mathematical statement or question that you need to solve, followed by five answer choices. Sometimes the problem will include a chart, graph, or geometric diagram. Your job, obviously, is to choose the right answer.

The MCs are split into two groups: 25 in one of the 30-minute math sections and 10 in the 15-minute section. Both groups are organized according to difficulty, so you know the first questions of each group will be easier while the last will be harder.

The procedure to follow for answering individual MCs is not that different than the one we described for answering sentence completions and analogies.

1. Read the question without looking at the answers. Determine what the question is asking and come to some conclusion about how to solve it. Do not look at the answers unless you decide that using the process of elimination is the best way to go (we describe how to use the process of elimination below).

2. If you think you can solve the problem, go ahead. Once you've derived an answer—and only then— see if your answer matches one among the choices.

3. Once you've decided on an answer, test it out to make sure it's correct and move on.

Working Backward: The Process of Elimination

If you run into difficulty while trying to solve an MC, you might want to try the process of elimination. On every question, the answer is right in front of you, hidden among those five answer choices. So if you can't solve the problem directly, you might be able to plug each answer into the question to see which one works.

Not only can this process help you when you can't figure out a question, there are times when it can actually be faster than setting up an equation, especially if you work strategically. Take the following example:

> A classroom contains 31 chairs, some which have arms and some of which do not. If the room contains 5 more armchairs than chairs without arms, how many armchairs does it contain?
>
> (A) 10
> (B) 13
> (C) 16
> (D) 18
> (E) 21

Given this question, you could build the equations:

$$\text{total chairs } (31) = \text{armchairs } (x) + \text{normal chairs } (y)$$
$$\text{normal chairs } (y) = \text{armchairs } (x) - 5$$

Then, since $y = x - 5$, you can make the equation:

$$31 = x + (x - 5)$$
$$31 = 2x - 5$$
$$36 = 2x$$
$$x = 18$$

This approach of building and working out the equations will produce the right answer, but it takes a long time. What if you strategically plugged in the answers instead? Since the numbers ascend in value, let's choose the one in the middle: (C) 16. This is a smart strategic move because if we plug in 16 and discover that it was too small a number to satisfy the equation, we can eliminate (A) and (B) along with (C). Alternatively, if 16 is too big, we can eliminate (D) and (E) along with (C).

So our strategy is in place. Now let's work it out. If you have 16 armchairs, then you would have 11 normal chairs and the room would contain 27 total chairs. We needed the total numbers of chairs to equal 31, so clearly (C) is not the right answer. But because the total number of chairs was too small, you can also eliminate (A) and (B), the answer choices indicating fewer numbers of armchairs. If you then plug in **(D)** 18, you have 13 normal chairs and 31 total chairs. There's your answer. In this instance, plugging in the answers takes less time and in general just seems easier.

Notice that the last sentence began with the phrase "in this instance." Working backward and plugging in is *not* always the best method. For the SAT, you will need to build up a sense of when working backward can help you most. A good rule of thumb for deciding whether to work backward is:

- Work backward when the question describes an equation of some sort and the answer choices are all rather simple numbers.

If the answer choices contain variables, working backward will often be quite difficult— more difficult than working out the problem would be. If the answer choices are complicated, containing hard fractions or radicals, plugging in might prove so complex that the process will be a waste of time.

Substituting Numbers

Substituting numbers is a lot like working backward, except the numbers you plug into the equation *aren't* in the answer choices. Instead, you have to strategically decide on numbers to substitute to take the place of variables. For example, take the question:

If p and q are odd integers, then which of the following must be odd?

$$(A) \quad p + q$$
$$(B) \quad p - q$$
$$(C) \quad p^2 + q^2$$
$$(D) \quad p^2 \times q^2$$
$$(E) \quad p + q^2$$

It might be hard to conceptualize how the two variables in this problem interact. But what if you chose two odd numbers, let's say 5 and 3, to represent the two variables? Once you begin this substitution it quickly becomes clear that:

$$(A) \quad p + q = 5 + 3 = 8$$
$$(B) \quad p - q = 5 - 3 = 2$$
$$(C) \quad p^2 + q^2 = 25 + 9 = 34$$
$$(D) \quad p^2 \times q^2 = 25 \times 9 = 225$$
$$(E) \quad p + q^2 = 5 + 9 = 14$$

By picking two numbers that fit the definition of the variables provided by the question, it becomes clear that the answer has to be **(D)** $p^2 \times q^2$ since the equation equals 225. (By the way, you could have answered this question without doing the multiplication since two odd numbers, such as 9 and 25, when multiplied, will always result in an odd number.)

Substituting numbers can help you transform problems from the abstract into the concrete. However, you have to remember to keep the substitution consistent. If you're using a 5 to represent p, don't suddenly start using 3. Also, when picking numbers to use as substitutes, pick wisely. Choose numbers that are easy to work with and that fit the definitions provided by the question.

Quantitative Comparisons

The 15 QC questions appear before the 10 grid-ins in one of the two 30-minute math sections. The QCs are arranged by order of difficulty, from least to most difficult.

QC Instructions

In addition to the directions provided above in general math instructions, Quantitative Comparisons have their own special instructions:

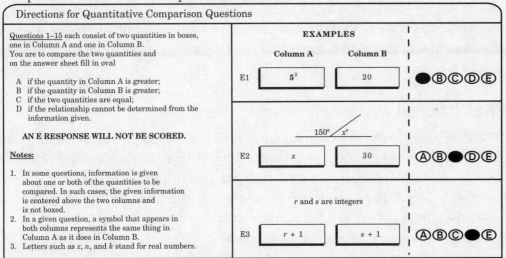

Directions for Quantitative Comparison Questions

Questions 1–15 each consist of two quantities in boxes, one in Column A and one in Column B. You are to compare the two quantities and on the answer sheet fill in oval

  A if the quantity in Column A is greater;
  B if the quantity in Column B is greater;
  C if the two quantities are equal;
  D if the relationship cannot be determined from the information given.

AN E RESPONSE WILL NOT BE SCORED.

Notes:

1. In some questions, information is given about one or both of the quantities to be compared. In such cases, the given information is centered above the two columns and is not boxed.
2. In a given question, a symbol that appears in both columns represents the same thing in Column A as it does in Column B.
3. Letters such as x, n, and k stand for real numbers.

Note that though QC questions have only four possible answer choices while the grid has five answer spaces. Know the instructions!

QC questions ask you to look at two expressions or mathematical statements and choose which is of greater value. For example:

Column A	Column B
2	4

Answering (A) means you think that the expression in Column A is bigger. Answering (B) means you think that the expression in Column B is bigger. If the two expressions are equal, answer (C). If the relative size of the two expressions can't be determined, then answer (D). The answer in the easy example above is (B), since 4 is bigger than 2.

In the example above, the values in Columns A and B were expressed by actual numbers. The columns might also contain:

	Column A	Column B
Expressions	$1 + \dfrac{1}{2}$	$\dfrac{1}{3} - \dfrac{1}{16} + \dfrac{1}{8}$
Simple Variables	x	y
Algebraic Expressions	$x + y$	$x - y$
Word problems	Jimmy's age	Mary's age
Geometric figures	Area of $ABCD$	Area of $EFGH$

Sometimes the values in the two columns will be represented in different ways. You may come upon a quantitative comparison that has an algebraic expression in Column A and a simple real number in Column B.

Given Information

When the values in the two columns contain variables, algebraic expressions, values derived from a word problem, or geometric information, the problem will often also include additional information that defines the expressions in the columns or gives them some context. For example, the statement "All variables represent positive numbers" would limit and define what numbers a variable can represent.

In fact, let's say you came upon the question:

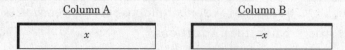

The answer to this question would have to be **(D)**, because if x = 0, then the two columns would be equal; if x = 1, then Column A would be greater; if x = –1, then Column B would be greater. But what if the question also included the following information?

All variables represent positive numbers.

From the information provided, you know that in this problem x can never equal 0 or any negative number. Instead, x must always be positive, which means that Column A will always be greater than Column B, making the answer to the question **(A).** Make sure to look at and understand the given information because it will always affect the outcome of the question.

The Difference Among A, B, C, and D

If you answer a quantitative comparison with choice (A), (B), or (C), you are implicitly stating that the value of the expressions in each column can be determined in some relative way. After all, you can only claim that one column is greater than the other or that the two columns are equal if you know the relative values of two columns *under every circumstance*. In contrast, if you select answer choice (D) you are claiming that there is no possible way to know the value of at least one of the columns under every circumstance.

This difference among (A), (B), (C), and (D) has two important ramifications.

- (D) can only possibly be an answer if you have a variable in one of the columns. If both columns hold numbers, you can't answer (D) because the value of each column is constant. (This won't happen much—it lets you get an answer too easily.)

- If you are able to show that it is possible for two different relationships to exist between the columns, the answer must be (D).

Column A	Column B
$x + y$	$x - y$

- At first glance, you might think that of course Column A is bigger than Column B because Column A involves addition while B uses subtraction. But what if y represents a negative number? Then everything gets flipped and Column B will be bigger than Column A. Depending on which number you plug into the variables, you will receive difference answers, so the answer must be **(D)**.

Note, however, that just showing that the value of one column *can* vary does not necessarily prove that the relative relationship between the two columns *must* vary. For example, let's say you can prove that Column A can be either 3 or 7 (and nothing else), while Column B will always be 2. Even though Column A changes in value, its relative value will still always be greater than Column B, and so the answer will be **(A)**.

Answering Quantitative Comparisons

Your job on QCs is to compare the relative size of the two columns, not the exact value of each column. While there will be many times when you do compute exact values to find the relative sizes, sometimes you won't have to do any calculations at all. Always remember your QC priorities: do enough work so that you can successfully compare the two columns but no more. Of course, you must make sure you do enough work to compare the two expressions in *every* possible circumstance. Below are some techniques to help you in your efforts.

Element by Element Comparison

Working out a problem can take quite a bit of time and often isn't necessary, as we just said. Take the following example:

Column A	Column B
$\frac{1}{2} + \frac{3}{8} + \frac{1}{4}$	$\frac{9}{16} + \frac{1}{2} + \frac{7}{8}$

To find the value of each of these expressions, you first would have to find a common denominator for each and then carry out the necessary steps. None of that is needed however, to quickly and accurately answer this question.

Since the only process in each expression is addition, you should automatically recognize that the column that contains bigger pieces will have the greater sum. Look at the pieces, and see if they can be easily compared. Both Column A and Column B have a ½, so at this point the columns are equal. The 7/8 in Column B is greater than the 3/8 in Column A. It is possible to then quickly calculate that the 1/4 in Column A is equal to 4/16, and then see that the 9/16 in Column B is larger. The fractions in Column B are all either larger or equal to their counterparts in Column A, so the value of Column B as a whole must also be larger. There's the answer, and without having to do any math more complicated than converting 1/4 to 4/16.

Perform the Same Operation on Each Column

In fact, the last problem could have been made even simpler. Instead of immediately comparing the two expressions, it would have been better to simplify the two columns by subtracting 1/2 from each side. Then you would only have to deal with two fractions on each side.

Column A	Column B
$\frac{3}{8} + \frac{1}{4}$	$\frac{9}{16} + \frac{7}{8}$

The simpler the expression, the more likely you are to see how to compare them quickly.

Make sure that when you employ this technique you do so evenly on each column. If you inadvertently perform an operation on only one column, you will not preserve the relative values of the two columns and you will get the question wrong.

Transform Apples and Oranges into Pears and Pears

As the cliché goes, you can't compare apples and oranges. But there are times in QCs comparisons when it seems as if you're being asked to do just that. In such situations, don't panic: these questions are designed so that by applying some knowledge of math you will be able to make the columns comparable. For example:

At first glance, these two columns look very different, and as if they can't be compared. But if you simply multiply out the first column, it will resemble the second:

Column A	Column B
$x^2 + ax$	$x^2 + ax$

Whenever you get into a situation in which you don't know how to compare the two columns, see if there might be a way for you to make the two columns similar.

Substituting Numbers QC Style

Sometimes the best way to compare two columns that have variables is to choose substitute numbers for those variables. Choosing the proper substitute numbers takes some skill and practice. First, you should try to use numbers that are easy to calculate. Second, you must make sure that the numbers you choose to substitute represent all possible circumstances. Remember, when you are answering QCs you are not trying to figure out a single answer. You must also figure out if you can arrive at a definitive answer. Take the following example:

$$p > q$$

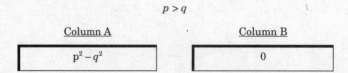

Let's plug in two easy-to-use numbers that fit the definition in the given information; how about 3 for p (which makes p2 = 9) and 2 for q (making q2 = 4)? Plugging the numbers into Column A, we get $9 - 4 = 5$. Column A is greater than Column B.

Before we congratulate ourselves, it's necessary to make sure that Column A is always larger than Column B, not just in this single instance with these particular numbers. Let's try negative numbers (remember, p has to be larger than q, meaning p has to be *less* negative than q). A good move is to take your original numbers and make them negative. In this case, we also have to remember to keep p greater than q, so we must also switch the numerical values of the two variables: $p = -2$ and $q = -3$. If we plug these new numbers into Column A we get $(-2)^2 - (-3)^2 = 4 - 9 = (-5)$. In this instance, Column A is *smaller* than Column B. In other words, Column A can be larger than Column B in some instances and smaller in others, meaning that there is no definite answer and the answer must be **(D).**

Whenever you plug in numbers for QCs, you must be aware that it is possible that other numbers might yield a different result. So, any time you plug in numbers, you must make certain to try all of the different possible numbers. Therefore, each time you plug in numbers make sure to:

- Use a number larger than 1.

- Use the number 1.

- Use a fraction.

- Use 0.

- Use a negative number.

If any of these options yields a comparative result different than the others, your answer should be **(D)**.

Guessing on QCs

Because QCs have four rather than five multiple-choice possibilities, ETS adjusted the guessing penalty so that you lose 1/3 of a point rather than 1/4 of a point for a wrong answer. This means that you still have to eliminate at least one possibility on a QC in order to make guessing worthwhile.

Sometimes eliminating an answer choice is easier than it looks. Remember that for the answer to be (D), you must not be able to find the exact value of either side. Therefore, if you know that each side has an exact value, even if you don't know how to determine what those values are, you *do* know that (D) cannot be the answer. At that point, the guessing odds are in your favor. Take the following example:

Column A	Column B
$\dfrac{17}{49}$	$\dfrac{22}{51}$

This is a pretty easy problem, but let's say that you didn't have enough time to cross-multiply and figure out that column (B) is greater. Even so, from looking at these two columns you should *instantaneously* know that their respective values are set in stone, meaning (D) cannot be the answer.

Time Management and QCs

The 15 QCs are found in the same 30-minute section as the 10 GIs. As you already know, both of these question-type groups are organized by difficulty. Depending on your target score, you can manage your time by skipping over questions that you just can't figure out. Remember, you should make sure to take a look at every problem in a section to see if you can answer it or put yourself in position to guess, but don't struggle to answer questions that are too difficult. You should use the location of a question as a hint of its probable difficulty, but you shouldn't just skip a question without ever looking at it. If you get to the end of the QCs and haven't answered a few questions, don't worry. Just move on to the GIs and answer what you can. If time allows, when you've answered everything you definitely can, then come back to the questions you skipped and give them another try.

Grid-Ins

Like the other types of SAT math questions, the 10 GIs are ordered from easiest to most difficult. Unlike every other type of question on the test, the 10 GIs are not multiple-choice. Instead, you have to generate your own answer and express this answer to the machine grading the test by filling in a special grid.

Directions for Student-Produced Response Questions

Each of the remaining 10 questions (16–25) requires you to solve the problem and enter your answer by marking the ovals in the special grid, as shown in the examples below.

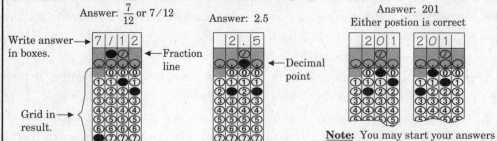

- Mark no more than one oval in any column.

- Because the answer sheet will be machine-scored, **you will receive credit only if the ovals are filled in completely.**

- Although not required, it is suggested that you write your answer in the boxes at the top of the columns to help you fill in the ovals accurately.

- Some problems may have more than one correct answer. In such cases, grid only one answer

- No question has a negative answer.

- **Mixed numbers** such as $2\frac{1}{2}$ must be gridded as 2.5 of 5/2. If $2\,1\,/\,2$ is gridded, it will be interpreted as $\frac{21}{2}$, not $2\frac{1}{2}$.)

Note: You may start your answers in any column, space permitting. Columns not needed should be left blank.

- **Decimal Accuracy:** If you obtain a decimal answer, **enter the most accurate value the grid will accommodate.** For example, if you obtain an answer such as 0.6666 . . . , you should record the result as .666 or .667. **Less accurate values such as .66 or .67 are not acceptable.** Acceptable ways to grid $\frac{2}{3} = .666$ . . .

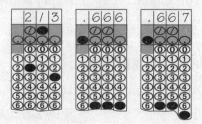

Grid-In Instructions: The Grid

ETS provides extensive instructions that describe how to fill in the grid. As always, memorize these instructions before you take the test. As you look at the instructions, note that for some questions you will be able to write your answer in more than one form.

Those directions are a little intense. Here's a summary:

The computer that grades the test can't read anything but the ovals. You don't actually have to write anything in the spaces at the top as long as you fill in the ovals correctly. However, filling in the spaces at the top might help you to avoid making careless mistakes. We recommend that you do write out your answers in the spaces: the increased accuracy is worth that extra bit of time. Whether you decide to write out your answers or not, make sure you don't forget to fill in the ovals!

The grid cannot accommodate any number longer than four digits or any decimal or fraction that includes more than three numbers. The grid also cannot indicate a negative sign. If the answer you come up with can't fit into the grid or if your answer is negative, then your answer is incorrect.

You can express a number as either a fraction or a decimal.

You must transform all mixed numbers to fraction form. For example, 4 1/2 must be written as 9/2. If you were to try to write 4 1/2 the dumb grading machine would read it as 41/2.

Sometimes the answer you come to will actually be a range of answers, such as "any number between 4 and 5." In those instances, you will be correct if you oval in any number that fits the criteria; 4.6, 4.2, 9/2. Remember, though: no mixed numbers.

No Tricks

Because GIs aren't multiple choice, there really aren't any strategies we can offer you to help you come to an answer on a particular question. Taking practice tests will help you to get comfortable with answering GIs in general, and studying those tests will help you learn how to answer the types of GI questions typically asked.

Grid-in Guessing

There's no guessing penalty for GIs because the likelihood of a person guessing correctly on a question is shockingly, amazingly, incredibly small. In most situations, guessing isn't worth the time it takes to fill out the ovals in the grid. However, if you're low on time and you've worked on a question and come to an answer that fits in the grid, it wouldn't hurt to fill in the grid.

SAT Arithmetic

Almost half of the 60 math questions on the SAT test basic arithmetic. The SAT does not cover *all* of arithmetic, however. In fact, the test covers only thirteen arithmetic topics, as you can see in the table of contents to the right. The SAT usually covers these 13 topics in very similar ways. Because the SAT is so focused in what it tests, we are too. We don't cover arithmetic. We explain *SAT arithmetic,* covering only the topics the SAT will test and explaining how the SAT will test those topics.

Order of Operations

The SAT does not often directly test the order of operations, but you must know the order in which mathematical operations should be performed in order to deal with many of the questions on the test. The best way to remember which operation gets performed before another is the acronym PEMDAS, which stands for:

Parentheses
Exponents
Multiplication
Division
Addition
Subtraction

If you come across an equation that contains any or all of these elements, you should carry out the math within the parentheses first, then work out the exponents, then do the multiplication, then the division, and finally the subtraction. Given the expression:

$$\frac{(18-3) \times 2^2}{5} - 7 + (6 \times 3 - 1)$$

You would first work out the math in the parentheses (following PEMDAS even within the parentheses, meaning do multiplication before subtraction):

$$\frac{15 \times 2^2}{5} - 7 + 17$$

Then work out the exponents:

$$\frac{15 \times 4}{5} - 7 + 17$$

Then do the multiplication:

$$\frac{60}{5} - 7 + 17$$

Then the division:

$$12 - 7 + 17$$

Then the addition:

$$12 - 24$$

Then the subtraction:

$$-12$$

Odd and Even Numbers

Again, you should already know about odd and even numbers and the difference between them. For this topic, however, we will provide a very quick review.

Even Numbers

Even numbers are numbers that are divisible by 2 with no remainder. Remember that 0 is included within this definition.

$$\ldots, -6, -4, -2, 0, 2, 4, 6, \ldots$$

Odd Numbers

Odd numbers are numbers that, when divided by 2, will leave a remainder of 1.

$$\ldots, -5, -3, -1, 1, 3, 5, \ldots$$

Operations and Odd and Even Numbers

There are a number of rules regarding operations and odd and even numbers that you should know instinctively.

Addition	Subtraction	Multiplication
Even + Even = Even	Even − Even = Even	Even × Even = Even
Odd + Odd = Even	Odd − Odd = Even	Odd × Odd = Odd
Even + Odd = Odd	Even − Odd = Odd	Even × Odd = Even

When the SAT tests your knowledge of odd and even numbers, which happens about once or twice a test, it will usually test your knowledge of these rules.

Odd and Even Numbers

1. For which of the following ordered pairs (a, b) is $a + 3b$ equal to an odd number?

    (A) $(2, 4)$
    (B) $(5, 1)$
    (C) $(3, 6)$
    (D) $(0, 8)$
    (E) $(4, 0)$

2. $0 < x < 6$, $4 < y < 10$. If both x and y are odd integers, what is the largest possible value of $x + y$?

    (A) 13
    (B) 14
    (C) 15
    (D) 16
    (E) 17

3. If x is an odd integer less than 10 and $y = 2x$, what is the largest possible value of y?

    (A) 11
    (B) 12
    (C) 16
    (D) 18
    (E) 20

4.

Column A	Column B
Remainder when a positive odd integer is divided by 2	Remainder when a positive even integer is divided by 2

5.   What is the product of the smallest even integer greater than 12 and the largest odd integer less than 80?

Answers

1.   **(C)**   Odd and Even Numbers   *Easy*
The easiest way to answer this question is to plug each answer choice into $a + 3b$ and see which one produces an odd number.

$\qquad$ (A) $(2, 4)$, $a = 2$, $b = 4$, $a + 3b = 2 + 3(4) = 14$

$\qquad$ (B) $(5, 1)$, $a = 5$, $b = 1$, $a + 3b = 5 + 3(1) = 8$

$\qquad$ (C) $(3, 6)$, $a = 3$, $b - 6$, $a + 3b = 3 + 3(6) = 21$

$\qquad$ (D) $(0, 8)$, $a = 0$, $b = 8$, $a + 3b + 0 + 3(8) = 24$

$\qquad$ (E) $(4, 0)$, $a = 4$, $b = 0$, $a + 3b = 4 + 3(0) = 4$

The only answer choice that produces an odd number is (C).

2.   **(B)**   Odd and Even Numbers   *Easy*
In order to make $x + y$ as large as possible, you need to choose the largest x value and the largest y value. Since x must be an odd number less than 6, you know that the largest possible value is $x = 5$. Since y must be an odd number less than 10, you know that the largest possible value is $y = 9$. Now add x plus y to find the answer: $5 + 9 = 14$.

3.   **(D)**   Odd and Even Numbers   *Easy*
In order to make y as large as possible, you need to choose the largest x value given the inequality. Since x must be an odd number less than 10, choose $x = 9$.

$$y = 2(9)$$

$$y = 18$$

4.   **(A)**   Odd and Even Numbers   *Easy*
When a positive odd integer is divided by 2, the remainder is 1. All positive even integers are divisible by 2; therefore, the remainder when a positive even integer is divided by 2 is 0. Since $1 > 0$, Column A is larger than Column B, and the correct answer is (A).

5.   **1106** Odd and Even Numbers   *Easy*

The smallest even integer greater than 12 is 14. The largest odd integer less than 80 is 79. Find the product of 14 and 79: $(14)(79) = 1106$.

Signed Numbers

The term "signed numbers" refers to numbers that include either a positive or negative sign, and are therefore marked as being either greater than 0 (positive) or less than 0 (negative). Zero has no sign. For our purposes, the term usually refers to negative numbers, since you already know instinctively how to think about positive numbers.

Here's a look at negative numbers on a number line:

$$\ldots, -5, -4, -3, -2, -1, \ldots$$

Students who are comfortable with positive numbers sometimes get confused when dealing with negative numbers. For example, while positive numbers become larger as they move farther away from 0, negative numbers become smaller: –10 is a smaller number than –1. When dealing with negative numbers, be careful not to see the 10 in –10 and just assume that it is a larger number than –1.

Negative Numbers and Operations

Negative numbers behave differently from positive numbers when you perform various operations on them. In terms of addition and subtraction, negative numbers invert the operations.

Adding Signed Numbers

When a negative number is added to another number, the sum will be a smaller number. In fact, adding a negative number is the same as subtracting a positive number of the same value.

$$3 + -2 = 1, \text{ just as } 3 - 2 = 1$$

Subtracting Signed Numbers

When a negative number is subtracted from another number, the difference will be a *larger* number. In fact, subtracting a negative number is the same as adding the inverse positive number.

$$3 - (-2) = 5, \text{ just as } 3 + 2 = 5$$

Negative numbers also follow different rules when you multiply or divide them.

Multiplying and Dividing with Negative Numbers

Negative numbers also follow different rules when you include them in multiplication or division.

Multiplying with Negative Numbers	Dividing with Negative Numbers
Positive × Positive = Positive	Positive ÷ Positive = Positive
Negative × Negative = Positive	Negative ÷ Negative = Positive
Positive × Negative = Negative	Positive ÷ Negative = Negative

Negative Numbers and Quantitative Comparisons

Because negative numbers act in such different ways from positive numbers, whenever you plug a positive number into a QC question to try to determine which of the two columns is bigger, you must also plug in a negative number. Often, you'll discover that positive and negative numbers will yield different answers, meaning that the relative size of the columns cannot be determined.

Signed Numbers

1. If the product of 3 and –8 is divided by the sum of 6 and –2, the result is

    (A)   6
    (B)   4
    (C)   2
    (D)   –2
    (E)   –6

2. If ab 0 and $a^3b^3 < 0$, which of the following <u>could</u> be true?

    (A) $a = 0$
    (B) $b = 0$
    (C) $a < 0$ and $b > 0$
    (D) $a < 0$ and $b < 0$
    (E) $a > 0$ and $b > 0$

3.   If $-1 < x < 0$, which of the following must be true?

       I. $x > x^3$
       II. $x^3 > x^2$
       III. $x > x^2$

(A)   None of the above
(B)   I only
(C)   II only
(D)   III only
(E)   I, II, and III

4.

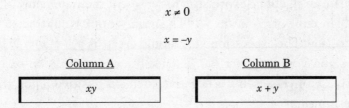

$$x \neq 0$$

$$x = -y$$

Column A	Column B
xy	$x + y$

5.

If the negative of x is subtracted from the cube of y, the result is 0.

Column A	Column B
x	y

Answers

1. **(E)** Signed Numbers   *Easy*

The product of 8 and -3 is -24, and the sum of 6 and -2 is 4. -24 divided by 4 is -6.

2. **(C)** Signed Numbers   *Difficult*

If ab 0, then neither a nor b could equal zero. The next step is to determine how to make a^3b^3 less than zero—in other words, how to make it a negative number. Notice that $a^3b^3 = (a^2)(a)(b^2)(b)$. You know that a^2 and b^2 are always positive. So, in order to make a^3b^3 negative, you would need the product $(a)(b)$ to be negative; in other words, either a or b needs to be positive but not both. The correct answer is (C), $a < 0$ and $b > 0$.

3. **(B)** Signed Numbers   *Difficult*

$-1 < x < 0$ indicates that x is a negative fraction (or decimal). When a negative fraction is squared, the result is positive and thus bigger than the original. When a negative fraction is cubed, the result is a negative fraction that is smaller than the original and smaller than the square of the original. Therefore, only the first statement (that $x > x^3$) is true, and choice (B) is the correct answer.

4.   **(B)**   Signed Numbers   *Moderate*
If $x = -y$, then x and y have the same absolute value, though one is positive and one is negative. Multiplying x and y yields a negative number. Adding x and y yields 0. Zero is greater than a negative value, so Column B is bigger than Column A.

5.   **(D)**   Signed Numbers   *Difficult*
You need to write an algebraic expression to represent the statement. "The negative of x" means $-x$. "The cube of y" means y^3. "The negative of x is subtracted from the cube of y" means $y^3 - (-x)$. The expression you should create is $y^3 - (-x) = 0$. If you simplify the operation signs, you get $y^3 + x = 0$. Then subtract x to get $y^3 = -x$. If x is positive, then y is negative. Conversely, if x is negative, then y is positive. Thus, the relationship cannot be determined.

Divisibility and Remainders

A number (x) is divisible by another number (y) if, when x is divided by y, the answer is a whole number. For example, 6 is divisible by 3 because $6 \div 3 = 2$, and 2 is a whole number. 6 is not divisible by 4, because $6 \div 4 = 1\,{}^2/_4 = 1\,{}^1/_2$, which is not a whole number. Another way of describing $6 \div 4$ is to say that you can make one complete division with a remainder of 2.

The SAT will sometimes test whether you can determine if one number is divisible by another. To check divisibility, you can always do the division by hand and see if the result is a whole number. However, if the number you have to divide is large, working out the problem by hand can be quite difficult. There are some divisibility rules that make this task much easier—these rules allow us to determine whether a number is divisible by another number without having to carry out the division.

Divisibility Rules

1.   All whole numbers are divisible by 1.

2.   All numbers with a ones digit of 0, 2, 4, 6, or 8 are divisible by 2.

3.   A number is divisible by 3 if its digits add up to a number divisible by 3. For example, 6,711 is divisible by 3 because $6 + 7 + 1 + 1 = 15$, and 15 is divisible by 3.

4.   A number is divisible by 4 if its last two digits are divisible by 4. For example, 780, 52, and 80,744 are divisible by 4, but 7,850 is not.

5.   A number is divisible by 5 if it ends in 0 or 5.

6.   A number is divisible by 6 if it is even and also divisible by 3.

7.   Sorry. There are no rules for 7.

8.   A number is divisible by 8 if its last three digits are divisible by 8. For example, 905,256 is divisible by 8 because 256 is divisible by 8. 74,513 is not divisible by 8 because 513 is not divisible by 8.

9.   A number is divisible by 9 if its digits add up to a number divisible by 9. For example, 1,458 is divisible by 9 because $1 + 4 + 5 + 8 = 18$ and 18 is divisible by 9.

10.   A number is divisible by 10 if it ends in 0.

Two Notes:

(1) Because a number divided by itself always yields 1, a number is always divisible by itself. For example, 7 is divisible by 7, and 8,374 is divisible by 8,374. **(2)** No number is divisible by a number greater than itself.

Divisibility and Remainders

1.   For which of the following values of n is $\frac{n}{12}$ in simplest reduced form?

   (A)   2
   (B)   3
   (C)   4
   (D)   5
   (E)   6

2.   If the remainder when 112 is divided by 3 is added to the remainder when 79 is divided by 6, the result is

   (A)   1
   (B)   2
   (C)   3
   (D)   4
   (E)   5

SAT Arithmetic

3. Let x^r be defined as the remainder when x is divided by r. If $x^{101} = 5$, which of the following could be the value of x?

    (A) 1
    (B) 2
    (C) 96
    (D) 106
    (E) 505

4. Balls that are numbered from 1 to 4 are to be packed into a large carton. The balls will be placed in the carton in numerical order: a ball numbered 1 will be put in first; a ball numbered 2 will be put in second; a ball numbered 3 will be put in third, a ball numbered 4 will be put in fourth, a ball numbered 1 will be put in fifth, a ball numbered 2 will be put in sixth, and so on.

Column A	Column B
The number on the 40th ball	The number on the 52nd ball

5. When x is divided by 4, the remainder is 3. What is the remainder when $2x + 1$ is divided by 8?

Answers

1. **(D)** Divisibility and Remainders   *Easy*
If the fraction $\frac{n}{12}$ cannot be reduced further, then you know that n and 12 do not have any common factors. Of the answer choices, only choice (D), 5, does not share a factor with 12.

2. **(B)** Divisibility and Remainders   *Moderate*
When 112 is divided by 3, the remainder is 1. When 79 is divided by 6, the remainder is 1. Add the two remainders together to find the answer: $1 + 1 = 2$.

3. **(D)** Divisibility and Remainders   *Difficult*
Understanding what this question is asking is the most difficult part of solving the problem. The question asks you to divide x by 101 to obtain a remainder of 5. The best way to answer this question is to divide each of the answer choices by 101 and see which division leaves a remainder of 5.

$1 \div 101 = 0$ remainder 1

$2 \div 101 = 0$ remainder 92

$96 \div 101 = 0$ remainder 96

$106 \div 101 = 1$ remainder 5

$505 \div 101 = 5$ remainder 0

Choice (D), 106, is the correct answer.

4.   **(C)**   Divisibility and Remainders   *Moderate*
The problem describes balls that are put into a carton as follows: #1, #2, #3, #4, #1, #2, #3, #4, etc . . . . The best approach to this problem is to divide the balls into groups of four. After placing the 40th ball in the carton, you have 10 groups of 4 balls, and the number on the 40th ball must be 4. After placing the 52nd ball in the carton, you have 13 groups of 4 balls, and the number on the 52nd ball must also be 4.

5.   **7**   Divisibility and Remainders   *Moderate*
If the remainder when x is divided by 4 is 3, then x can be represented by $4n + 3$, where the integer n represents the number of times 4 goes into x. You are given the expression $2x + 1$ and asked to find the remainder when this expression is divided by 8. Let $x = 4n + 3$. If you plug this expression for x into $2x + 1$, You now have:

$$2(4n + 3) + 1$$

$$8n + 6 + 1$$

$$8n + 7$$

When $8n + 7$ is divided by 8, the remainder is 7.

Multiples, Factors, and Primes

SAT questions on multiples, factors, and primes can be difficult simply because of all the terminology they so freely throw around. Below, we give you the definition for these three mathematical concepts. You don't have to love them, but you should know them.

Multiples

The multiple of a number is the product generated when that number is multiplied by an integer. The first five multiples of 7 are 7, 14, 21, 28, and 35 since $7 \times 1 = 7$; $7 \times 2 = 14$; $7 \times 3 = 21$; $7 \times 4 = 28$; $7 \times 5 = 35$.

The Least Common Multiple

The least common multiple (LCM) is the name given to the lowest multiple that two particular numbers share. For example, the multiples of 6 and 8 are:

Multiples of 6:

$$6, 12, 18, 24, 30, 36, 42, 48, 54, \ldots$$

Multiples of 8:

$$8, 16, 24, 32, 40, 48, 56, 64, 72, \ldots$$

As the two lists show, 6 and 8 both have 24 and 48 as multiples (they also share many other multiples, such as 72, 96, . . .) Because 24 is the lowest in value of these shared multiples, it is the least common multiple of 6 and 8.

Being able to figure out the least common multiple of two numbers can prove quite handy on the SAT, especially for questions in which you have to add or subtract two fractions with unlike denominators, which we'll explain later in this chapter.

Factors

A factor of a number is the quotient produced when that number is divided by an integer. For example, 2, 3, 4, and 6 are all factors of 12 because $12 \div 6 = 2$; $12 \div 4 = 3$; $12 \div 3 = 4$; and $12 \div 2 = 6$. Factors, then, are related to multiples. A given number is a multiple of all its factors: 2 and 6 are factors of 12, so 12 is a multiple of both 2 and 6.

The Greatest Common Factor

The Greatest Common Factor (GCF) of two numbers is the largest factor that the two numbers share. For example, the GCF of 18 and 24 is 6, since 6 is the largest number that is a factor for both 18 and 24.

Primes

A prime number is divisible by only 1 and itself (the number 1 itself is not considered prime). For example, 17 is prime because it is divisible by only 1 and 17. The first few primes, in increasing order, are:

$$2, 3, 5, 7, 11, 13, 17, 19, 23, 29, 31, 37, 41, 43, 47, 53, \ldots$$

Let's say the SAT asks you whether 91 is prime. You should try to answer this question by showing that 91 is not prime. You can do this pretty quickly if you understand the rules above. Here is the strategic way to check whether 91 is prime:

1. Is 91 divisible by 2? No, it does not end with an even number.

2. Is 91 divisible by 3? No, $9 + 1 = 10$, which is not divisible by 3. You don't have to check if 91 is divisible by 4, because you already know that is isn't divisible by 2. No number that isn't divisible by 2 will be divisible by 4.

3. Is 91 divisible by 5? No, 91 does not end with 0 or 5. You don't have to check if 91 is divisible by 6, because you already know that is isn't divisible by 2 or 3.

4. Is 91 divisible by 7? Yes! $^{91}/_7 = 13$.

Therefore, 91 is not prime.

Multiples, Factors, and Primes

1. Let P be the set of positive factors of 12. What is the sum of the elements of set P?

    (A) 6
    (B) 12
    (C) 28
    (D) 33
    (E) 36

2. If y is a factor of 100 and $x = y + 1$, what is the largest prime value of x?

    (A) 3
    (B) 11
    (C) 23
    (D) 51
    (E) 101

3.

Column A	Column B
The largest prime factor of 14	The smallest prime factor of 77

4.

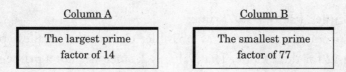

$$x = 10y$$

$$y > 3$$

Column A	Column B
The largest prime factor of x	The largest prime factor of y

5. If x is a prime number between 1 and 12, and $y = 6$, what is the smallest possible value of xy?

6. The number $n = 23,571,113$ was created by listing the first 6 prime numbers in order from left to right. If a similar number is created listing the first 18 prime numbers, how many times will the digit "1" appear in the new number?

Answers

1. **(C)** Multiples, Factors, and Primes   *Easy*
Set P includes all of the factors of 12: $\{1, 2, 3, 4, 6, 12\}$. Add the elements of P to find the correct answer: $1 + 2 + 3 + 6 + 12 = 28$.

2. **(E)** Multiples, Factors, and Primes   *Moderate*
List the factors of 100: y = 1, 2, 4, 5, 10, 25, 50, 100. Since x is equal to y + 1, list all possible values of x: x = 2, 3, 5, 6, 11, 26, 51, 101. The largest prime number in this list is 101.

3. **(C)** Multiples, Factors, and Primes   *Moderate*
List the factors of 14: 1, 2, 7, 14. Now list the factors of 77: 1, 7, 11, 77. The largest prime factor of 14 is 7, and the smallest prime factor of 77 is 7, so Column A and Column B are equal.

4. **(D)** Multiples, Factors, and Primes   *Difficult*
Try plugging in different values for x and y. When y = 4, x = 40. The largest prime factor of 40 (the x value) is 5. The largest prime factor of 4 (the y value) is 2. In this example, Column A is greater than Column B. When y = 5, x = 50. The largest prime factor of 50 (the x value) is 5. The largest prime factor of 5 (the y value) is also 5. In this case, Column A is equal to Column B. Therefore, the relationship between the two columns cannot be determined.

5. **12** Multiples, Factors, and Primes   *Moderate*
To make the product xy as small as possible, choose the smallest prime number between 1 and 12 for the x value. That value is 2, since 1 is not a prime number. Since you know that x = 2 and y = 6, you can find the answer: xy = 12.

6. **8** Multiples, Factors, and Primes   *Difficult*
Create the new number: 2357111317192329313741434753596l. The number 1 appears 8 times in this number.

Fractions, Decimals, and Percents

The SAT focuses far more closely on fractions, decimals, and percents than on any other arithmetic topic. In fact, almost 14 percent of all SAT math questions require some knowledge of fractions, decimals, or percents. On a single SAT, 7 to 8 questions will deal with this topic. Because fractions encompass such a large part of the test, knowing your stuff here can really help your final score.

Fractions

A fraction describes a part of a whole. The number on the bottom of the fraction is called the denominator, and it denotes the number of equal parts into which the whole is divided. The number on the top of the fraction is called the numerator, and denotes how many of those equal parts the fraction has. For example, the fraction ³/₄ denotes "3 of 4 equal parts," 3 being the numerator and 4 being the denominator.

You can also think of fractions as similar to division. In fact, ³/₄ means the same thing as 3 ÷ 4.

Equivalent Fractions

Two fractions are equivalent if there is a number by which both the numerator and the denominator of one fraction can be multiplied or divided to yield the other fraction. For example, ²/₃ is equivalent to ⁴/₆ because if you multiply the numerator and denominator of ²/₃ by 2, you get ⁴/₆:

$$\frac{2 \times 2}{2 \times 3} = \frac{4}{6}$$

Equivalent fractions are equivalent in value. When you multiply or divide both the numerator and denominator of a fraction by the same number, *you will not change the overall value of the fraction.* Because fractions represent a part of a whole, if you increase both the part and whole by the same multiple, you will not change the relationship between the part and the whole. See how ⅓ of a pizza is exactly the same as ³/₉?

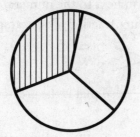 

Reducing Fractions

On the SAT, you will sometimes encounter fractions involving large, unwieldy numbers, such as ¹⁸/₁₀₂. It would probably be hard (and time consuming) for you to work with ¹⁸/₁₀₂, just because the numbers in the numerator and denominator are so big. When faced with such cases, it is always a good idea to see if the fraction can be reduced, or simplified.

The fastest way to simplify a fraction is to divide both the numerator and denominator by their Greatest Common Factor (GCF). In the case of ¹⁸/₁₀₂, the GCF of 18 and 102 is 6, leaving you with ³/₁₇. With your knowledge of divisibility rules, you should be able to see that both the numerator and denominator are divisible by 6. Had you not immediately seen that 6 was the GCF, you could have divided both numbers by 2 and gotten $\frac{9}{51}$. From there, it would have been pretty obvious that both numerator and denominator are also divisible by 3, yielding $\frac{3}{17}$.

On the SAT, when you encounter a fraction that involves big numbers, very often that fraction can be reduced. And because the SAT is in part a test of speed, any knowledge you have that lessens the time it takes to answer a question is very important. You need to get skilled not only at reducing fractions, but also at recognizing when a fraction can be reduced.

Comparing Fractions

Particularly on quantitative comparison questions, you may be asked to compare two fractions. If either the denominators or the numerators of the two fractions are the same, that comparison is easy. $\frac{8}{9}$ is obviously greater than $\frac{5}{9}$, and $\frac{5}{9}$ is greater than $\frac{5}{17}$. Just remember, if the denominators are the same, the fraction with the larger numerator is bigger. If the numerators of the two fractions are the same, the fraction with the smaller denominator is bigger.

If the two fractions don't lend themselves to immediate easy comparison, don't fret. There is a trick that allows you to compare fractions: cross-multiplication. To cross-multiply, multiply the numerator of each fraction by the denominator of the other. Write the product of each multiplication next to the numerator you used to get it. The greater product will be next to the greater fraction. For example:

$$32 = \frac{4}{7} \; > \times < \; \frac{5}{8} = 35$$

35, the greater product, is next to the fraction $\frac{5}{8}$, so that is the greater fraction.

Adding and Subtracting Fractions

There are two different types of fractions that the SAT might ask you to add or subtract. It might ask you to work with two fractions that have the same denominator. Or it might ask you to handle two fractions with different denominators.

If fractions have the same denominator, adding them is extremely easy. All you have to do is add up the numerators:

$$\frac{1}{20} + \frac{3}{20} + \frac{13}{20} = \frac{17}{20}$$

Subtraction works similarly. If the denominators of the fractions are equal, then you simply subtract one numerator from the other:

$$\frac{13}{20} - \frac{2}{20} = \frac{11}{20}$$

If the fractions do not have equal denominators, the process is somewhat more involved. The first step is to make the denominators the same. To set the denominators of two fractions equal, find the Least Common Denominator (LCD), which is simply the Least Common Multiple (LCM) of the two denominators. For example, 18 is the LCD of $\frac{1}{6}$ and $\frac{4}{9}$, since 18 is the smallest multiple of both 6 and 9.

Setting the denominators of two fractions equal to each other is a two-step process. First, find the LCD. Second, write each fraction as an equivalent fraction with the LCD as the new denominator, remembering to multiply the numerator by the same multiple as the denominator. For example, if you wanted to add $\frac{5}{12}$ and $\frac{4}{9}$, you would do the following:

I. Find the LCD

1. Factor the denominators. $12 = 2 \times 2 \times 3$ and $9 = 3 \times 3$.

2. Find the LCM of the denominators. $2 \times 2 \times 3 \times 3 = 36$.

3. The LCD is 36.

II. Write each fraction as an equivalent fraction with the LCD as the new denominator.

1. Multiply the denominator and numerator of the first fraction by the LCD.

$$\text{denominator } = 12 \times 3 = 36$$
$$\text{numerator } = 5 \times 3 = 15$$

The new fraction is, therefore, $\frac{15}{36}$.

2. Multiply the denominator and numerator of the second fraction by the LCD.

$$\text{denominator } = 9 \times 4 = 36$$
$$\text{numerator } = 4 \times 4 = 16$$

The new fraction is $\frac{16}{36}$.

Now that the fractions have the same denominator, you can quickly add the numerators to get the final answer. $15 + 16 = 31$, so the answer is $\frac{31}{36}$.

If you think it will take you too long to figure out the LCD, you can always multiply the denominators together to get a common denominator that isn't the least common denominator. For example, if the two denominators are 6 and 8, you can use 48 as your common denominator just as easily as 24 (the LCD). There are two drawbacks to not using the LCD. First, you will have to work with larger numbers. Second, because the answer choices will appear as reduced fractions, you will have to reduce your answer at the end.

Multiplying Fractions

Multiplying fractions is quite easy. Simply multiply the numerators together and the denominators together, as seen in the example below.

$$\frac{4}{5} \times \frac{2}{7} \times \frac{1}{3} = \frac{4 \times 2 \times 1}{5 \times 7 \times 3} = \frac{8}{105}$$

Canceling Out

You can often make multiplying fractions even easier by canceling out. If the numerator and denominator of any of the fractions you need to multiply share a common factor, you can divide by the common factor to reduce both numerator and denominator. For example, the fraction:

$$\frac{4}{5} \times \frac{1}{8} \times \frac{10}{11}$$

can be rewritten, after canceling out the 4, 8, 5, and 10, as:

$$\frac{\cancel{4}^{1}}{\cancel{5}^{1}} \times \frac{1}{\cancel{8}^{2}} \times \frac{\cancel{10}^{2}}{11} = \frac{1}{1} \times \frac{1}{2} \times \frac{2}{11}$$

then, canceling the 2's, you get:

$$\frac{1}{1} \times \frac{1}{\cancel{2}^{1}} \times \frac{\cancel{2}^{1}}{11} = \frac{1}{1} \times \frac{1}{1} \times \frac{1}{11}$$

Though multiplying fractions is fairly easy mechanically, it is a little tricky intuitively. You are probably used to the product of multiplication being bigger than the numbers that are being multiplied. But when dealing with a fraction, the product of two numbers is *smaller*. Note that this phenomenon only occurs in reference to fractions smaller than one, in which the numerator is smaller than the denominator.

Dividing Fractions

Multiplication and division are inverse operations. It makes sense, then, that to perform division with fractions, all you have to do is invert (flip over) the dividing fraction and then multiply.

$$\frac{\frac{1}{4}}{\frac{5}{8}} = \frac{1}{4} \times \frac{8}{5}$$

Also note that just as multiplication of fractions that are smaller than one results in an even smaller product, division of fractions smaller than one results in a *larger* product.

Converting Mixed Numbers to Fractions

A mixed number is composed of a whole number and a fraction: $6\frac{2}{3}$, for example, is a mixed number because 6 is a whole number and $\frac{2}{3}$ is a fraction. For the SAT, it is very important that you be able to convert a mixed number into a fraction. Whenever you are asked to perform an operation of any sort on a mixed number, you will first have to convert it to fraction form. Also, for GI questions you will have to convert any mixed numbers to fractions before gridding them in.

To convert a mixed number into a fraction, multiply the whole number by the denominator and add the result to the numerator. Do not change the denominator.

For example, $6\frac{2}{3}$ can be converted into a fraction in the following way: multiply the whole number, 6, by the denominator, 3, and then add the yielded product to the original numerator, 2. $(6 \times 3) + 2 = 20$. The denominator remains the same, so the answer is $\frac{20}{3}$.

Decimals

Decimals are simply another way to express fractions. To get a decimal, divide the numerator of a fraction by the denominator. For example, if you take the fraction $\frac{2}{5}$ and divide 2 by 5 you would get .4.

Place Value and Decimals

Normally, numbers get bigger when they involve more numerals. The number 4000, for example, is obviously bigger than 4. However, with decimals, more zeros often means less: .4 is larger than .004. If you remember that decimals are just another way to express fractions, the reason for this difference in size is easy to see. .4 is equivalent to the $\frac{4}{10}$, while .004 is equivalent to $\frac{4}{1000}$.

The SAT will occasionally try to trip you up by asking you to compare a decimal such as .002 with the decimal .0008. Because you aren't so used to looking at decimals and 8 is obviously a larger integer than 2, you may be tempted to overlook that the second decimal includes an additional 0 and choose it as the larger decimal. To avoid such mistakes, all you have to do is be careful. One way to insure that you're being careful is to line up the decimal points of the two decimals. While .0008 might seem larger than .002,

.0008 will always seem smaller than
.002

To make the situation even more obvious, you can add an extra zero to the bottom decimal to make it just as long as the upper

.0008
.0020

Now you are comparing $^8/_{1000}$ to $^{20}/_{1000}$, and $^{20}/_{1000}$ is clearly the bigger of those two numbers. If numbers are being added to the right of the decimal number, then it's a different story.

.0008 is smaller than
.000819

Operations, Decimals, and Calculators

The processes of addition, subtraction, multiplication, and division for decimal numbers are quite similar to the rules of those same operations for integers. However, we're not going to delve into the specifics of those rules right now for a very simple reason: when dealing with the addition, subtraction, multiplication, or subtraction of decimals, it is almost always faster and more accurate to use a calculator. If you type in the correct decimals to begin with, your calculator will always come out with the right answer.

Percents

Percents are just another way to talk about a specific type of fraction (which also means that percents are also just another way to talk about a specific type of decimal). *Percent* literally means "of 100" in Latin, so when you have 25 percent of all the money in the world, that means you have $^{25}/_{100}$ (or .25) of the world's money.

But, sadly, you don't have that much money, and you have to take the SAT. So let's look at an example question: 4 is what percent of 20? This question presents you with a whole, 20, and then asks you to determine how much of that whole 4 represents in percentage form. To come to the answer, you have to set up an equation that sets the fraction $^4/_{20}$ to $^x/_{100}$:

$$\frac{4}{20} = \frac{x}{100}$$

if you then cross-multiply to solve for x, you get $20x = 400$, meaning $x = 20$. Therefore, 4 is 20% of 20. You also might realize that instead of working out all this cross multiplication, you could simply cancel out the 20 and the 100 to get

$$\frac{4}{20} \times 100 = 4 \times 5 = 20$$

Converting Percents into Fractions or Decimals

Converting percents into fractions and decimals will almost surely come up on the SAT. To convert from a percent to a fraction, all you have to do is take the percentage number and place it as a numerator over the denominator 100. If you have 88 percent of something, then you can quickly convert it into the fraction $^{88}/_{100}$.

To convert from a percent to a decimal, you must take a decimal point and insert it into the percent number two spaces from the right. 79% therefore becomes .79, while 350% becomes 3.5.

To convert from either a fraction or decimal back to a percent, perform the processes in reverse: multiply the fraction by 100 or move the decimal point two spaces to the left.

To save time while taking the SAT, you should memorize some of the conversions between common fractions, decimals, and percents.

$$\frac{1}{2} = 50\% = .5$$

$$\frac{1}{4} = 25\% = .25$$

$$\frac{1}{5} = 20\% = .2$$

$$\frac{1}{10} = 10\% = .1$$

$$\frac{1}{20} = 5\% = .05$$

$$\frac{1}{25} = 4\% = .04$$

Part Versus Whole Problems

Percentage problems on the SAT can often be hard but not because the math they use is confusing. Instead, it is the words the problems use that can cause difficulties. To combat this verbal nastiness, we're going to look at a sample question and explain where and why it is tricky.

What percent of 2 is 5?

When you see a percentage question, your first goal should always be to determine which number represents the whole and which the part. Intuitively, when you see the question above, you will probably think that 2 is the part, since 2 is smaller than 5, and how can you have a part that's bigger than the whole? But you can calculate the percentage when the part is bigger than the whole: the answer will simply be bigger than 100%. Now, let's break down the question. What percent of 2 is 5? This question could be written: 5 is what percent of 2? Once we've reorganized the question, it should be obvious that the "of 2" marks the 2 as the whole and the 5 as the part. We can then set up the fraction $^5/_2 \times 100 = 250\%$.

Remember the most important lesson of percents: before beginning a problem, always identify which number represents the whole and which represents the part.

Important Percent Terms

Percent terminology can be a little tricky, so here is a very short dictionary of terms:

- Percent more—if Max has 50% more children than Chris does, then Max has the same number of children as Chris *plus* an additional 50%.

- Percent increase—percent increase means the same thing as percent more. If the price of a $10 shirt increases 10%, the new price is the original $10 plus 10% of the $10 original.

- Percent decrease—the opposite of percent increase. This term means you subtract the specified percent of the original value from the original value.

Sometimes students see these terms and figure out what the 10% increase or decrease is, but then forget to carry out the necessary addition or subtraction. The SAT writers know about this tendency and will try to use it to trick you:

A shirt originally cost $20, but during a sale its price was reduced by 15%. What is the current price of the shirt?

(A) $3
(B) $5
(C) $13
(D) $17
(E) $23

To answer this question, you should multiply $20 by .15 to see what the change in price was:

$$\$20 \times .15 = \$3$$

Once you know that price change, then you need to subtract it from the original price, since the question asks you to find the *reduced* price of the shirt:

$$\$20 - \$3 = \$17$$

The answer is **(C)**. But if you only finished the first part of this question and looked at the answers, you might see the $3 at answer (A) like a big affirmation of correctness and be tempted to choose it without finishing the calculation.

Double Percents

Some SAT questions will ask you to determine a percent of a percent. For example, take the question:

The original price of a banana in a store is $2. During a sale, the store reduces the price by 25% and Joe buys the banana. Joe then meets his friend Sam who is faint with hunger.

Seeing an opportunity, Joe raises the price of the banana 10% from the price at which he bought it and sells it to Sam. How much does Sam pay for the banana?

In this question, you are being asked to determine the cumulative effect of two percent changes. The key to solving this type of problem is to realize that each percentage change is dependent on the last. In other words, you have to work out the effect of the first percentage change, come up with a value, and then use that value to determine the effect of the second percentage change. When you are working on a percentage problem that involves a series of percentage changes, you should follow the same basic procedure that we explained for one percentage change, except in this case you should follow the procedure twice. For the first percentage change, figure out what is the whole, calculate the percentage of the whole, make sure to perform addition or subtraction if necessary, then take the new value and put it through these same steps for the second percentage change.

To answer the problem, you should first find 25% of the original price:

$$\frac{25}{100} \times \$2 = \frac{50}{100} = \$.50$$

Now subtract that .50 from the original price:

$$\$2 - \$.5 = \$1.50$$

Then we use $1.50 and increase it by 10%:

$$\frac{10}{100} \times \$1.50 = \frac{15}{100} = \$.15$$

Therefore, Sam buys the banana at a price of $1.50 + $.15 = $1.65.

When dealing with double-percent questions, some students are tempted to simply combine the two percentage changes. But you *cannot* simply add or subtract the two percent changes and then find that percent of the original value. If you tried to answer the question above by reasoning that the first percentage change lowered the price 25% and the second raised the price 10%, meaning that the total change was −15%, you would get the question wrong:

$$\frac{15}{100} \times \$2 = \frac{30}{100} = \$.30$$

Now subtract that .30 from the original price:

$$\$2 - \$.30 = \$1.70$$

We *promise* you that when the SAT gives you a double-percent problem they will include this sort of wrong answer among the choices as a distraction. Don't fall for the trick. Don't give them the satisfaction.

Fractions, Decimals, and Percents

1. What is $\frac{2}{3}$ of $\frac{3}{4}$?

    (A) $\frac{1}{12}$

    (B) $\frac{1}{2}$

    (C) $\frac{5}{7}$

    (D) $\frac{8}{9}$

    (E) 2

2. Which of the following decimals has the greatest value?

    (A) 0.6
    (B) 0.12
    (C) 0.5
    (D) 0.199
    (E) 0.32567

3. In Town A, there is a 10% tax on luxury gift items. What would be the total cost, including tax, of a luxury gift item purchased in Town A, if the marked price is $775.00?

    (A) $785.00
    (B) $787.75
    (C) $800.00
    (D) $825.50
    (E) $852.50

4. What is the average of $\frac{1}{2}, \frac{1}{3}$, and $\frac{1}{4}$?

    (A) $\frac{1}{9}$

    (B) $\frac{1}{3}$

    (C) $\frac{7}{20}$

    (D) $\frac{13}{36}$

    (E) $\frac{9}{24}$

5.   If the tic marks on line segment $\overline{AB}$ are evenly spaced, what is the value of $\dfrac{AP}{AB}$?

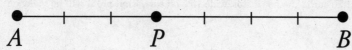

(A) $\dfrac{1}{7}$

(B) $\dfrac{2}{7}$

(C) $\dfrac{3}{7}$

(D) $\dfrac{4}{7}$

(E) $\dfrac{5}{7}$

6.   If Janet completed one half of a job and Evan completed one third of the same job, what fraction of the job remains unfinished?

(A) $\dfrac{1}{6}$

(B) $\dfrac{1}{12}$

(C) $\dfrac{5}{12}$

(D) $\dfrac{5}{6}$

(E) $\dfrac{11}{12}$

7.   What percent of 12 is 8?

(A) $33\dfrac{1}{3}\%$

(B)   50%

(C) $66\dfrac{2}{3}\%$

(D)   81%

(E)   150%

8.   If 3% of the bulbs in every shipment arrive broken, how many broken bulbs will there be in a shipment of 1200 bulbs?

(A)   12

(B)   25

(C)   36

(D)   120

(E)   360

9. Mr. Tee sells small brackets at his hardware store. He buys the brackets for $0.75 each and sells them at $1.20 each. If he has a storewide 10% off sale, what profit will he make on each bracket sold?

   (A) $0.12
   (B) $0.25
   (C) $0.29
   (D) $0.33
   (E) $1.08

10.

Column A	Column B
$\dfrac{9}{11}$	$\dfrac{8}{12}$

11.

   Store A is having a 25%-off sale.

   Store B is having a 20%-off sale.

Column A	Column B
The cost of a coat marked $80 in store A	The cost of a coat marked $75 in store B

12.

   Richard does a job in 3 hours.

   Marvin does the same job in 4 hours.

Column A	Column B
The number of hours required to complete the job if they work together	2

13. There are 14 girls and 16 boys in Mr. Lordeb's class. If of the girls are absent and of the boys are absent, what fraction of the total class is absent?

14. If the product of 0.632 and 1.479 is rounded to the nearest thousandth, what is the number in the thousandths place?

15. Points $A, B, C,$ and D are located on a line in that order. If B is the midpoint of AC and $AB = CD$, what percent of AC is AD?

Answers

1.   **(B)**   Fractions, Decimals, and Percents   *Easy*

$\frac{2}{3}$ of $\frac{3}{4}$ means $\left(\frac{2}{3}\right)\left(\frac{3}{4}\right)$. Multiply the fractions together to find the answer:

$\left(\frac{2}{3}\right)\left(\frac{3}{4}\right) = \frac{6}{12} = \frac{1}{2}$.

2.   **(A)**   Fractions, Decimals, and Percents   *Easy*

When comparing decimals, you must look at the digit in the left-most position – (in other words, the digit right after the decimal point). Of the choices offered, the largest number in tenths place is 6, so (A), 0.6, has the greatest value.

3.   **(E)**   Fractions, Decimals, and Percents   *Easy*

If there is a 10% tax on an item marked $775.00, you need to calculate the amount of the tax by taking 10% of 775. Change 10% to 0.10 and multiply by 775: (.10)(775) = 77.50. The total cost of the item is the marked price plus the tax: $775.00 + $77.50 = $825.50.

4.   **(D)**   Fractions, Decimals, and Percents   *Easy*

To average three values, you need to add them and then divide the result by 3:

$\frac{1}{2} + \frac{1}{3} + \frac{1}{4} = 1\frac{1}{12}$. divided by 3 $= \frac{13}{36}$.

5.   **(C)**   Fractions, Decimals, and Percents   *Easy*

AP is 3 segments long, and AB is 7 segments long. So $\frac{AP}{AB} = \frac{3}{7}$.

6.   **(A)**   Fractions, Decimals, and Percents   *Easy*

First add one half to one third to find out what fraction of the job has been completed

by Janet and Evan: $\frac{1}{2} + \frac{1}{3} = \frac{5}{6}$. Subtract this fraction from 1 to figure out what fraction

of the job has not been done: remains unfinished.

7.   **(C)**   Fractions, Decimals, and Percents   *Easy*

In percent questions phrased like this, the number that follows "of" represents the

whole and the number that follows "is" represents the part. In this case, 12 is the

whole, and 8 is the part. To find what percent 8 is of 12, use the formula $\frac{part}{whole} \times 100$.

Plug 8 and 12 into this formula: $\frac{8}{12} \times 100 = 66\frac{2}{3}\%$.

8. **(C)** Fractions, Decimals, and Percents   *Moderate*
You need to calculate 3% of 1200. 3% of 1200 means (.03)(1200) = 36.

9. **(D)** Fractions, Decimals, and Percents   *Difficult*
When the store has a 10%-off sale, the bracket priced at $1.20 will be sold for 10% less.
10% of $1.20: (1.20)(0.10) = $0.12. You need to subtract $0.12 from $1.20 in order to
find the sale price: 1.20 − 0.12 = 1.08.

    Mr. Tee's profit is equal to the sale price minus his cost (in other words, the price at
which he bought the bracket): $1.08 − $0.75 = $0.33.

10. **(A)** Fractions, Decimals, and Percents   *Easy*
One way to compare fractions is to change them into decimals through division.

$$\frac{9}{11} = 9 \div 11 = .8181$$

$$\frac{8}{12} = 8 \div 12 = .666$$

0.8181 is larger than 0.666, so column A is larger than column B.

11. **(C)** Fractions, Decimals, and Percents   *Moderate*
For Column A, you need to calculate 25% of the $80.00 coat. Change 25% to 0.25 and
multiply: (0.25)(80) = 20. Therefore, the coat will cost $80 − $20 = $60. For Column B,
you need to calculate 20% of the $75.00 coat. Change 20% to 0.20 and multiply:
(0.20)(75) = 15. Therefore, the coat will cost $75 − $15 = $60. The new costs of the coats
are equal, so (C), the columns are equal in value, is the correct answer.

12. **(B)** Fractions, Decimals, and Percents   *Difficult*
If it takes Richard 3 hours to do the job, then he does $\frac{1}{3}$ of the job per hour. And likewise, Marvin does $\frac{1}{4}$ of the job per hour, since it takes him 4 hours to complete the job.
Together, they do $\frac{1}{3} + \frac{1}{4} = \frac{7}{12}$ of the job per hour. Therefore, they need $\frac{12}{7}$ hours to complete the job together. $\frac{12}{7}$ is less than 2, so column B is larger than column A.

13. **2/15** Fractions, Decimals, and Percents   *Moderate*
$\frac{1}{7}$ of the 14 girls are absent from school: $\frac{1}{7} \times 14 = 2$ girls are absent.

    $\frac{1}{8}$ of the 16 boys are absent from school: $\frac{1}{8} \times 16 = 2$ boys are absent.

    The total number of students in the class is: 14 + 16 = 30.

    The fraction of the class that is absent is equal to the number of absent students

divided by the total number of students, or: $\frac{4}{30} = \frac{2}{15}$.

14. **5**   Fractions, Decimals, and Percents   *Moderate*

The product of 0.632 and 1.479 is: (0.632)(1.479) = 0.934728. The names for the decimal places, beginning at the left, are: tenths, hundredths, thousandths. 0.934728 rounded to nearest thousandth is 0.935, and the number in the thousandths place is 5.

15. **150** Fractions, Decimals, and Percents   *Difficult*

Draw a diagram of the number line.

All segments on this line are equal in length. AC = 2 segments, and AD = 3 segments.

To find what percent AD is of AC, you first need to figure out which is the part and which is the whole. The phrase "of AC" indicates that AC is the whole and, thus, that AD is the part. Plug AC = 2 and AD = 3 into the formula $\frac{\text{part}}{\text{whole}} \times 100 : \frac{3}{2} \times 100 = 150\%$.

Ratios

Ratios can look a lot like fractions, and they are related to fractions, but they differ in important ways. Whereas a fraction describes a part out of a whole, a ratio compares two separate parts of the same whole.

A ratio can be written in a variety of ways. Mathematically it can appear as $^3/_1$ or as 3:1. In words, it would be written out as the ratio of 3 to 1. Each of these three forms of the ratio 3:1 mean the same thing, that there are three of one thing for every one of another. If you have three red marbles and one blue marble, then you would have a ratio of 3:1 for red marbles to blue marbles. For the SAT, you must remember that ratios compare *parts to parts*, rather than parts to a whole. The SAT will ask you questions like this:

> Of every 40 games a baseball team plays, it loses 12 games. What is the ratio of the team's losses to wins?
>
> (A)   3:10
> (B)   7:10
> (C)   3:7
> (D)   7:3
> (E)   10:3

The key to this sort of ratio question is to see that the question is stated in terms of a whole to a part but asks for a part to part answer. The questions tells you the team loses

12 of every 40 games, but it asks you for the ratio of losses : *wins* not losses : *games*. So the first thing you have to do is find out how many games the team wins in 40 games:

$$40 - 12 = 28$$

The team wins 28 games for every 40. So for every 12 losses, the team wins 28 games or 12:28. You can reduce this ratio by dividing both sides by 4 to get 3 losses for every 7 wins, or 3:7. Answer **(C)** is correct. If you didn't realize that the losses to games was a part to whole, you might have just reduced the ratio 12:40 to 3:10, and then chose answer (A). You can bet that on this sort of ratio problem the SAT will include the incorrect *part:whole* answer to try to trip you up.

Proportions

If you have a ratio of 3 red marbles to 1 blue, that doesn't necessarily mean that you have exactly 3 red marbles and 1 blue one. It could also mean that you have 6 red and 2 blue marbles or that you have 240 red and 80 blue marbles. In other words, ratios compare only *relative* size. In order to know how many of each color marble you actually have, in addition to knowing the ratios, you also need to know how many total marbles there are.

The SAT will often ask questions testing your ability to figure out a quantity based on the given information of a ratio between items and the total number of all items. For example:

> You have red, blue, and green marbles in the ratio of 5:4:3, and you have a total of 36 marbles. How many blue marbles do you have?

The information given states that for each group of 5 red marbles, you have a corresponding group of 4 blue marbles, and a group of 3 green marbles. The ratio therefore tells you that out of every 12 marbles (since $5 + 4 + 3 = 12$) 4 of them will be blue. The question also tells you that you have 36 total marbles.

Since the ratio of blue marbles will not change no matter how many marbles you have, we can solve this problem by setting up a proportion, which is an equation that states that two ratios are equal. In this case, we are going to set equal 4:12 and x:36, with x being the number of blue marbles that we would have if we had 36 total marbles. To do math with proportions, it is most useful to set up proportions in fraction form:

$$\frac{4}{12} = \frac{x}{36}$$

Now you just need to isolate x by cross-multiplying, and then you can solve.

$$12x = 4 \times 36$$
$$12x = 144$$
$$x = 12$$

When you are dealing with ratio questions of this sort, you should always set up an equation of equivalent fractions and cross-multiply.

Ratio and Proportion

1.   If the ratio of 3 to x is the same as the ratio of 7 to 14, what is the value of x?

   (A)   4
   (B)   5
   (C)   6
   (D)   7
   (E)   10

2.   An inheritance was split among three cousins in a ratio of 2:3:5. If the person with the largest share received $3,000, how much did the cousin with the smallest share receive?

   (A) $180
   (B) $300
   (C) $600
   (D) $1,200
   (E) $4,200

3.   One bag of cat food feeds 12 cats for 2 weeks. For how many days would the same bag feed 8 cats?

   (A)   3
   (B)   9
   (C)   15
   (D)   18
   (E)   21

4.   Oliver reads p pages in h hours. In terms of p, h, and m, how many pages does he read in m minutes?

   (A) $\dfrac{pm}{60h}$

   (B) $\dfrac{60m}{ph}$

   (C) $\dfrac{60h}{pm}$

   (D) $\dfrac{60hm}{p}$

   (E) $\dfrac{hp}{60m}$

SAT Arithmetic

5. The ratio of juniors to seniors at Ellis School is the same as the ratio of freshmen to sophomores at Duncan School. If the number of juniors at Ellis School is twice the number of freshmen at Duncan School, and there are 120 sophomores at Duncan School, how many seniors are there at Ellis School?

(A) 60
(B) 80
(C) 180
(D) 240
(E) 300

6.

A bag contains white marbles and red marbles.
The ratio of white marbles to red marbles is 5:7.

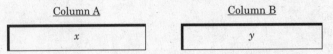

Column A	Column B
The total number of marbles	12

7.

The ratio of x to y is the same as the ratio of x to $\sqrt{2}$.

Column A	Column B
x	y

8.

A bowl contains red, white, and blue disks.
The ratio of red disks to white disks is 3:4,
and the ratio of white disks to blue disks is 2:5.

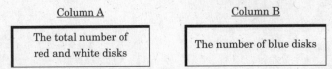

Column A	Column B
The total number of red and white disks	The number of blue disks

9. If 3 apples cost $0.69, how many apples can Sue get for $2.76?

10. A 15-foot tree casts an 8-foot shadow at the same time that a boy casts a 3-foot shadow. To the nearest tenth of a foot, how tall is the boy?

Answers

1. **(C)** Arithmetic: Ratio and Proportion   *Easy*
Set up the following ratio: $\dfrac{3}{x} = \dfrac{7}{14}$. Cross-multiply the sides to get: $(3)(14) = (7)(x)$, which becomes $42 = 7x$ when you multiply out each side. Divide both sides by 7 to find: $6 = x$.

2. **(D)** Arithmetic: Ratio and Proportion   *Moderate*
Ratios describe relative amounts. The ratio 2:3:5 means that the smallest share of the inheritance could be $2x$, the middle share could be $3x$, and the largest share could be $5x$, where x is a constant multiplier. Since the largest share is equal to \$3000, you can figure out the value of x by writing the equation $5x = 3000$. When you divide by 5, you find that $x = 600$. To find the smallest share, multiply 2 by 600: $2x = 2(600) = \$1200$.

3. **(E)** Arithmetic: Ratio and Proportion   *Moderate*
The total amount of food in the bag is equal to 12 cats multiplied by 14 days. If one bag of food feeds 12 cats for 14 days, the same bag will feed 8 cats for x days. Since the amount of food in the bag remains the same, you can set up the following equation to find the value of x:

$$(12 \text{ cats})(14 \text{ days}) = (8 \text{ cats})(x \text{ days})$$

$$(12)(14) = (8)(x)$$

$$168 = 8x$$

$$21 = x$$

4. **(A)** Arithmetic: Ratio and Proportion   *Difficult*
The question says that Oliver reads p pages in h hours; in other words, he reads at a rate of p/h pages per hour. Since the question wants to find his reading rate in terms of minutes, your first step should be to convert h hours to minutes. There are 60 minutes in an hour, so h hours = $60h$ minutes. Now set up a proportion to figure out how many pages Oliver reads in m minutes: $\dfrac{m}{60h} = \dfrac{x}{p}$, where x represents the number of pages he reads in m minutes. Cross-multiply the equation to get: $mp = 60h(x)$. Divide both sides of the equation by $60h$ to find the value of x: $x = \dfrac{mp}{60h}$.

5. **(D)** Arithmetic: Ratio and Proportion   *Difficult*
Based on the information given in the question, you can set up the following ratio:

$$\frac{(EJ)\,\text{Ellis Juniors}}{(ES)\,\text{Ellis Seniors}} = \frac{(DF)\,\text{Duncan Freshmen}}{(DS)\,\text{Duncan Sophomores}} = \frac{EJ}{ES} = \frac{DF}{DS}$$

Cross-multiply to get: $(EJ)(DS) = (ES)(DF)$. Since $EJ = 2DF$, you can substitute $2DF$ into the equation: $(2DF)(DS) = (ES)(DF)$. Divide both sides of the equation by DF: $2DS = ES$. If $DS = 120$, then $ES = 2(120) = 240$.

6.   **(D)**   Arithmetic: Ratio and Proportion   *Easy*
Since the ratio of white marbles to red marbles is 5 to 7, you can represent the number of white marbles as $5x$ and the number of red marbles as $7x$. Therefore, the total number of marbles is $12x$. Since x can have any value, the number of marbles could be any multiple of 12 (for example, 12, 24, or 36) and the relationship between the two columns cannot be determined.

7.   **(D)**   Arithmetic: Ratio and Proportion   *Moderate*
You can set up the following proportion based on the information in the question: $\frac{x}{y} = \frac{\pi}{\sqrt{2}}$. The question asks you to compare the values of x and y. You may be tempted to say that x is greater than y since π is greater than $\sqrt{2}$, but that would be true only if x and y are positive. If x and y are negative, then y is greater in value than x. Therefore, the relationship between the two columns cannot be determined.

8.   **(B)**   Arithmetic: Ratio and Proportion   *Difficult*
The ratio of red to white disks is 3:4, and the ratio of white to blue disks is 2:5. You need to find a way to compare these two ratios. If you double the ratio of white to blue disks, you get 4:10. Since the ratio of red to white disks is 3:4 and the ratio of white to blue disks is 4:10, the ratio of red to white to blue disk is 3:4:10. Column A is the total number of red and white disks, or $7x$. Column B is the total number of blue disks, or $10x$. Since x is a constant number, Column B is greater than Column A.

9.   **12**   Arithmetic: Ratio and Proportion   *Easy*
Set up a direct proportion using the information given in the question.

$$\frac{3\,\text{apples}}{\text{how many apples}(x)} = \frac{\$0.69}{\$2.76}$$

$$\frac{3}{x} = \frac{69}{276}$$

Cross multiply the equation to get: $(3)(276) = (69)(x)$. Multiply out both sides to get: $828 = 69x$. Finally, divide both sides by 69 to find x: $12 = x$.

10.   **5.6**   Arithmetic: Ratio and Proportion   *Moderate*
Set up a proportion to find the height of the boy: $\frac{15'\ \text{tree}}{8'\ \text{shadow}} = \frac{x'\ \text{boy}}{3'\ \text{shadow}}$. Cross multiply to get: $(15)(3) = (8)(x)$. Multiply out both sides to get: $45 = 8x$. Then divide both sides of the equation by 8 to find the height of the boy: $5.625 = x$. Finally, round the boy's height to the nearest tenth of a foot: the boy is approximately 5.6 feet tall.

Rates

Rates are a special kind of ratio that deal with related quantities that have different units. The relationship between these two different quantities is defined by a rate:

$$\frac{\text{quantity 1 (measured in } x \text{ units)} \times \text{rate (measured in } \frac{y}{x} \text{ units)}}{\text{quantity 2 (measured in } y \text{ units)}}$$

That equation might seem a little complicated, but it will seem much simpler once we give some concrete examples. The most common rate questions on the SAT deal with speed, work, or price, so we'll use those.

Speed

In rate questions dealing with speed, you will usually find the first quantity measured in time, the second measured in distance, and the rate in distance covered per second, minute, or hour, a unit known as speed. If you traveled for 7 hours at 30 miles per hour, then:

$$7 \text{ hours} \times 30 \frac{\text{miles}}{\text{hour}} = 210 \text{ miles}$$

Notice how the units of "hour" canceled out, since the hour in the rate is at the bottom of the fraction, while the unit for the time is a normal number (meaning it could also be written as 7 $^{\text{hours}}/_1$).

Work

In rate questions dealing with work, you will usually find the first quantity measured in time, the second quantity measured in work done, and the rate in measured in work done per time. If you worked for 5 hours and dug 3 ditches an hour, then:

$$5 \text{ hours} \times 3\frac{\text{ditches}}{\text{hour}} = 15 \text{ ditches}$$

Notice how the "hour" units canceled out.

Price

In rate questions dealing with price, you will usually find the first quantity measured in numbers of items, the second measured in price, and the rate in price per item. Let's say you had 6 cucumbers, and you knew that cucumbers cost $.50 each.

$$6 \text{ cucumbers} \times \$0.50 \text{ rate } \frac{\text{price}}{\text{cucumber}} = 3 \text{ price}$$

Notice how the units of "cucumber" canceled out.

Simple Rate Problems

Simple SAT rate problems might test your ability to solve for any one of the three aspects of a rate equation: quantity 1, quantity 2, or the rate. The key to solving any rate problem is determining which values fit into which of the categories. Once you've figured out which information the question is giving you, all you have to do is plug in the numbers and work out the equation.

Take a look at the following example of a simple rate problem:

A car salesmen sells cars at the rate of .3 per hour. How many cars will the salesmen sell in 15 days if he works 8 hours a day?

To answer this question let's first define what we know:

- **Quantity 1:** 15 days, since that is how much time the salesmen puts into his work in this problem.

- **Rate:** .3 cars sold per hour.

- **Quantity 2:** x cars sold?

First off, this problem contains a little trick. Did you notice that the units of time in the rate and input are not the same? The question states that the salesman sells .3 cars per *hour*, while asking you to figure out how many cars he will sell in 15 *days*. We included this trick in this sample problem because it is one that the SAT occasionally likes to play. So when you see rate questions dealing with time, be careful.

Before beginning to solve the problem, you must equalize the time units of hours and days. Since the salesman works 8 hours a day:

$$15 \text{ days} \times \frac{8 \text{ hours}}{\text{day}} = 120 \text{ hours}$$

Now that the units are equalized, the problem can be answered using the rate equation:

$$\text{quantity } 1 \times \text{rate} = \text{quantity } 2$$

so

$$120 \text{ hours} \times \frac{0.3 \text{ cars}}{\text{hour}} = 36 \text{ cars}$$

The salesmen sold 36 cars. Notice that in this problem, the hours unit for quantity 1 cancels with the $^{\text{cars}}/_{\text{hours}}$ unit in the rate, yielding the proper unit of cars. If the units do not work out when you get your answer, you've probably made a mistake.

Complicated Rate Problems

Complicated SAT rate problems can involve more than one rate. Such problems might ask you to compare in some way two different objects moving at a different rate or to determine the distance traveled by an object going at two different rates. There is no way for us to cover every single example of a complicated rate problem in this section. We will provide one good example here, but you should also pay attention to these rate problems when you come upon them in practice tests.

> It took Griselda 5 hours to walk from her house to the supermarket and then back to her house by the same route. While going to the store, she walked at a rate of 3 kilometers per hour. Returning home, she was carrying heavy groceries, so her speed was reduced to 2 kilometers per hour. How many miles was the supermarket from Griselda's house?

We know Griselda traveled at a rate of 3 km/hr on the way to the store and 2 km/hr back from the store. We also know it took her a total of 5 hours to make the trip. Finally, since the distance between the store and Griselda's house remained constant for the trip there and back, we know that she must have spent a different amount of time traveling to the store and back. In fact, we know precisely the ratio between the time she spent walking to the store and the time she spent walking back. Since Griselda walked $^3/_2$ as fast on the way to the store as she did on the way back, we know (because she traveled the same distance on each trip) that she must have spent only $^2/_3$ as much time walking to the store as she spent walking back. Therefore, since we know she spent a total of 5 hours walking to and from the store, we can set up the equation:

$$y + \frac{2}{3}y = 5$$

where y stands for the number of hours Griselda spent walking home from the store. Now, to solve the equation for y

$$y + \frac{2}{3}y = 5$$

$$\frac{3y}{3} + \frac{2y}{3} = 5$$

$$\frac{5y}{3} = 5$$

$$5y = 15$$

We now know Griselda spent 3 hours walking home from the store. If we plug that 3 into the equation for her walk home we get:

$$3 \text{ hr} \times 2\frac{\text{km}}{\text{hr}} = \text{distance between store and house}$$

$$6 \text{ km} = \text{distance between store and house}$$

You can check this answer by looking back at the original question and making sure that the distance of 6 km works out. We know Griselda was walking at the speed of 3 km/hr to the store, and that the distance to the store was 6 km. Therefore, it took her 2 hours to walk to the store. We also know Griselda walked at the speed of 2 km/hr back from the store. Since the distance was 6 kilometers, it must have taken her 3 hours to walk back. In sum, then, it took her 5 hours to walk to and from the store, which fits the question perfectly.

Rate Problems with Variables

The SAT will occasionally ask rate problems using variables rather than numbers. These questions can be difficult because the variables can make it hard for you to figure out what refers to quantity 1, quantity 2, and the rate, and also because they can cause some confusion about what the question is asking you to do.

> A company produces soap at the rate of b bars in h hours. If the company can sell each bar of soap for 3 dollars, how many dollars worth of soap does it produce in x hours?
>
> (A) $3b/h$
> (B) $bx/3h$
> (C) $3h/bx$
> (D) $3bx/h$
> (E) $3bh/x$

Many test-prep books recommend that you try to answer this question by substituting in numbers for the variables and then working out all the answer choices to see which one works. This method will work, but it's slow and laborious, and if you have a good understanding of rates, you would be better off just dealing with the variables directly. We'll cover both methods here.

Dealing Directly with the Variables

The key to answering this question is figuring out what the question wants and then figuring out how to give it what it wants. Looking at this question, we can see that the question is asking for the total value of the soap produced in x hours. Now, since we know that each bar of soap is worth 3 dollars, you know that the total value of soap produced in x hours is equal to:

$$\text{total worth} = 3 \times \text{the number of bars of soap produced}$$

Now all you have to do is figure out how many bars of soap are produced in x hours and multiply that expression by 3. To figure out the expression for soap produced in hours, you just need to identify what all those variables mean. Since the rate equation is:

$$\text{quantity 1} \times \text{rate} = \text{quantity 2}$$

we just have to figure out what variables go where. This is pretty easy. The question explicitly says that the rate is "b bars in h hours," which means that the rate is b/h. Also, since you know you are looking for bars of soap produced, you can substitute the variable for hours worked, x, in for quantity 1.

$$x \times \frac{b}{h} = \text{soap produced}$$

You already know that **total worth** = 3 × **soap produced**, so you just have to substitute to get:

$$\text{total worth} = 3 \times \text{soap produced}$$
$$\text{total worth} = 3 \times \frac{xb}{h}$$
$$\text{total worth} = \frac{3xb}{h}$$

(D) is the right answer. Now, all that looks like a lot of work, but please note that we explained every possible step to teach you how to answer this question. If you were really good at rates, you probably could have done many of those steps in your head and just written this:

$$\text{soap produced} = \frac{bx}{h}$$
$$\text{value of soap} = 3 \times \text{soap produced}$$

and then substituted to get:

$$\text{soap produced} = \frac{3bx}{h}$$

See? Very quick.

Answering By Plugging In

If you aren't so comfortable with rates, your best bet is to substitute numbers in for the variables and then try to work out the question. We'll make $b = 4$, $h = 2$, and $x = 5$. So the question that once read:

> A company produces soap at the rate of b bars in h hours. If the company can sell each bar of soap for 3 dollars, how many dollars worth of soap does it produce in x hours?

now reads as:

> A company produces soap at the rate of 4 bars in 2 hours. If the company can sell each bar of soap for 3 dollars, how many dollars worth of soap does it produce in 5 hours?

With the variables gone, the question immediately becomes much less difficult to comprehend. You can see that the rate is $^4/_2 = 2$ bars per hour. And you can see that to find out the total numbers of bars produced, you just have to multiply the rate by the hours given:

$$\text{Soap produced} = 2 \text{ bars per hour} \times 5 \text{ hours} = 10$$

Then just multiply those 10 bars by the \$3 charged per bar, and you get \$30. To find the answer, you need to substitute the numbers into the answer choices and see which works out to \$30:

- (A) $^{3b}/_h = {}^{3 \times 4}/_2 = {}^{12}/_2 = 6$

- (B) $^{bx}/_{3b} = {}^{4 \times 5}/_{3 \times 2} = {}^{20}/_6 = 3^1/_3$

- (C) $^{3h}/_{bx} = {}^{3 \times 2}/_{4 \times 5} = {}^6/_{20} = {}^3/_{10}$

- (D) $^{3bx}/_h = {}^{3 \times 4 \times 5}/_2 = {}^{60}/_2 = 30$

- (E) $^{3bh}/_x = {}^{3 \times 4 \times 2}/_5 = {}^{24}/_5$

(D) is still the right answer. This method is conceptually easier than the last, but you must do all the math to use this method, which makes it take quite some time.

Rates

1. The distance from Reading to Carmel is 1,720 miles. If an airplane travels at 500 miles per hour, which of the following is the closest approximation of the number of hours required for the airplane to make the trip?

    (A) 3

    (B) $3\frac{1}{2}$

    (C) 4

    (D) $4\frac{1}{2}$

    (E) 5

2. Megan is reading a 225-page book at a rate of 50 pages per hour. If she has been reading for hours, how much longer must she read to finish her book?

    (A) 0.75 hours
    (B) 1 hour
    (C) 1.5 hours
    (D) 2 hours
    (E) 2.5 hours

3. A wheel makes 100 revolutions per minute. If one revolution covers 6 inches on the ground, how many feet does the wheel travel in 5 minutes?

    (A) 100
    (B) 250
    (C) 500
    (D) 600
    (E) 3000

4. Lauren bikes for 2 hours and travels 14.5 miles. She then walks for $3\frac{1}{2}$ hours, covering another 10.25 miles. What is her average speed, in miles per hour (mph), for the entire trip?

    (A) 15 mph
    (B) 12 mph
    (C) 8.5 mph
    (D) 5 mph
    (E) 4.5 mph

5.

James walks twice as fast as Murphy.

Column A	Column B
The time it takes James to walk from home to school.	The time it takes Murphy to walk from home to school.

Answers

1. **(B)** Arithmetic: Rates *Easy*

The formula to use is (Rate)(Time) = Distance: (500)(time) = 1720. Divide both sides of the equation by 500 to find how long it takes the airplane to fly the distance: Time = 3.44. The answer choice that is the best approximation of this time is $3\frac{1}{2}$, or 3.5.

2. **(B)** Arithmetic: Rates *Easy*

To figure out the total amount of time Megan needs to finish the book, rewrite the standard rate formula as: $\frac{\text{number of pages}}{\text{pages per hour}}$ = number of hours. Plug the numbers given in the question into this formula: it would take her $\frac{225}{50}$ = 4.5 hours to read the whole book. Subtract the number of hours she has already spent reading from the total number of hours she needs to read the whole book: 4.5 – 3.5 = 1 hour more to finish the book.

3. **(B)** Arithmetic: Rates *Moderate*

In 1 revolution, the wheel rolls 6 inches, or 0.5 feet. To find out how far the wheel rolls after completing 100 revolutions, multiply 100 by 0.5 feet: (100)(0.5) = 50 feet. To find out how far the wheel rolls in 5 minutes, multiply 50 feet by 5 (since the wheel makes 100 revolutions per minute): 5(50) = 250 feet.

4. **(E)** Arithmetic: Rates *Difficult*

Use the following formula to find Lauren's average speed:

$$\text{Average speed} = \frac{\text{Total Distance}}{\text{Total Time}}$$

The total distance is the number of miles Lauren biked plus the number of miles she walked. The total time is the number of hours Lauren biked plus the number of hours Lauren walked:

$$\text{Average Speed} = \frac{14.5 + 10.25}{2 + 3.5} = \frac{24.75}{5.5} = 4.5$$

5. **(D)** Arithmetic: Rates *Moderate*

The answer cannot be determined, because you do not know how far James and Murphy need to walk. Although James walks twice as fast as Murphy, James may need to walk more than twice as far.

Arithmetic Mean, Median, and Mode

The arithmetic mean, median, and mode are all different ways to describe a group or set of numbers. The three concepts are related, and some questions on the SAT will test your knowledge of two or even three of them in conjunction. Here, we will cover each individually and then look at how they overlap.

Arithmetic Mean, a.k.a Average

The arithmetic mean, which also goes by the names *average* and *mean,* is the most important and most commonly tested of these three mathematical concepts. The basic rules of finding an average are not very complicated. To find an average of a set of n numbers, you need to find the sum of all the numbers and divide that sum by n.

For example, the average of the set 9, 8, 13, 10 is equal to the sum of those four numbers divided by 4:

$$\frac{9 + 8 + 13 + 10}{4} = \frac{40}{4} = 10$$

Occasionally, the SAT will test your knowledge of averages in a straightforward manner, giving you a bunch of numbers and asking you to find their average. More often, the SAT will find some roundabout way to test your knowledge of averages. The SAT might give you three numbers of a four-number set, the average of that set, and then ask you to find the fourth number in the set:

> If the average of four numbers is 22, and three of the numbers are 7, 11, and 18, then what is the fourth number?

There are two ways to solve this type of problem, and both are fairly simple. To use the first method, you have to realize that if you know the average of a group and also know how many numbers are in the group, you can calculate the sum of the numbers in the group. In the question asked above, you know that the average of the numbers is 22 and that there are four numbers. The four numbers, when added together, must equal $4 \times 22 = 88$. From the information given in the problem and our own calculations, we know three of the four numbers in the set, and the total sum of the numbers in the set:

$$7 + 11 + 18 + \text{unknown number} = 88$$

Solving for the unknown number is easy. All you have to do is subtract the sum of 7, 11, and 18 from 88: $x = 88 - (7 + 11 + 18) = (88 - 36) = 52$.

All average problems on the SAT cover these, and basically only these, fundamental points. Difficult problems simply cover them in a trickier manner.

For example:

> The average of a set of 7 numbers is 54. The average of three of those seven numbers is 38.
> What is the average of the other four numbers?

This question seems really tough, since it keeps splitting apart this theoretical set of seven numbers and you have no idea what the numbers in the set are. Often, when students can't say exactly what numbers are in a set, they panic. But for this problem you don't have to know the exact numbers in the set. All you have to know is how averages work. So let's solve the problem.

There are 7 numbers in the entire set and the average of those numbers is 54. The sum of the seven numbers in the set is therefore: $7 \times 54 = 378$. Now, as the problem states, if we take three particular numbers from the set, their average is 38. We can calculate that the the sum of those three numbers is: $3 \times 38 = 114$. Suddenly, we can calculate the sum of the four remaining numbers, since that value must be the total sum of the set of seven minus the sum of the mini-set of three, $378 - 114 = 264$. Now, since we know the total sum of the four numbers, to get the average of those numbers, all we have to do is divide that by 4: $264 \div 4 = 66$.

Median

The median is the number whose value is in the middle of the numbers in a particular set. Take the set: $\{6, 19, 3, 11, 7\}$. If we arrange the numbers in order of value, we get:

$$\{3, 6, 7, 11, 19\}$$

When we list the numbers in this order, it becomes clear that the middle number in this group is 7, making 7 the median.

The set we just looked at contained an odd number of items, but in a set with an even number of items it's impossible to isolate a single number as the median. Let's add one number to the set from the previous example:

$$\{3, 6, 7, 11, 19. 20\}$$

In this case, we find the median by taking the two most middle numbers and finding their average. The two middle numbers in this set are 7 and 11, so the median of the set is $(7+11)/2 = 9$.

Mean and Median on the SAT

As we said earlier, some SAT questions might test your knowledge of mean and median in conjunction. For example, a question might show you five sets and ask you to pick the set in which the average is greater than the median. For these questions, there are a few things you should know:

1. The median and mean of a set do not have to be equal. In fact, they very seldom will be equal. The median might be larger or smaller than the mean in any set with more than two numbers. For example, take a set of three numbers where the mean is 10. The numbers could be {9, 10, 11}, which means the median and mean would be equal. The set could be {7, 8, 15}, which means the mean is larger than the median. Finally, the set could be {1, 14, 15}, and the median would be larger than the mean.

2. If you have a set of consecutive numbers, then the median and the mean will always be equal. This rule is true no matter how many numbers are in the set. In a set with five consecutive numbers, such as {7, 8, 9, 10, 11}, both mean and median are 9. In a set with four consecutive numbers, such as {7, 8, 9, 10}, both mean and median are 8.5. This rule comes up in questions fairly regularly on the SAT.

Mode

The mode is the number within a set that appears most frequently. In the set {10, 11, 13, 11, 20}, the mode is 11 since it appears twice and all the others appear just once. In a set where more than one number appears at the same highest frequency, there can be more than one mode: the set {2, 2, 3, 4, 4} has modes of 2 and 4. In a set such as {1, 2, 3, 4, 5}, where all of the numbers appear an equal number of times, there is no mode.

Mean, Median, and Mode

1. For a set of numbers {4, 6, 7, 8, 10}, what is the result when the median of the set is subtracted from the average?

   (A) −1
   (B) 0
   (C) 1
   (D) 2
   (E) 3

2. For the set of numbers {2, 3, 4, 4, 6, 7, 12}, which of the following must be true?

   I.   The median = the mode
   II.   The average is greater than the median
   III. The average is less than the mode

   (A) I, II, and III
   (B) I only
   (C) I and II only
   (D) II and III only
   (E) None of the above

3.   If the average of x, y, and z is 27, and the average of x and y is 22, what is the value of z?

    (A)   5
    (B)   22
    (C)   27
    (D)   37
    (E)   44

4.   The average weight of 3 boys is 130 pounds. If no boy weighs less than 90 pounds, what is the maximum that any one boy could weigh?

    (A)   200 pounds
    (B)   205 pounds
    (C)   210 pounds
    (D)   215 pounds
    (E)   220 pounds

5.

Let P be the set of even integers from 10 to 22, inclusive.

Column A	Column B
The average of the elements of P	The median of the elements of P

6.   Oliver's average on four tests is 80. What grade must he get on the fifth test to raise his average to 82?

7.   For a set of numbers $\{a, a, a, b, c\}$, the average is equal to five times the mode. If $b + c = 66$, what is the value of a?

Answers

1.   **(B)**   Arithmetic: Mean, Median, and Mode   *Easy*
First calculate the average of the set by summing the elements of the set and dividing the sum by the number of elements: $\dfrac{4+6+7+8+10}{5} = \dfrac{35}{5} = 7$. The median is the middle number of a set; in this case, the median is 7. Subtract the median from the average: $7 - 7 = 0$.

2.   **(C)**   Arithmetic: Mean, Median, and Mode   *Moderate*
First calculate the average of the set of numbers: $\dfrac{2+3+4+4+6+7+12}{7} = \dfrac{38}{7} = 5.4$. The median of this set is the middle number: 4. The mode is the number that appears most often in the set; in this case, the mode is also 4. Since the median is equal to the mode, option I is true. Since the average is greater than the median, option II is also true. Since

the average is larger than the mode, option III is false. The correct answer is (C), which says that options I and II only are true.

3. **(D)** Arithmetic: Mean, Median, and Mode   *Moderate*
The average of x, y, and z is 27, so the sum of x, y, and z is 3(27) = 81. The average of x and y is 22, so the sum of x and y is 2(22) = 44. Subtract 44 from 81 to find the value of z: $z = 81 - 44 = 37$.

4. **(C)** Arithmetic: Mean, Median, and Mode   *Difficult*
If the average weight of 3 boys is 130 pounds, the sum of the weights of the 3 boys is 3(130) = 390. If you want to find out the maximum weight of one boy, you need to make the other boys' weights as low as possible. According to this question, the minimum weight of any of the boys is 90 pounds. If two of the boys weigh 90 pounds, you can find the weight of the third boy by subtracting the two boys' weights from the total weight of 390: 390 – 90 – 90 = 210.

5. **(C)** Arithmetic: Mean, Median, and Mode   *Easy*
Set P consists of the following integers: {10, 12, 14, 16, 18, 20, 22}. Calculate the average of the integers in the set: $\frac{10+12+14+16+18+20+22}{7} = \frac{112}{7} = 16$. The median, or the value in the exact middle of a set's number, is 16 for Set P. Since the average and the median of this set are the same, the columns are equal in value, and the correct answer is (C).

6. **90** Arithmetic: Mean, Median, and Mode   *Moderate*
If Oliver has an average of 82 after taking 5 tests, then his total score on all five tests is equal to the number of tests he's taken multiplied by his average score, or 5(82) = 410. The question says that Oliver has an average of 80 after 4 tests. His total score on those four tests is 4(80) = 320. In order to raise his average score to 82, he needs to have a total score of 410; in other words, he needs to score 410 – 320 = 90 points on the fifth test.

7. **3** Arithmetic: Mean, Median, and Mode   *Difficult*
The mode is the value that appears most often in a set. The mode of the set given in the question is a. The question says that the average of the set is five times the mode, so you know the average of the set is $5a$. Since the average is also equal to the sum of the elements in the set divided by the number of elements in the set, you can set up the fol-

lowing equation: $5a = \dfrac{a + a + a + b + c}{5}$. The question tells you that $b + c = 66$, so you can

substitute 66 into the equation to get: $5a = \dfrac{3a + 66}{5}$. When you cross multiply, you end

up with: $25a = 3a + 66$. Subtract $3a$ from both sides of the equation to get: $22a = 66$.

Divide by 22 to solve the problem: $a = 3$.

Exponents

Exponents are a shorthand method of describing how many times a particular number is being multiplied by itself. To write $3 \times 3 \times 3 \times 3 \times 3$ in exponent form, we would simply count out how many 3s were being multiplied together (in this case five), and then write 3^5. In written or verbal form, 3^5 is stated as: "three to the fifth power."

There are a number of exponent terms that are important to know. The SAT will not directly test you on this knowledge, but you should know these terms if you are going to discuss or learn about exponents.

- **Base.** The base refers to the 3 in 3^5. In other words, the base is the number that is being multiplied by itself, however many times specified by the exponent.

- **Exponent.** The exponent is the 5 in 3^5. In other words, the exponent tells how many times the base is to be multiplied with itself.

- **Squared.** Saying that a number is squared is a common code word to say that it has been raised to the second power, i.e., that it has an exponent of 2. In the expression 6^2, 6 has been squared.

- **Cubed.** Saying that a number is cubed is a common code word to say that it has been raised to the third power, i.e., that it has an exponent of 3. In the expression 4^3, 4 has been cubed.

When you take the SAT, you should already know the squares of numbers 1 through about 15. Memorizing this little chart can save you a lot of time on the test.

Number	Square	Number	Square
1	1	9	81
2	4	10	100
3	9	11	121
4	16	12	144
5	25	13	169
6	36	14	196
7	49	15	225
8	64		

You should also know that 2 cubed (2^3) = 8 and that 3^3 = 27, and—just to be safe—that 4^3 = 64 and 5^3 = 125.

Adding and Subtracting Numbers with Exponents

Actually, you can't add or subtract numbers with exponents. Instead, you have to work out each exponent to find its value and then add the two numbers. For example, to add $3^3 + 4^2$, you must work out the exponents to get $(3 \times 3 \times 3) + (4 \times 4)$ and then calculate 27 + 16 = 43. (You probably don't need to write out the whole first step when doing a problem like this one. We included it just to be complete.) Often, you can work out exponents on your calculator, so figure out how to use your calculator's exponent functions before the test. It can save you time and increase your accuracy.

Multiply and Dividing Numbers with Exponents

To multiply two base exponential numbers that have the same base, all you have to do is add the exponents together:

$$3^6 \times 3^2 = 3^{(6+2)} = 3^8$$

To divide two same-base exponential numbers, just subtract the exponents.

$$\frac{3^6}{3^2} = 3^{(6-2)} = 3^4$$

If you need to multiply or divide two exponential numbers that do not have the same base or exponent, you'll just have to do your work the old-fashioned way: multiply the exponential numbers out and multiply or divide them accordingly.

Raising an Exponent to an Exponent

Occasionally you might see an exponent raised to another exponent, as seen in the following format $(3^2)^4$. In such cases, multiply the exponents:

$$(3^2)^4 = 3^{(2 \times 4)} = 3^8$$

Exponents and Fractions

To raise a fraction to an exponent, raise both the numerator and denominator to that exponent:

$$\left(\frac{1}{3}\right)^3 = \frac{1}{27}$$

Exponents and Negative Numbers

When you multiply a negative number by a negative number, you get a positive number, and when you multiply a negative number by a positive number, you get a negative number. These rules affect how negative numbers function in reference to exponents.

- **A negative number raised to an even-number exponent results in a positive number.** For example $(-2)^4 = 16$. To see why this is so, let's break down the example. $(-2)^4$ means $(-2) \times (-2) \times (-2) \times (-2)$. When you multiply the first two −2s together, you get positive 4 because you are multiplying two negative numbers. Then when you multiply the (+4) by the next (−2), you get (−8), since you are multiplying a positive number by a negative number. Finally, you multiply the (−8) by the last (−2) and get (+16), since you're once again multiplying two negative numbers.

- **A negative number raised to an odd power results in a negative number.** To prove this to yourself all you have to do is look at the example above and stop the process at (−8), which equals $(-2)^3$.

Square Roots

The square root of a number is the number that, when squared (multiplied by itself), is equal to the given number. For example, the square root of 16 is 4, because $4^2 = 4 \times 4 = 16$. A perfect square is a number whose square root is an integer.

The sign denoting a square root is $\sqrt{}$. To use the previous example, $\sqrt{16} = 4$. As with exponents, you need to know how to multiply and divide square roots.

Multiplication and Square Roots

$$\sqrt{4}\sqrt{6} = \sqrt{24}$$

As the example shows, to multiply two square roots, you should multiply the numbers within each individual square root and place the product under a single square root.

This rule also works in reverse, so you can take a number within a $\sqrt{}$ and factor it into perfect squares.

$$\sqrt{48} = \sqrt{16}\sqrt{3} = 4\sqrt{3}$$

Notice in this example that once we separated out 16 from 48, we could change the $\sqrt{16}$ into 4. This skill is important for the SAT. When dealing with square roots, you may get an answer that looks quite different from any of the answer choices. In such situations, you probably have just neglected to reduce the number within the square-root sign.

Division and Square Roots

Just as when you multiply square roots, when you divide them, you can divide the numbers and place them under a single square root.

$$\frac{\sqrt{20}}{\sqrt{16}} = \sqrt{\frac{20}{16}} = \sqrt{\frac{5}{4}}$$

Fractions and Square Roots

To find the square root of a fraction, take the square root of both the numerator and the denominator. For example, $\sqrt{1/16} = 1/4$. In some instances, either the numerator or denominator might not be a perfect square. In these instances, you won't be able to get rid of the $\sqrt{}$ sign. For example, $\sqrt{4/17} = 2/\sqrt{17}$.

Exponents and Square Roots

1. Solve for x if $x^4 = 81$.

    (A) 1
    (B) 2
    (C) 3
    (D) 4
    (E) 5

2. If $\sqrt{x} + \sqrt{y} = 7$, then $(x, y) =$

    (A) $(3, 4)$
    (B) $(2, 5)$
    (C) $(1, 7)$
    (D) $(9, 16)$
    (E) $(1, 49)$

3. $3^x \cdot 3^y = 3^w$. Express w in terms of x and y.

    (A) $x + y$
    (B) xy
    (C) $3x + 3y$
    (D) $3xy$
    (E) $x + 3y$

4. Express $\sqrt{32x^2 y^2}$ in its simplest form.

    (A) $5xy$

    (B) $8xy$

    (C) $2xy\sqrt{3}$

    (D) $3xy\sqrt{2}$

    (E) $4xy\sqrt{2}$

5. If 4^m divided by 4^n equals 16, express m in terms of n.

    (A) $n - 2$
    (B) $n + 2$
    (C) $n - 4$
    (D) $n + 4$
    (E) $2n$

6.

$$x > 1$$

Column A	Column B
$\dfrac{\sqrt{x+1}}{\sqrt{x}}$	1

7.

$$0 < x < 1$$

Column A	Column B
x	$\sqrt{x}$

8. If $x = \sqrt{30}$, what is the value of $\dfrac{\sqrt{4nx^2 + n}}{\sqrt{n}}$?

Answers

1.   **(C)**   Arithmetic: Exponents and Square Roots   *Easy*
If $x^4 = 81$, you can solve for x by raising each side of the equation to the $\frac{1}{4}$ power.

$$(x^4)^{\frac{1}{4}} = 81^{\frac{1}{4}}$$
$$x = 3$$

2.   **(D)**   Arithmetic: Exponents and Square Roots   *Easy*
An easy way to solve this problem is to plug each of the answer choices into the equation until you find an (x, y) pair that produces the answer 7.

(A) $\sqrt{3} + \sqrt{4} = 1.7 + 2 = 3.7$

(B) $\sqrt{2} + \sqrt{5} = 1.4 + 2.2 = 3.6$

(C) $\sqrt{1} + \sqrt{7} = 1 + 2.6 = 3.6$

(D) $\sqrt{9} + \sqrt{16} = 3 + 4 = 7$

(E) $\sqrt{1} + \sqrt{49} = 1 + 7 = 8$

Choice (D) is the correct answer.

3.   **(A)**   Arithmetic: Exponents and Square Roots   *Moderate*
The rules of exponents state that $3^x \cdot 3^y = 3^{x+y}$. Since the question tells you that $3^x \cdot 3^y = 3^w$, you know that $w = x + y$.

4.   **(E)**   Arithmetic: Exponents and Square Roots   *Moderate*
To simplify this radical, you need to express it as the product of several simpler radicals. Since $32 = 16 \cdot 2$, you can rewrite the original radical as: $\sqrt{32x^2 y^2} = \sqrt{16}\sqrt{2}\sqrt{x^2}\sqrt{y^2}$. Since $\sqrt{16} = 4$, $\sqrt{x^2} = x$, and $\sqrt{y^2} = y$, you can simplify the radical to $\sqrt{32x^2 y^2} = 4xy\sqrt{2}$.

5.   **(B)**   Arithmetic: Exponents and Square Roots   *Difficult*
The question says that $\frac{4^m}{4^n} = 16$. The trick to solving this problem is recognizing that 16 $= 4^2$, which allows you to rewrite the equation as $\frac{4^m}{4^n} = 4^2$. According to the rules of exponents, $\frac{4^m}{4^n} = 4^{m-n}$; therefore, $m - n = 2$. If you add n to both sides of the equation, you get $m = n + 2$.

6. **(A)** Arithmetic: Exponents and Square Roots *Easy*
Rewrite Column A so the expression is under one radical sign: $\frac{\sqrt{x+1}}{\sqrt{x}} = \sqrt{\frac{x+1}{x}}$. Since x > 1, $\frac{x+1}{x}$ is greater than 1. The square root of a value greater than 1 is also greater than 1; therefore, Column A, $\frac{\sqrt{x+1}}{\sqrt{x}}$, is greater than Column B, 1.

7. **(B)** Arithmetic: Exponents and Square Roots *Moderate*
If $0 < x < 1$, then x is a decimal. Since the square root of a decimal value is larger than its original value, $\sqrt{x}$ is larger than x, and Column B is greater than Column A.

8. **11** Arithmetic: Exponents and Square Roots *Difficult*

Rewrite under one radical sign: $\frac{\sqrt{4nx^2+n}}{\sqrt{n}} = \sqrt{\frac{4nx^2+n}{n}}$. Next, factor out the n in the numerator $\sqrt{\frac{n(4x^2+1)}{n}}$; the expression simplifies to $\sqrt{(4x^2+1)}$. If $x = \sqrt{30}$, then $x^2 = 30$, and $\sqrt{4x^2+1} = \sqrt{4(30)+1} = \sqrt{121} = 11$.

Probability

Usually, about two questions on each SAT cover the topic of probability. To begin to deal with these questions you first have to understand what probability is:

$$\frac{\text{chance of a particular outcome}}{\text{total number of possible outcomes}}$$

For example, let's say you're on a game show and are shown three doors. Behind one door there is a prize while behind the other two doors are big piles of nothing. The probability that you will choose the door with the prize is ⅓, because out of the three possibilities, there is one chance that you will pick the correct door.

How about a more detailed example?

Joe has 3 green marbles, 2 red marbles, and 5 blue marbles, and if all the marbles are dropped into a dark bag, what is the probability that Joe will pick out a green marble?

There are 3 ways for Joe to pick a green marble (since there are 3 different green marbles), but there are 10 total possible outcomes (one for each marble in the bag). Therefore the probability of picking a green marble is

$$\text{Probability} = \frac{\text{particular outcomes}}{\text{total outcomes}}$$
$$= \frac{\text{green marbles}}{\text{total marbles}}$$
$$= \frac{3}{10}$$

When you calculate probability, always be careful to divide by the total number of chances. In the last example, you may have been tempted to leave out the three chances of picking a green marble from the total possibilities, yielding the incorrect equation $P = \frac{3}{7}$.

Backward Probability

The SAT might also ask you a "backward" probability question. For example, if you have a bag holding twenty marbles, and you have a $\frac{1}{5}$ chance of picking a blue marble, how many blue marbles are in the bag? All you have to do is set up the proper equation, following the model of $P = \frac{m}{n}$:

$$\frac{1}{5} = \frac{x}{20}$$

and x is the variable denoting the number of blue marbles. Cross-multiplying through the equation, you get $5x = 20$, , which reduces to $x = 4$.

Combinations

Combination questions are more rarely found on the SAT than probability questions. Still, they do occasionally show up, so we cover them here. You can think of combination problems as half-probability problems. These questions give you a situation and ask you to figure out the total number of outcomes that can arise from that situation. Whereas for probability questions you have to figure out the likelihood of one outcome in comparison to the total outcomes, in combination problems you only have to figure out the total number of outcomes. For example:

> Imagine a man (or, if you want, a woman). To make things interesting, let's make him a naked man who wants to put on a pair of pants and a shirt. He has 6 pairs of pants and 3 shirts. How many different outfits does he have to choose from?

To answer this question you have to figure out how many different combinations of shirts and pants the man can make. To do this, multiply the total number of object 1 (6 pants) by the total number of object 2 (3 shirts). Total outfits = 3×6 = 18.

If the man also had 4 hats, to calculate the total number of outfits he could make you would multiply $3 \times 6 \times 4 = 72$ total outfits—that's over two months of outfits!

Probability

1. If two standard dice, each numbered 1 through 6, are rolled, what is the probability that the outcome of the roll will be two even numbers?

    (A) $\dfrac{1}{2}$

    (B) $\dfrac{1}{3}$

    (C) $\dfrac{1}{4}$

    (D) $\dfrac{1}{9}$

    (E) $\dfrac{1}{12}$

2. A box contains red marbles and blue marbles. The probability of randomly choosing a red marble is $\dfrac{2}{3}$. If 12 blue marbles are added to the box, the probability of choosing a blue marble becomes $\dfrac{1}{2}$. How many marbles were in the box before the extra 12 blue marbles were added?

    (A)   42
    (B)   36
    (C)   30
    (D)   24
    (E)   18

3. Each house number on Main Street has 4 digits. All of the houses look identical. Tim wants to visit his friend, and he remembers the first 2 digits of his friend's address. However, he has forgotten the last 2 digits, but he does remember that his friend's house number is odd. If he chooses a house based on what he knows about the address, what is the probability that Tim will choose his friend's house?

    (A) $\dfrac{1}{5}$

    (B) $\dfrac{1}{14}$

    (C) $\dfrac{1}{15}$

    (D) $\dfrac{1}{45}$

    (E) $\dfrac{1}{50}$

4.   A bowl contains red, green, and white balls. The probability of choosing a red ball is $\frac{1}{3}$. There are 5 more green balls than red balls, and there are 12 white balls total. What is the probability of choosing a white ball?

(A) $\frac{4}{17}$

(B) $\frac{22}{51}$

(C) $\frac{7}{12}$

(D) $\frac{12}{17}$

(E) $\frac{17}{22}$

5.   A dish contains both chocolate and vanilla candy. There are 22 pieces of candy total, and 12 of them are chocolate. What is the probability of choosing a piece of vanilla candy from the dish?

Answers

1.   **(C)**   Arithmetic: Probability   *Moderate*

There are six possible outcomes when you roll a die: {1, 2, 3, 4, 5, 6}. Of these outcomes, three are even numbers, so the probability of getting an even number on a single roll is $\frac{3}{6}$. Since you have two dice and you want to know the probability of rolling two even numbers, you should multiply the probability of rolling an even number on a single roll by itself: $\frac{3}{6} \times \frac{3}{6} = \frac{9}{36} = \frac{1}{4}$.

2.   **(B)**   Arithmetic: Probability   *Difficult*

You need to set up two equations in order to answer this question. The first equation should describe the probability of picking a red marble out of the box before the 12 blue marbles are added: $P(red) = \frac{r}{r+b} = \frac{2}{3}$, where r is the number of red marbles and b is the number of blue marbles. The second equation should describe the probability of picking a blue marble after the 12 blue marbles are added: $P(blue) = \frac{b+12}{r+b+12} = \frac{1}{2}$. Cross multiply the first equation to get:

$$2(r+b) = 3r$$

$$2r + 2b = 3r$$

$$2b = r$$

Now solve for the red marbles in the second equation. Cross multiply to get:

$$r + b + 12 = 2(b + 12)$$

$$r + b + 12 = 2b + 24$$

$$r = b + 12$$

Since you have two equations equal to r, you can set $2b$ equal to $b + 12$:

$$2b = b + 12$$

$$b = 12$$

If you plug $b = 12$ into $r = 2b$, you get $r = 24$. Since there were 12 blue marbles and 24 red marbles in the box before the extra 12 blue marbles were added, the original number of marbles in the box was 36.

3. **(E)** Arithmetic: Probability   *Difficult*

You can ignore the first two digits of the address when solving this problem since Tim remembers what they are. The digits that matter are the last two. The first of these two digits is one of 10 possible numbers: {0, 1, 2, 3, 4, 5, 6, 7, 8, 9}. The second of these digits is one of 5 possible numbers, since Tim remembers that the number is odd: {1, 3, 5, 7, 9}. Multiply 10 by 5 to figure out how many combinations of the last two digits there are: 10(5) = 50 possible combinations. Of these combinations, only one is the correct address, so the probability that Tim will pick the correct address is $\frac{1}{50}$.

4. **(A)** Arithmetic: Probability   *Difficult*

The probability of choosing a red ball from the bowl is equal to the number of red balls divided by the total number of balls, so you can set up the following equation: $P(red) = \frac{r}{r + w + g} = \frac{1}{3}$, where r is equal to the number of red balls, w the number of white balls, and g the number of green balls. The question tells you that there are five more green balls than red balls (or $g = r + 5$), and that there are twelve white balls total (or $w = 12$). Substitute these expressions into the probability equation to get: $\frac{1}{3} = \frac{r}{r + r + 5 + 12}$. If you multiply out this equation, you get:

$$r + r + 5 + 12 = 3r$$

$$2r + 17 = 3r$$

$$17 = r$$

You now know that there are 12 white balls and 17 red balls; you just need to figure out how many balls there are total. Since there are 5 more green balls than red balls, you know there are 22 green balls total. The total number of balls in the bowl is $17 + 22 + 12 = 51$. The probability of picking a white ball from the bowl is equal to the number of white balls divided by the total number of balls: $P(white) = \frac{12}{51} = \frac{4}{17}$.

5.   **5/11** Arithmetic: Probability   *Easy*
Since you know that there are 22 pieces of candy in the bowl and that 12 of these pieces are chocolate, you can figure out the number of vanilla pieces by subtracting 12 from 22: $22 - 12 = 10$ pieces of vanilla candy. The probability of choosing a piece of vanilla candy from the bowl is equal to the number of vanilla pieces divided by the number of total pieces of candy: $P(vanilla) = \frac{10}{22} = \frac{5}{11}$.

Series

A series is a sequence of numbers that proceed one after another according to some pattern. Usually the SAT will give you a few numbers in a series and ask you to specify what number should come next. For example,

$$-1, 2, -4, 8, -16$$

is a series. Can you figure out which number should come after the −16? Well, in this series, each number is multiplied by −2 to yield the next number. Therefore, 32 is the number in the series after −16. These types of questions ask you to be able to recognize patterns and then apply them. Learning to recognize the patterns is key. When you look at a pattern, try to think whether it is changing by addition or subtraction, multiplication or division, or by exponents. There isn't one tried-and-true way to find a pattern. Just think critically, and use your intuition and trial and error.

Series Problems that Seem Harder than They Are

Sometimes the SAT might show you a series and ask you to identify the 50th number in the series or to calculate the sum of the first 24 numbers in the series. These questions seem difficult and time-consuming, so many students skip them. Other students write out the series and do the math, which does take a bit of time. Whenever you see such a question, you should assume that there is some shortcut to the answer. For example, on a question that asks for the 50th term in the series, see if the series begins to repeat itself. Take the following problem:

> The first two numbers of a series are 1 and 2. All the numbers in the series after that are produced by subtracting from the previous term the term before that. What is the fiftieth term in the sequence?

To answer this question, start writing out the sequence

$$1, 2, 1, -1, -2, -1, 1, 2, 1, \ldots$$

By this time you should see that the pattern has begun to repeat itself: the 1st term is the same as the 7th, the 2nd is the same as the 8th . . . Since you know the sequence repeats, you can extrapolate into the future. If the 1st term is the same as the 7th, it will also be the same as the 14th, 21st, 28th, 35th, 42nd, and 49th. This repetion means that the second term must be equal to the 50th term, so the answer is 2.

If you were given the same question but asked to figure out the sum of the first 35 terms, you would do basically the same thing. Once you discovered that the sequence repeats every seven terms, you would know that the value of the first 24 terms is equal to 4 × the sum of the first six terms, since terms 1–6, 7–12, 13–18, and 19–24 will all be identical. The sum of the first 6 terms is:

$$1 + 2 + 1 + (-1) + (-2) + (-1) = 0$$

So the sum of the first 24 terms is equal to 0.

Series

1.   What is the fifth term in the series 5, 1, –3, –7, …?

    (A)   –3
    (B)   –6
    (C)   –8
    (D)   –11
    (E)   –12

2. The first term in a series is 1, and the second term is 2. Each successive term is created by adding the two previous terms together. What is the tenth term in the series?

   (A) 55
   (B) 89
   (C) 90
   (D) 143
   (E) 144

3. Let *A* represent the sum of all integers from 1 to 100, inclusive. Let *B* represent the sum of all integers from 6 to 95, inclusive. What is the value of *A* – *B*?

   (A) 201
   (B) 205
   (C) 501
   (D) 505
   (E) 600

4.

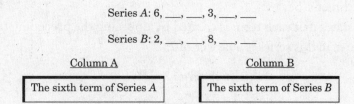

Series *A*: 6, ___, ___, 3, ___, ___

Series *B*: 2, ___, ___, 8, ___, ___

Column A	Column B
The sixth term of Series *A*	The sixth term of Series *B*

5.

2, 4, 8, 16, ...

In the series above, each term is created by doubling the previous term. What is the tenth term in the series?

Answers

1. **(D)** Arithmetic: Series   *Easy*
Each term in this series is created by subtracting 4 from the previous term. To create the fifth term, you need to subtract 4 from the fourth term: –7 – 4 = –11.

2. **(B)** Arithmetic: Series   *Moderate*
The question says that starting with the third term, each term is created by adding together the two previous terms. Since the first term is 1 and the second term is 2, the third term in this series is 1 + 2 = 3. To create the fourth term, add the second and third terms together: 2 + 3 = 5. Continue this process until you get to the tenth term. The series up to the tenth term is: {1, 2, 3 (1 + 3), 5 (2 + 3), 8 (3 + 5), 13 (5 + 8), 21 (8 + 13), 34 (13 + 21), 55 (21 + 34), 89 (34 + 55)}.

3.   **(D)** Arithmetic: Series   *Difficult*

Notice the similarity between the integers you are adding to create A and the integers you are adding to create B. B includes all of the integers in A except $\{1, 2, 3, 4, 5\}$ and $\{96, 97, 98, 99, 100\}$. To find the difference between A and B, all you need to do is add $1 + 2 + 3 + 4 + 5 + 96 + 97 + 98 + 99 + 100$, since all of the other numbers will cancel each other out when sum B is subtracted from sum A. The difference between A and B is 505.

4.   **(D)** Arithmetic: Series   *Difficult*

The question does not give you enough information to complete Series A or Series B. The blanks in each series could be filled in with any number, so you cannot determine the relationship between Columns A and B based on the information given in the question.

5.   **1024** Arithmetic: Series   *Easy*

The question states that each term is created by doubling the preceding term. In other words, each term in this series is a power of 2:

$$1^{\text{st}} \text{ term: } 2 = 2^1$$

$$2^{\text{nd}} \text{ term: } 4 = 2^2$$

$$3^{\text{rd}} \text{ term: } 8 = 2^3$$

$$4^{\text{th}} \text{ term: } 16 = 2^4$$

Based on this pattern, you should be able to see that the tenth term in this series is $2^{10} =$ 1024.

Sets

Sets are discrete groups of items. For example, the number of people who received a B in Mr. Japlonski's chemistry class can be considered a set. A set contains only those things that can fit its definitions. If a student got an A in Mr. Japlonski's class, he cannot be in the set of students who got Bs. If you have a set that is defined as $(1, 2, \sqrt{7})$, then the only things that can be in that set are $(1, 2, \sqrt{7})$. Really, on the SAT, sets don't get much more complicated than that.

The One Exception

That is, set questions don't get more complicated except for one specific type of question. In this question, the SAT will describe two sets and a few people who fit into both sets. Then it will ask how many total people are in the two sets. For example:

Of the lions at the zoo, 13 eat zebra meat, 11 eat giraffe meat, and 7 eat both. How many total lions are there in the zoo?

When you read it, this question just feels like it's going to be very hard. A lot of students will therefore not even try to answer it. So what does that mean to you? It's a chance for you to gain points in comparison to other students. Luckily, this type of question is actually quite simple to answer, as long as you know and use the following formula:

Total = number in set 1 + number in set 2 – number common to set 1 and 2

To answer the question about the lions, write:

Total lions = 13 zebra eaters + 11 giraffe eaters – 7 eaters of both
Total lions = 17

Once you know the formula, all you have to do is figure out which numbers in the word problem define set 1, which define set 2, and which define the overlap set. After that, you just have to plug in the numbers and do some simple addition and subtraction.

Sets

1. Set P: $\{-1, 0, 1, 2, 3\}$ Set Q: $\{-3, -2, -1, 0, 1\}$ How many terms are common to Set P and Set Q?

    (A) 1
    (B) 2
    (C) 3
    (D) 4
    (E) 5

2. Set A is the set of all positive integers of the form $2n + 1$, where $0 \le n \le 10$. What is the sum of the 2 largest elements of Set A?

    (A) 40
    (B) 41
    (C) 42
    (D) 43
    (E) 44

3.

Set Q: $\{3, 4, 5\}$

Column A	Column B
The product of the elements of Set Q	12

4.

$$\text{Set } P: \{1, 2, 3, 4, 5, 6, 7, 8, 9, 10, 11, 12\}$$

$$\text{Set } Q: \{-5, -4, -3, -2, -1, 0, 1, 2\}$$

x is an element of Set P.

y is an element of Set Q.

Column A	Column B
The largest value of $x - y$	17

Answers

1. **(C)** Arithmetic: Sets   *Easy*
Three of the terms in Set P are also in Set Q.

2. **(A)** Arithmetic: Sets   *Difficult*
Since the question asks you to find the sum of the two largest elements in Set A, all you need to do is find the two largest values in the set; you don't need to worry about the set's other elements. The question says that Set A is the set of all positive integers of the form $2n + 1$, where $0 \le n \le 10$, so you get the two largest elements in the set when $n = 9$ and $n = 10$. You get the second largest element when $n = 9$: $2(9) + 1 = 19$. You get the largest element when $n = 10$: $2(10) + 1 = 21$. Add these two elements together to get the answer: $19 + 21 = 40$.

3. **(A)** Arithmetic: Sets   *Easy*
The product of the elements of Set Q is $3 \cdot 4 \cdot 5 = 60$. Since $60 > 12$, Column A is greater than Column B, and (A) is the correct answer.

4. **(C)** Arithmetic: Sets   *Moderate*
To make $x - y$ as large as possible, choose the largest x-value in Set P ($x = 12$) and the smallest element in Set Q ($y = -5$). When you subtract y from x, you get: $12 - (-5) = 12 + 5 = 17$. Since both Column A and Column B have the same value, (C) is the correct answer to this question.

SAT Arithmetic

SAT Unit Test–Arithmetic

1. What is the sum when the largest even number less than 14 is added to the smallest odd number great than 20?

   (A) 32
   (B) 33
   (C) 34
   (D) 35
   (E) 36

2. If $x > -6$ and if x is an integer, what is the smallest possible value of x?

   (A) -8
   (B) -7
   (C) -5
   (D) -4
   (E) 0

3. What is the remainder when 17 is divided by 4?

   (A) 1
   (B) 3
   (C) 8
   (D) 13
   (E) 21

4. What is the least common multiple of the prime factors of 18?

   (A) 4
   (B) 6
   (C) 7
   (D) 8
   (E) 10

5. What percent of 10 is 16?

   (A) 37.5%
   (B) 60%
   (C) 62.5%
   (D) 140%
   (E) 160%

6. On a class trip, 2 chaperones are needed for every 10 students. If there are 55 students, how many chaperones are needed?

   (A) 5
   (B) 10
   (C) 11
   (D) 12
   (E) 20

SAT Arithmetic

7. Car 1 uses gasoline at a rate of 30 miles per gallon. Car 2 uses gasoline at a rate of 25 miles per gallon. If each car travels 150 miles, how many more gallons of gasoline will be used by Car 2 than by Car 1?

    (A) 1
    (B) 2
    (C) 3
    (D) 4
    (E) 5

8. Debra's grades on her five math tests were 82, 91, 75, 94 and 85. If her teacher drops the lowest grade before calculating her average, what will Debra's average be?

    (A) 70
    (B) 82
    (C) 85
    (D) 87
    (E) 88

9. Of the juniors at Pleasant Valley High, 23 have brown hair, 31 have blue eyes, and 7 have both. If all of the juniors at Pleasant Valley fall into these categories, how many juniors are there total?

    (A) 46
    (B) 47
    (C) 54
    (D) 61
    (E) 63

10. 1, –2, 3, –4, 5, –6, … The series above is created by listing consecutive integers and by alternating positive and negative signs. What is the sum of the first one hundred elements in this series?

    (A) –100
    (B) –50
    (C) 0
    (D) 50
    (E) 100

11. A bowl contains 4 walnuts and 2 almonds. A nut is randomly selected from the bowl, and then it is put back into the bowl. Then another nut is randomly selected. What is the probability that both nuts selected are walnuts?

    (A) 0

    (B) $\dfrac{1}{9}$

    (C) $\dfrac{4}{9}$

    (D) $\dfrac{2}{3}$

    (E) 1

12.   If $9(3^x) = 3^y$, then what is y in terms of x?

(A) $x + 2$
(B) $x + 3$
(C) $2x$
(D) $3x$
(E) $9x$

13.   Pat's average after four tests is 78. If her next test raises her average to 80, what grade did she get on the fifth test?

(A)   82
(B)   84
(C)   86
(D)   88
(E)   90

14.   Jane ran from her home to the grocery store at an average speed of 15 miles per hour. She walked home along the same route at an average speed of 5 miles per hour. If her total time making the trip to the store and back was 1 hour, how many <u>minutes</u> did it take Jane to drive from her home to the store?

(A)   12
(B)   15
(C)   20
(D)   40
(E)   45

15.   If y is a positive integer and $x = 2y + 1$, which of the following could be true?

I. x is an even integer.
II. x is an odd integer.
III. $x = 0$.

(A)   None of the above
(B)   I only
(C)   II only
(D)   III only
(E)   I, II, and III

16.   If the difference between two negative numbers is 5, and the sum of the two numbers is –7, what is the value of the larger number?

(A)   –1
(B)   –2
(C)   –4
(D)   –5
(E)   –6

17. Villanova School had 550 students at the beginning of the year and 605 students at the end of the year.By what percentage did the number of students increase during the year?

    (A) 5%
    (B) 10%
    (C) 15%
    (D) 85%
    (E) 90%

18. A stand in the street sells lemonade and iced tea and nothing else.For every l cups of lemonade, the girl operating the stand makes t cups of iced tea.One day the girl makes a total of 25 cups.How many cups of lemonade does she make in terms of l and t?

    (A) $\dfrac{25}{l+t}$

    (B) $\dfrac{l+t}{25t}$

    (C) $\dfrac{25l}{l+t}$

    (D) $25-t$

    (E) $\dfrac{25-t}{l}$

19. The average of five distinct integers is 100.If none of the integers is less than 50, what is the greatest possible value of one of the integers?

    (A) 280
    (B) 284
    (C) 290
    (D) 294
    (E) 300

20. If $(x+y)^2 = 19$ and $x^2 + y^2 = 9$, then what is the value of xy?

    (A) 2
    (B) 5
    (C) 10
    (D) 28
    (E) 171

Quantitative Comparisons

21.

$$x^2 = y = \sqrt{6}$$

Column A	Column B
x	y

22.

$$\frac{1}{5} < j + \frac{1}{9} < \frac{1}{3}$$

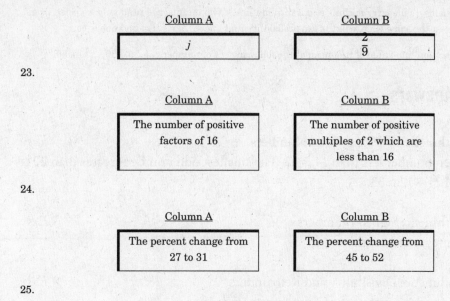

23.

Column A	Column B
j	$\dfrac{2}{9}$

24.

Column A	Column B
The number of positive factors of 16	The number of positive multiples of 2 which are less than 16

25.

Column A	Column B
The percent change from 27 to 31	The percent change from 45 to 52

The number of female cats at a pet store was fewer in January than it was in March, but the total number of cats remained constant.

Column A	Column B
The number of male cats in the pet store in March.	The number of male cats in the pet store in January.

Grid Questions

26. What is the probability of selecting a king from a standard deck of cards?

27. Mr. Richards is in school from 8am to 3pm Monday through Friday. Most of his time is spent teaching, but the following chart shows the number of hours he does NOT teach each day:

Monday	1
Tuesday	1
Wednesday	2
Thursday	1
Friday	1

What is the average number of hours per day that Mr.Richards spends teaching?

28. A recipe calls for 4 teaspoons of flour per 1 cup of liquid. Lauren does not have a teaspoon available to measure the flour, so she uses a tablespoon instead. If one tablespoon is equal to 3 teaspoons and Lauren plans to use 3 cups of liquid, how many tablespoons of flour will she need?

29.   A basket holds 4 blueberry muffins and 2 corn muffins. If two muffins are randomly selected from the basket at the same time, what is the probability that one is blueberry and one is corn?

30.   What is the absolute value of the mean of the following set of numbers: {–55, –50, …, 45, 50}?

Unit Test–Answers

1.   **(B)**   Arithmetic: Odd and Even Numbers   *Easy*
The largest even number less than 14 is 12. The smallest odd number greater than 20 is 21. The sum of 21 + 12 is 33.

2.   **(C)**   Arithmetic: Signed Numbers   *Easy*
The smallest integer greater than –6 is –5.

3.   **(A)**   Arithmetic: Divisibility and Remainders   *Easy*
17 divided by 4 yields a quotient of 4 with a remainder of 1.

4.   **(B)**   Arithmetic: Multiples, Factors and Primes   *Easy*
First find the prime factors of 18: $18 = 2 \times 3 \times 3$. The prime factors of 18 are 2 and 3.

Now find their least common multiple, or in other words, the smallest number that is evenly divisible by 2 and 3. The least common multiple of 2 and 3 is 6.

5.   **(E)**   Arithmetic: Fractions, Decimals and Percents   *Easy*
In percent questions phrased like this, the number that follows "of" represents the whole and the number that follows "is" represents the part. In this case, 10 is the whole, and 16 is the part. To find what percent 16 is of 10, use the formula $\frac{part}{whole} \times 100$. Plug 10 and 16 into this formula: $\frac{16}{10} \times 100 = 160\%$.

6.   **(C)**   Arithmetic: Ratio and Proportion   *Easy*
The question says that 2 chaperones are needed for every 10 students. Set up the following proportion to figure out how many chaperones you need for 55 students:

$$\frac{2 \text{ chaperones}}{10 \text{ students}} = \frac{x \text{ chaperones}}{55 \text{ students}}$$

Now cross multiply:

$$(2)(55) = (10)(x)$$

$$110 = 10x$$

$$11 = x$$

7. **(A)** Arithmetic: Rates   *Easy*

To figure out how many gallons of gas each car uses, divide the distance the car travels by its mileage per gallon.

$$\text{Car \#1:} \frac{150\,\text{miles}}{30\,\text{miles per gallon}} = 5\,\text{gallons}$$

$$\text{Car \#2:} \frac{150\,\text{miles}}{25\,\text{miles per gallon}} = 6\,\text{gallons}$$

The difference between the number of gallons used by each car is: 6 – 5 = 1 gallon.

8. **(E)** Arithmetic: Mean, Median, and Mode   *Easy*

Debra's teacher drops her lowest grade, 75. To find Debra's average test grade, calculate the average of the remaining four grades: $\frac{82 + 91 + 94 + 85}{4} = \frac{352}{4} = 88$.

9. **(B)** Arithmetic: Sets   *Moderate*

There are two sets of juniors at Pleasant Valley: those with brown hair and those with blue eyes. There's also a group of people who fall into both sets. To find the total number of juniors, add the number of people in set 1 (brown hair) to the number of people in set 2 (blue eyes); then subtract the number of people who fall into both sets (brown hair and blue eyes). Total juniors = 23 brown hair + 31 blue eyes – 7 brown hair and blue eyes, or total juniors = 47.

10. **(B)** Arithmetic: Series   *Moderate*

If you add the first two numbers in the series, 1 and –2, the sum is –1. If you add the third and fourth numbers, 3 and –4, the sum is also –1. If you add the fifth and the sixth numbers, 5 and –6, you again get the sum of –1. Adding together consecutive pairs in this pattern always produces the sum of –1. Since there are fifty pairs of numbers in the first 100 terms of the series, you get the sum of –1 fifty times; thus the sum of the first 100 terms is 50(–1) = –50.

11. **(C)** Arithmetic: Probability   *Moderate*

There are 4 walnuts out of a total of 6 nuts, so the probability of selecting a walnut in a single drawing is $\frac{4}{6} = \frac{2}{3}$. Because the first drawing is independent of the second, the probability of both events occurring is simply the product of their independent probabilities: $\frac{2}{3} \times \frac{2}{3} = \frac{4}{9}$.

12. **(A)** Arithmetic: Exponents and Square Roots *Moderate*

You're given the equation $9(3^x) = 3^y$ and asked to solve for y. First you should recognize that $9 = 3^2$, so you can rewrite the equation as $3^2(3^x) = 3^y$. Then using the rules of exponents, you can rewrite the equation as $3^{2+x} = 3^y$. Since the bases of the terms in this equation are equal, their exponents must also be equal: $2 + x = y$.

13. **(D)** Arithmetic: Mean, Median, and Mode *Moderate*

If Pat's test average after four tests is 78, then she scored a total of $4(78) = 312$ points on the tests. If her average after five tests is 80, then she scored a total of $5(80) = 400$ points on the five tests. To find the grade she got on the fifth test, take the difference between the two total scores: $400 - \frac{3}{2} = 88$ points.

14. **(B)** Arithmetic: Rates *Difficult*

You know that Jane ran to the store at a rate of 15 miles per hour and that she walked back from the store at a rate of 5 miles per hour. You also know that making the total trip took Jane 1 hour. What you want to find out is how long it took Jane to get from her home to the store; you can call this unknown amount of time x.

If you multiply Jane's traveling rate by the time she spends traveling, you can find her distance: $\frac{\text{miles}}{\text{hour}} \times \text{hours} = \text{miles}$. Since the distance between the store and the home is constant, you can write two equations for the distance and set them equal to each other. In the first equation, multiply Jane's running rate, 15 miles per hour, by her traveling time, x. In the second equation, multiply Jane's walking rate, 5 miles per hour, by her traveling time, $(1 - x)$. You end up with two equations for the distance between the store and the house:

$$\text{Distance} = \frac{15 \text{ miles}}{\text{hour}} \times x \text{ hours}$$
$$\text{Distance} = \frac{5 \text{ miles}}{\text{hour}} \times (1 - x) \text{ hours}$$

Since the distance is the same, you can set the two equations equal to each other:

$$15x = 5(1 - x)$$

$$15x = 5 - 5x$$

$$20x = 5$$

$$x = \frac{1}{4} \text{ hour}$$

Since the question asks you for the time in minutes, you need to convert $\frac{1}{4}$ hour to 15 minutes.

15. **(C)**   Arithmetic: Odd and Even Numbers   *Moderate*

The product of 2 and any positive integer is always even, and the sum of 1 and any even integer is always odd. Since $x = 2y + 1$, you know that x must be odd. Option II, which says that x is an odd integer, must be true, and option I, which says that x is an even integer, must be false. If $x = 0$, then y must be equal to $-1/2$, which is not an integer; therefore, option III cannot be true either. Choice (C), II only, is the correct answer to this question.

16. **(E)**   Arithmetic: Signed Numbers   *Difficult*

Call the two negative numbers x and y. Since the difference between the two numbers is 5, you can write the following equation: $x - y = 5$. Since their sum is -7, you can write another equation: $x + y = -7$. Add the two equations together:

$$(x - y) + (x + y) = 5 + (-7)$$

$$2x = -2$$

$$x = -1$$

Plug $x = -1$ into one of the equations above to find the value of y:

$$-1 - y = 5$$

$$y = -6$$

17. **(B)**   Arithmetic: Fractions, Decimals, and Percents   *Difficult*

Use the following formula to find the percent increase of students at Villanova School:

$$\% \text{ increase} = \frac{\text{amount of increase}}{\text{original amount}} \times 100$$

The amount of increase is equal to the difference between the new number of students, 605, and the initial number of students, 550:

$$\% = \frac{605 - 550}{550} \times 100$$

$$\% = \frac{55}{550} \times 100$$

$$\% = 0.1(100)$$

$$\% = 10$$

The number of students at the school increased by 10%.

18. **(C)** Arithmetic: Ratio and Proportion   *Difficult*

The girl makes cups of lemonade and iced tea in the ratio of $l : t$. If she makes 25 cups total one day, you can write the equation $lx + tx = 25$, where lx is the number of cups of lemonade, tx is the number of cups of iced tea, and x is a common multiple. To answer this question in terms of l and t, you need to solve first for x. First factor out the x, so you have: $x(l + t) = 25$. Then divide both sides by $(l + t)$: $x = 25/(l + t)$. Since you're looking for the number of cups of lemonade, you need to multiply both sides of this equation by l to get: $lx = \frac{25l}{l+t}$.

You can also answer this question by finding the fraction of the cups that have lemonade. There are l cups of lemonade out of every $(l + t)$ cups; in other words, $\frac{l}{l+t}$ cups are lemonade. Thus the number of cups of lemonade among 25 cups is $\frac{25l}{l+t}$.

19. **(D)** Arithmetic: Mean, Median and Mode   *Difficult*

If the average of five integers is 100, then the sum of the five integers is 500. To make one of the integers as big as possible, you need to make the other four as small as possible. Since the integers are all distinct (in other words, they are not the same as each other) and since they are greater than or equal to 50, the four smallest integers you can have are 50, 51, 52, and 53. To find the fifth integer, subtract these four numbers from the total sum, 500: $500 - 50 - 51 - 52 - 53 = 294$ is the fifth integer.

20. **(B)** Arithmetic: Exponents and Square Roots   *Difficult*

You need an expression that has xy in it: $(x + y)^2 = (x + y) \times (x + y) = x^2 + 2xy + y^2$. If $(x + y)^2 = 19$, then $19 = x^2 + 2xy + y^2$. Since the question says that $x^2 + y^2 = 9$, you can substitute 9 in for $x^2 + y^2$ in the equation $19 = x^2 + 2xy + y2$. You end up with the new equation $19 = 9 + 2xy$. Subtract 9 from both sides of the equation to get: $10 = 2xy$. Then divide each side of the equation by 2: $5 = xy$

21. **(B)** Arithmetic: Exponents and Square Roots   *Easy*
In order to answer this question, you need to solve for x and y. First solve for y:

$$y = \sqrt{16}$$

$$y = 4$$

Then solve for x:

$$x^2 = y$$

$$x^2 = 4$$

$$x = \pm 2$$

The value of y, 4, is greater than either value of x, –2 or 2, so Column B is greater than Column A.

22. **(B)** Arithmetic: Fractions, Decimals, and Percents   *Moderate*
First isolate j in the inequality by subtracting $\frac{1}{9}$ from each term. To make the subtraction easier, you can rewrite the fractions so they share a common denominator. The least common multiple of 3, 6, and 9 is 18, so you should make 18 the new denominator. After subtracting, you end up with the inequality $\frac{1}{18} < j < \frac{4}{18}$. Column B, $\frac{2}{9}$, is the same as $\frac{4}{18}$, so Column B is greater than Column A.

23. **(B)** Arithmetic: Multiples, Factors, and Primes   *Moderate*
There are five positive factors of 16: {1, 2, 4, 8, 16}. There are seven positive multiples of 2 that are less than 16: {2, 4, 6, 8, 10, 12, 14}. Column B, 7, is greater than Column A, 5.

24. **(A)** Arithmetic: Fractions, Decimals and Percents   *Difficult*
Use the following formula to calculate percent change: percent of increase = $\frac{\text{amount of increase}}{\text{original amount}} \times 100$. Column A is the percent change from 27 to 31, so the amount of increase is 31 – 27 = 4. Plug these numbers into the formula above: % change = $\frac{4}{27} \times 100 = 14.81$. Column B is the percent change from 45 to 52, so the amount of increase is 52 – 45 = 7: % change = $\frac{7}{45} \times 100 = 15.55$. 15.55% is greater than 14.81%, so Column B is greater than Column A.

25. **(B)** Arithmetic: Sets   *Easy*
The total number of cats in the store is equal to the number of female cats plus the number of male cats. If the number of female cats increased between January and March but the total number of cats remained constant, then the number of male cats must have decreased from January to March. Thus Column B, the number of male cats in January, is greater than Column A, the number of male cats in March.

26. **1/13** Arithmetic: Probability   *Easy*
There are 4 kings in a standard 52-card deck, so the probability of picking a king from the deck is equal to the number of kings divided by the total number of cards: $\frac{4}{52} = \frac{1}{13}$.

27. **5.4** Arithmetic: Fractions, Decimals, and Percents   *Moderate*
The easiest way to find the average number of hours Mr. Richards spends teaching each day is to find the total amount of hours he teaches per week and divide that number by the number of days he spends at school per week. To figure out how many hours Mr. Richards teaches per week, subtract the time he doesn't teach from the total amount of time he spends at school. Mr. Richards is in school 7 hours per day for 5 days a week, or 35 hours total. Now add up the hours he doesn't teach: $1\frac{1}{2} + 1\frac{1}{4} + 2 + 1\frac{3}{4} + 1\frac{1}{2} = 8$ hours.

So Mr. Richards spends $35 - 8 = 27$ hours teaching. To calculate the average number of hours he teaches per day, divide 27 by 5: $\frac{27}{5} = 5.4$.

28. **4**   Arithmetic: Ratio and Proportion   *Moderate*
The recipe calls for 1 cup of liquid, but Lauren is going to use 3 cups, which means that she's tripling the recipe. Since she's tripling the recipe, she needs to use three times as much flour as called for in the recipe, so she needs to use 12 teaspoons of flour instead of 4 teaspoons. The question, however, doesn't ask how many *teaspoons* of flour Lauren needs; it asks how many *tablespoons* she needs. You're told that one tablespoon is equal to 3 teaspoons, so you can set up the following proportion:

$$\frac{1 \text{ tablespoon}}{3 \text{ teaspoons}} = \frac{x \text{ tablespoons}}{12 \text{ teaspoons}}$$
$$(1)(12) = (3)(x)$$

$$4 = x$$

Lauren needs 4 tablespoons of flour.

29. **8/15** Arithmetic: Probability $\hspace{2cm}$ *Difficult*

Simultaneously taking two muffins from the basket is the same as taking one muffin out and then taking another one out of the remaining muffins. In other words, you take the second muffin out without replacing the first. The question asks you for the probability of withdrawing one blueberry and one corn muffin. This result can arise in two ways: one, if you first withdraw a blueberry muffin and then a corn muffin, or two, if you first withdraw a corn muffin and then a blueberry muffin.

In the first case, the probability of withdrawing a blueberry muffin first is $\frac{4}{6} = \frac{2}{3}$, since there are 4 blueberry muffins out of a total 6 muffins. The probability of withdrawing a corn muffin second is $\frac{2}{5}$ because there are 2 corn muffins out of the remaining 5 muffins. The probability of both events happening is equal to the product of their individual probabilities: $\frac{2}{3} \times \frac{2}{5} = \frac{4}{15}$.

In the second case, the probability of taking a corn muffin first is $\frac{2}{6} = \frac{1}{3}$, since there are 2 corn muffins out of a total 6 muffins. The probability of taking a blueberry muffin second is $\frac{4}{5}$ because there are 4 blueberry muffins out of the remaining 5 muffins. The probability of both events happening is $\frac{1}{3} \times \frac{4}{5} = \frac{4}{15}$.

Since both of these cases produce 1 blueberry and 1 corn muffin, you need to add together the likelihood of each event occurring to solve the problem: $\frac{4}{15} + \frac{4}{15} = \frac{8}{15}$.

30. **2.5** Arithmetic: Mean, Median, and Mode $\hspace{2cm}$ *Difficult*

There are faster ways of answering this question than summing all of the terms in this set. Every negative term except for –55 has a corresponding positive term, and each pair of negative and positive numbers adds to 0: –50 + 50 = 0, –45 + 45 = 0, for example. The only terms that do not have pairs are –55 and 0, so the sum of all the numbers in the set is –55. Since there are ten pairs of numbers and the two unpaired numbers, you can figure out that there are 22 elements in the set. If the sum of the set is –55 and the number of elements in the set is 22, then the average of the set is –55/22 = –2.5.

You can also solve this problem using the first and last items in the set. For any set where the elements differ by a constant term (in this case, 5), the average of the outermost elements is the same as the average of the entire set. The average of –55 and 50 is $\frac{(-55+50)}{2} = -2.5$.

The question asks for the absolute value of the set's mean. The absolute value of –2.5 is 2.5.

SAT Algebra

Almost a third of the questions on the math portion of the SAT deal with algebra. This news strikes fear into the hearts of many students who associate algebra with intense and difficult math. But take heart: the algebra tested on the SAT is not very difficult. The equations on the test are fairly simple, and the questions asked about particular topics of algebra are often quite similar.

In this section we will cover the seven major algebraic topics covered by the SAT: substitution, building expressions and equations, simplifying and manipulating expressions, solving linear equations, solving systems of equations, solving inequalities, and multiplying binomials and polynomials

Before covering these topics, however, we will address a question brought up by the teachings of some other test prep companies.

To Algebra or Not to Algebra

There are many ways to answer most algebra problems. You can use algebra—setting up and working out equations. You can plug numbers into equations to try and avoid using algebra. In some cases, you might even be able to solve a question by being a particularly intuitive genius and finding a magnificent shortcut.

We want to stress that none of these methods is necessarily better than another. Which method is best for you relies on your math ability and your target score. Trying to solve problems with algebra is more conceptually demanding, but can take less time. Plugging in numbers makes questions easier to understand but will likely take more time. In general, if you are uncomfortable with algebra, you should generally try to use plugging in. If you are comfortable with algebra, using it is probably the best way to go. Still, these suggestions are not hard and fast rules. If you are generally comfortable with algebra but come upon a question that is stumping you, try plugging in answers. If you usually prefer plugging in answers but come upon a question you can solve using algebra, then use algebra. When you study your practice tests, while looking at the algebra questions you got wrong, you should think about the method you employed. Did you plug in when you should have used algebra? Did you use algebra when you should have plugged in? As for being an intuitive math genius, it can't just be taught—though we will show you how one might think.

Here's an example algebra question:

A man flipped a coin 162 times. The coin landed with heads side up 62 more times than it landed with tails up. How many times did the coin land heads?

(A)   100
(B)   104
(C)   108
(D)   112
(E)   116

Solving by Algebra

If you answer this question with algebra, you realize that if heads are represented by the variable x, then tails are represented by $(x - 62)$. Therefore,

$$x + (x - 62) = 162$$
$$2x - 62 = 162$$
$$2x = 224$$
$$x = 112$$

As you can see, there's simply less math to do for this problem when you use algebra. Using algebra will only take you longer than plugging in if you have trouble coming up with the equation $x + (x - 62) = 162$.

Therefore, if you can quickly come up with the necessary equation, then use algebra to solve algebra problems. If you have the sense that it will take you a while to figure out the correct equation, then plug in.

Solving by Plugging In

If you were to answer this problem by plugging in, you would pick (C) 108 as the first number to try, since if it does not happen to be the answer, you can still discard either the numbers smaller than it or larger than it. So, if the coin came up heads 108 times, then how many times did it land tails? It landed tails 162 – 108 = 54. Is 108 heads landings 62 more than 54 tails landings? No, 108 – 54 = 54. In order for the problem to work out you need more head landings. You can eliminate (A) and (B) as possibilities. Let's say we choose (D) 112 as our next plug in number. $162 - 112 = 50$. Does $112 - 50 = 62$? Yes. **(D)** is the answer.

Solving by Being an Amazing Genius

It is quite possible that you just looked at this problem and said to yourself, "Other than the 62 more heads, all the other flips were equally heads and tails. So: if you take the 62 out of the total of 162, then you know that the other 100 flips were 50 heads and 50 tails. Now I can just add $62 + 50 = 112$. Man, I am an amazing genius!"

The Bottom Line on Using Algebra

Hopefully, our example has convinced you that there isn't any "right way" to answer a question dealing with algebra. There are faster ways and slower ways, and it always benefits you to use the faster way if you can, but the most important thing is getting the question right. Therefore, when you come to a question, don't insist on using only one method to try to answer it. Just do what you have to in order to answer the question correctly in as little time as possible.

Now we'll cover the topics of algebra tested by the SAT.

Substitution

Substitution questions are some of the simplest algebra questions on the SAT. These questions provide you with an algebraic expression and give you the value of one of the variables within the equation. For example:

> If $2y + 8x = 11$, what is the value of $3(2y + 8x)$?

You might see this equation filled with variables and panic. You shouldn't. The problem is immensely simple. Since $2y + 8x = 11$, all you have to do is substitute 11 in for $2y + 8x$ in the expression $3(2y + 8x)$, and you get $3(11) = 33$.

Some substitution questions are a tad more complicated. For these, you might have to do some simple math either before or after the substitution.

Math Before Substitution

> If $3x - 7 = 8$, then $23 - 3x =$

In this problem you have to find what $3x$ equals before you can substitute that value into the expression $23 - 3x$. To find $3x$, simply take

$$3x - 7 = 8$$

and add 7 to both sides, giving:

$$3x = 15$$

Now we can substitute that 15 into $23 - 3x$:

$$23 - 15 = 8$$

Math After Substitution

If $a + b = 7$ and $b = 3$, then $4a = ?$

Here we first have to solve for a by substituting 3 for b:

$$a + b = 7$$
$$a + 3 = 7$$
$$a = 4$$

Once you know that $a = 4$, just substitute into $4a$:

$$4 \times 4 = 16$$

Substitution

1.   If $x = 7$, what is the value of y in the equation $3x + 2y = 31$?

    (A)   3
    (B)   5
    (C)   10
    (D)   11
    (E)   26

2.   If $x = 2y$, $y = 2z$, and $z = 5$, what is the value of x?

    (A)   1.25
    (B)   2.5
    (C)   5
    (D)   10
    (E)   20

3.   If $a = 2$ and $b = -3$, what is the value of ab^3?

    (A)   −216
    (B)   −54
    (C)   −1
    (D)   54
    (E)   216

4.   If $v = w - 6$ and $w = 2v - 9$, what is the value of w?

    (A)   5
    (B)   11
    (C)   15
    (D)   21
    (E)   24

5.

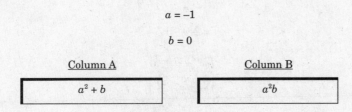

$$a = -1$$

$$b = 0$$

Column A	Column B
$a^2 + b$	$a^2 b$

6.

$$w = bx + a$$

$$y = ax + b$$

Column A	Column B
$\dfrac{w - a}{b}$	$\dfrac{y - b}{a}$

7.   Evaluate $3xy$ when $x = \sqrt{16}$ and $y = \sqrt{36}$

8.   The cube of 2 is equal to the square root of x. If $y = x^2$, what is the value of y?

Answers

1.   **(B)**   Algebra: Substitution   *Easy*

This question asks you to do simple substitution. Substitute 7 for x in the given equation:

$$3(7) + 2y = 31$$

$$21 + 2y = 31$$

Now isolate y on one side of the equation. First subtract 21 from both sides to get: $2y = 10$. Then divide both sides by 2: $y = 5$.

2.   **(E)**   Algebra: Substitution   *Easy*

Since $x = 2y$, you need to figure out the value of y before you can find x. Substitute 5 for z in $y = 2z$: $y = 2(5)$, so $y = 10$. Now substitute 10 for y in $x = 2y$: $x = 2(10)$, so $x = 20$.

3. **(B)** Algebra: Substitution   *Easy*
Substitute 2 for a and -3 for b in ab^3: $(2)(-3)^3 = (2)(-27) = -54$.

4. **(D)** Algebra: Substitution   *Moderate*
Since you want to find the value of w, you should make w the only variable in the equation. Substitute $w - 6$ for v in the equation $w = 2v - 9$.

$$w = 2(w - 6) - 9$$
$$w = 2w - 12 - 9$$
$$w = 2w - 21$$
$$-w = -21$$
$$w = 21$$

5. **(A)** Algebra: Substitution   *Easy*
Plug $a = -1$ and $b = 0$ into the expressions in Columns A and B. In Column A, $(-1)^2 + 0 = 1 + 0 = 1$. In Column B, $(-1)^2(0) = (1)(0) = 0$. 1 is greater than 0, so Column A is greater than Column B.

6. **(C)** Algebra: Substitution   *Moderate*
Since x does not appear in Column A or Column B, solve for x in the two equations. In the first equation,

$$w = bx + a$$
$$w - a = bx$$
$$\frac{w - a}{b} = x$$

In the second equation,

$$y = ax + b$$
$$y - b = ax$$
$$\frac{y - b}{a} = x$$

Each of the columns is equal to x, so the correct answer is (C), the columns are equal in value.

7. **72** Algebra: Substitution   *Easy*
Plug $x = \sqrt{16} = 4$ and $y = \sqrt{36} = 6$ into $3xy$: $3(4)(6) = 72$.

8. **4096** Algebra: Substitution   *Difficult*

The cube of 2 is 8, and the square root of x is $\sqrt{x}$, so you can write $8 = \sqrt{x}$. If you square both sides of this equation, you get $64 = x$. Now, substitute 64 for x in the equation $y = x^2$:

$$y = (64)^2$$
$$y = 4096$$

Building Expressions and Equations

Occasionally the SAT will ask a word problem, and you will have to write out an expression that describes the word problem, and perhaps simplify it. For example:

> Mary poured g cups of water into a bucket, leaving the bucket with a total of f cups in it. Mary then removed $(g - 3)$ cups of water from the bucket. How many cups of water remain in the bucket?

To answer this question, you have to interpret the word problem. In other words, you have to figure out what is important in the word problem and how it fits into the expression you need to build. In this question, you are asked to generate an expression that describes how many cups of water there are in the bucket after Mary removes $(g - 3)$ cups. It doesn't matter what g actually equals, because we don't care how much water was in the bucket before Mary added g cups. The question only includes that detail to trick you. As far as we're concerned the problem might as well have been:

> There were f cups of water in a bucket. Mary then removed $(g - 3)$ cups of water from the bucket. How many cups of water remain in the bucket?

To work out the equation, we take the number of cups in the bucket and subtract what was removed:

$$f - (g - 3) = f - g + 3$$

The equation to state how many cups of water are in the bucket is: total cups $= f - g + 3$.
    ETS often deliberately writes equations less clearly than it could. Instead of writing:

> Mark collects worms, frogs, and toasters. He has 6 more toasters than frogs, and 3 times as many frogs as worms.

ETS would probably write:

> Mark collects worms, frogs, and toasters. The number of toasters he has is 6 more than the number of frogs, and the number of frogs is 3 times as large as the number of worms.

The ETS writers do this simply to confuse you, which seems rather juvenile of them. But you should still be ready for it.

These types of questions usually appear in the last, difficult third of SAT math sections. If you are looking to score above a 600, you should definitely make sure that you know how to answer them.

Building Expressions and Equations

1. Which of the following expressions represents the statement "x increased by the square of x"?

   (A) $x - x^2$
   (B) $x + x^2$
   (C) $x - \sqrt{x}$
   (D) $x + \sqrt{x}$
   (E) $x \cdot x^2$

2. When a certain number is doubled and then decreased by 5, the result is the same as when the original number is increased by 7. What is the number?

   (A) 2
   (B) 4
   (C) 6
   (D) 12
   (E) 17

3. Grant buys p apples for c cents each. He also buys b bananas. If a banana costs 5 cents less than an apple, express the amount of money that Grant spends, in terms of p, b, and c, to buy p apples and b bananas.

   (A) $c(p + b) - 5b$
   (B) $pc + 5b$
   (C) $pbc - 5$
   (D) $b(c - 5) + p$
   (E) $c(p + b + 5)$

4. If one half of x is equal to 15 less than x, what is the value of x?

Answers

1. **(B)** Algebra: Building Expressions and Equations   *Easy*
The "square of x" is x^2, and "x increased by the square of x" is $x + x^2$.

2. **(D)** Algebra: Building Expressions and Equations   *Moderate*
You can write two expressions based on the information in the question. If n is the number you want to find, then $2n - 5$ represents what happens when you double the number and decrease it by 5. The expression $n + 7$ represents the number increased by 7. You can set these two expressions equal to each other and solve for the number, n:

$$2n - 5 = n + 7$$
$$n - 5 = 7$$
$$n = 12$$

3.　**(A)**　Algebra: Building Expressions and Equations　　　　　*Difficult*
If each apple costs c cents, then p apples cost pc cents. If each banana costs $(c - 5)$ cents, then b bananas cost $b(c - 5)$ cents. Add these two expressions together to find how much Grant spends: $(p)(c) + (b)(c - 5) = pc + bc - 5b = c(p + b) - 5b$

4.　**30**　Algebra: Building Expressions and Equations　　　　　*Moderate*
Based on the information given in the question, you can write the following equation:
$\frac{1}{2}x = x - 15$. to solve for x, first multiply both sides of the equation by 2: $1x = 2x - 30$.
Then subtract $2x$ from both sides: $-1x = -30$. Finally, divide both sides by -1: $x = 30$.

Simplifying and Manipulating Expressions

Simplifying Algebraic Expressions

Often the SAT will ask a question about an equation that seems impossibly complicated. In such cases, simplifying the equation can often reveal the answer more clearly or make calculating the answer a less harrowing task. There are two primary ways to simplify an equation, factoring and combining like terms.

Factoring and Expansion

Factoring an algebraic expression means finding factors common to all the terms in an expression and dividing them out. For example, to factor $3a + 3b$, divide out the three to get $3(a + b)$. Factoring is merely reversing the distributive property of multiplication. Below are some examples of factoring:

$$6y + 8x = 2(3y + 4x)$$
$$8b + 24 = 8(b + 3)$$
$$3(x + y) + 4(x + y) = (3 + 4)(x + y) = 7(x + y)$$
$$\frac{2x + y}{x} = \frac{2x}{x} + \frac{y}{x} = 2 + \frac{y}{x}$$

Expansion involves taking a factored expression, such as $8(b + 3)$, and distributing one term to the other(s) by multiplying them: $8b + 24$.

Combining Similar Terms

If an expression contains like terms you can combine those terms and simplify the equation. Like terms are identical variables that have the same exponential value.

$$x^2 + 8x^2 = 9x^2$$
$$y^{13} + 754y^{13} = 755y^{13}$$
$$m^3 + m^3 = 2m^3$$

As long as two terms have the same variable and the same exponential value, you can combine them. Note that when you combine like terms, the variable doesn't change.

Variables that have different exponential values are not like terms and cannot be combined. Two terms that do not share a variable are also not like terms, and cannot be combined regardless of their exponential value.

$$\text{You can't combine: } x^4 + x^2 =$$
$$y^2 + x^2 =$$

Manipulating Equations

A number of SAT questions will provide you with an equation such as $x = yz$ and then ask you to show what that equation looks like in terms of y. The secret to answering such questions is a simple rule: you can perform any operation on one side of the equation as long as you perform the same operation on the other side of the equation. For the question described above, you need to isolate y from the other two variables. To do so, all you have to do is divide both sides of the equation by z.

$$x = yz$$
$$\frac{x}{z} = y$$

A more difficult SAT question might ask:

If $x - 2 = z$ and $y = 7$, then $xy = ?$

To answer this question, you have to isolate x, multiply both sides of the new equation by y, and then substitute 7 for y on the right side.

$$x - 2 = z$$
$$x = z + 2$$
$$xy = y(z + 2)$$
$$xy = 7(z + 2)$$
$$xy = 7z + 14$$

Simplifying and Manipulating Expressions

1. $3m + 4n - 6 + 2m - 4n$ Which of the following expressions is the same as the expression above?

    (A) $5mn - 6$
    (B) $m - 6$
    (C) $mn - 6$
    (D) $6m$
    (E) $5m - 6$

2. Simplify: $3(2a^2 + 6b) - 2(a^2 - b)$.

    (A) $4(a^2 + 4b)$
    (B) $4(a^2 + 5b)$
    (C) $3a^2 + 5b$
    (D) $a^2 + 5b$
    (E) $8(a^2 + b)$

3. If and b - 0, which of the following expressions is equivalent to $\frac{ax + b}{b}$?

    (A) by

    (B) $\frac{y}{b}$

    (C) $y + 1$

    (D) $y + b$

    (E) $\frac{b}{y}$

4.

Column A	Column B
$3(x + y) - y$	$2(x + y) + x$

5.

$$xy = 1$$

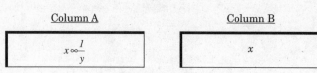

Column A	Column B
$x \infty \dfrac{1}{y}$	x

6.   For which positive value of x is $\dfrac{(x-7)(x+1)}{(x+6)(x-2)}$ undefined?

Answers

1.   **(E)**   Simplifying and Manipulating Expressions   *Easy*
To answer this problem, all you need to do is combine like terms. You end up with
$3m + 4n - 6 + 2m - 4n = 5m - 6$.

2.   **(B)**   Simplifying and Manipulating Expressions   *Moderate*
First distribute the 3 and the 2 to get: $6a^2 + 18b - 2a^2 + 2b$. If you combine like terms in
the equation, you end up with: $4a^2 + 20b$. Finally factor 4 from each term: $4(a^2 + 5b)$.

3.   **(C)**   Simplifying and Manipulating Expressions   *Difficult*
Simplify the expression $\dfrac{ax+b}{b}$:
$$\frac{ax+b}{b} = \frac{ax}{b} + \frac{b}{b} = \frac{ax}{b} + 1$$
Since $\dfrac{ax}{b} = y$, you know that $\dfrac{ax+b}{b} = y + 1$.

4.   **(C)**   Simplifying and Manipulating Expressions   *Easy*
First simplify Column A: $3(x + y) - y = 3x + 3y - y = 3x + 2y$. Then simplify Column B:
$2(x + y) + x = 2x + 2y + x = 3x + 2y$. The columns are equal, so (C) is the correct answer.

5.   **(D)**   Simplifying and Manipulating Expressions   *Difficult*
Using the equation $xy = 1$, you can simplify the expression in Column A. Divide both
sides of $xy = 1$ by y; you end up with the equation $x = \dfrac{1}{y}$. Plug this value for $\dfrac{1}{y}$ into
Column A: $x \infty \dfrac{1}{y} = x \infty x = x^2$. Since Column A is x^2 and Column B is x, you may be
tempted to say that Column A is greater than Column B. However, if x is a fraction
such as $\dfrac{1}{2}$, then x^2 will be smaller than x: $\left(\dfrac{1}{2}\right)^2 = \dfrac{1}{4}$. The relationship between the columns cannot be determined, and the answer is (D).

6.   **2**   Simplifying and Manipulating Expressions   *Easy*

A fraction is undefined when its denominator equals zero. The denominator of this expression is equal to zero when $x = -6$ or $x = 2$. The correct answer to this question is 2 because 2 is the positive value of x that makes the fraction equal to zero.

Solving Linear Equations

You can always solve linear equations on the SAT by isolating the variable whose value you are trying to determine on one side of the equation. However, if you stay alert, you can often find shortcuts that will save you time without affecting your accuracy. Let's look at an easy example:

> If $6p + 2 = 20$, then $6p - 3 = ?$

This is an easy problem to solve through the normal algebraic method. First solve for p:

$$6p + 2 = 20$$
$$6p = 18$$
$$p = 3$$

and then we plug 3 into the second equation:

$$6p - 3 =$$
$$6(3) - 3 =$$
$$18 - 3 = 15$$

But it's possible to answer this question much more quickly. The secret to this question is that you don't have to solve for p at all. Instead, you have to notice that both equations contain $6p$ and that the value of $6p$ will not change. Therefore, all you have to do in the first equation is solve for $6p$. And as you can see above, that simply means subtracting 2 from 20 to get 18. Once you know $6p$ is 18, you can plug 18 in for $6p$ in the second equation and get your answer of 15.

When you come upon an algebra question asking you to solve an equation, you should always take a moment to look for shortcuts. Look for equations that not only have the same variables, but the same coefficients attached to that variable (such as $6p$ and $6p$). ETS puts these shortcuts into their questions on purpose. They believe that if you're knowledgeable enough about math to see shortcuts, then you deserve the extra time those shortcuts will give you on the test. Since you now know that the shortcuts are there, you might as well take advantage of them.

SAT Algebra

Solving Linear Equations

1. If $3x + 7 = x + 25$, what is the value of x?.

    (A)   6
    (B)   7
    (C)   8
    (D)   9
    (E)   10

2. If $3(x + 1) = 4(x - 10)$, what is the value of x?

    (A)   34
    (B)   37
    (C)   43
    (D)   46
    (E)   50

3. If $3x + 7 + 2x = 52$, what is the value of $5x$?

    (A)   9
    (B)   30
    (C)   45
    (D)   225
    (E)   295

4. If $x = 22 + \frac{1}{2}x$, then $x =$

    (A)   11
    (B)   14
    (C)   26
    (D)   38
    (E)   44

5. If $ax - bc = x$, what is x in terms of a, b, and c?

    (A) $\dfrac{bc}{a-1}$

    (B) $a - bc$

    (C) $a + bc$

    (D) $\dfrac{bc}{a}$

    (E) $\dfrac{a+1}{bc}$

6. Solve for x if $\sqrt{x} + 2x = \sqrt{x} - (x - 3)$.

    (A)   0
    (B)   1
    (C)   3
    (D)   5
    (E)   9

SAT Algebra

7.

$$2x + y = 6$$

Column A	Column B
x	y

8.

$$\frac{1 - 3x}{7} + 3 = 2 - x$$

Column A	Column B
x	$2x$

9   If $3x + 6 = 12$, what is the value of $6x$?

10. $x - 3 = \dfrac{2x + 5}{5}$

What is the value of x in the equation above?

Answers

1.   **(D)**   Algebra: Solving Linear Equations   *Easy*
To solve this problem, isolate x on one side of the equation:

$$3x + 7 = x + 25$$

$$2x + 7 = 25$$

$$2x = 18$$

$$x = 9$$

2.   **(C)**   Algebra: Solving Linear Equations   *Easy*
Your first step should be to distribute the 3 and the 4 in $3(x + 1) = 4(x - 10)$: $3x + 3 = 4x - 40$. Then subtract $3x$ from each side to get: $3 = x - 40$. Finally, add 40 to find x: $43 = x$.

3.   **(C)**   Algebra: Solving Linear Equations   *Easy*
Combine like terms in the equation $3x + 7 + 2x = 52$ to get $5x + 7 = 52$. If you subtract 7 from both sides of the equation, you'll $5x = 45$

4.   **(E)**   Algebra: Solving Linear Equations   *Moderate*
In order to get rid of the fraction in the equation, you need to multiply the equation by 2:

$$2\left(x = 22 + \frac{1}{2}x\right)$$

$$2x = 44 + 1x$$

Subtract $1x$ from both sides of the equation to get: $x = 44$.

5.   **(A)**   Algebra: Solving Linear Equations   *Difficult*
To solve for x in terms of a, b, and c, you need to isolate x on one side of the equation.

$$ax - bc = x$$
$$ax = x + bc$$
$$ax - x = bc$$
$$x(a - 1) = bc$$
$$x = \frac{bc}{(a-1)}$$

6.   **(B)**   Algebra: Solving Linear Equations   *Difficult*
The square root in the equation makes this question seem more complicated than it is. You can get rid of the square root by subtracting $\sqrt{x}$ from both sides of the equation:

$$\sqrt{x} + 2x = \sqrt{x} - (x - 3)$$
$$2x = -(x - 3)$$
$$2x = -x + 3$$
$$3x = 3$$
$$x = 1$$

7.   **(D)**   Algebra: Solving Linear Equations   *Easy*
There are an infinite number of x and y values that could work in the given equation; therefore, the relationship between the columns cannot be determined.

8.   **(A)**   Algebra: Solving Linear Equations   *Difficult*
In order to get rid of the fraction on the left side of the equation, you need to multiply the equation by 7.

$$7\left(\frac{1 - 3x}{7} + 3 = 2 - x\right)$$
$$1 - 3x + 21 = 14 - 7x$$
$$1 + 21 = 14 - 4x$$
$$1 + 21 - 14 = -4x$$
$$8 = -4x$$
$$-2 = x$$

If $x = -2$, then $2x = -4$. Since $-2 > -4$, Column A is greater in value than Column B.

9. **12** Algebra: Solving Linear Equations   *Easy*
First solve for x:

$$3x + 6 = 12$$
$$3x = 6$$
$$x = 2$$

Now multiply x by 6 to find: $6x = 12$.

10. **20/3 or 6.66 or 6.67** Algebra: Solving Linear Equations   *Moderate*
Multiply the equation by 5 to get rid of the fraction on the right side:

$$x - 3 = \frac{2x + 5}{5}$$
$$5x - 15 = 2x + 5$$
$$3x - 15 = 5$$
$$3x = 20$$
$$x = \frac{20}{3}$$

Solving Systems of Equations

Occasionally the SAT will give you two equations and ask you to determine the value of a particular variable or some other equation or expression. For example, the SAT might ask:

If $3x + 4y = 32$ and $2y - x = 6$, then $x - y = ?$

The best way to answer this type of question is to use a type of substitution method: solve for one variable and then substitute that value into the other equation. Since the x in the second equation has no coefficient next to it, it will be easier to solve for that variable. All it takes is a little reorganizing:

$$2y - x = 6$$
$$2y - 6 = x$$
$$x = 2y - 6$$

Now, all we have to do is plug $2y - 6$ into the value for x in the first equation:

$$3(2y - 6) + 4y = 32$$

Now, we have only one variable to deal with in the equation, and we can easily solve for it:

$$6y - 18 + 4y = 32$$
$$10y = 50$$
$$y = 5$$

Once we know the value of y, we can plug that value into either equation to solve for x.

$$x = 2y - 6$$
$$x = 2(5) - 6$$
$$x = 4$$

Since $y = 5$ and $x = 4$, $x - y = 4 - 5 = -1$.

When you solve problems that deal with systems of equations, always be careful of two things.

- Make sure you solve for the first variable in its lowest form (solve for x rather than $2x$).

- Answer the question the SAT asks. For example, in the sample above, the question asked for the value of x – y. But it's certainly possible that after doing all the work and figuring out that x = 4, you might forget to carry out the final simple operation 4 – 5 = –1 and think that the answer is 4. You can be sure that the test will try to trick you by including 4 as one of its answer choices.

Solving Systems of Equations

1. If $x + y = 4$ and $x - y = 6$, what is the value of x?

    (A)   1
    (B)   2
    (C)   5
    (D)   10
    (E)   12

2.
$$y - 7 = x$$
$$7x + 6 - y = 3x$$

In the system of equations above, what is the value of x?

(A) $\dfrac{1}{3}$

(B) 1

(C) 3

(D) 5

(E) 7

3. $2x + 3y = 5$
    $3x + 2y = 25$

What is the average of x and y?

(A) 1

(B) 2

(C) 3

(D) 6

(E) 10

4. $3x + y = z - 1$
    $x + y = z - 11$

What is the value of x?

(A) -5

(B) -2

(C) 0

(D) 2

(E) 5

5.

$$x + y = 5$$

$$x + w = 7$$

Column A	Column B
y	w

6. Mary has 15 more marbles than John has. If Mary buys an additional 35 marbles, she will have twice as many as John. How many marbles does Mary have?

Answers

1. **(C)**   Algebra: Solving Systems of Equations   *Easy*
Since one of the equations has y and the other has $-y$, you can add the two equations to eliminate y:

$$x + y = 4$$
$$\underline{\pm\, x - y = 6}$$
$$2x = 10$$
$$x = 5$$

2. **(A)**   Algebra: Solving Systems of Equations   *Moderate*
Add the two equations to eliminate y.

$$y - 7 = x$$
$$\underline{+\, 7x + 6 - y = 3x}$$
$$7x + 6 + y - y - 7 = 4x$$
$$-1 = -3x$$
$$\frac{1}{3} = x$$

3. **(C)**   Algebra: Solving Systems of Equations   *Difficult*
Add the two equations:

$$2x + 3y = 5$$
$$\underline{+\, 3x + 2y = 25}$$
$$5x + 5y = 30$$

Notice that you can divide through this equation by 5 to get:

$$\frac{5x + 5y = 30}{5}$$
$$x + y = 6$$

If x and y add up to 6, their average is 3, since the average of two numbers is equal to their sum divided by 2.

4. **(E)**   Algebra: Solving Systems of Equations   *Difficult*
You cannot eliminate any of the variables by adding these equations, so you should try subtracting them instead:

$$3x + y = z - 1$$
$$\underline{-\,(x + y = z - 11)}$$
$$2x \qquad = \qquad -1 - (-11) = -1 + 11$$

$$2x = 10$$

$$x = 5$$

5. **(B)** Algebra: Solving Systems of Equations *Easy*

Since x increased by w yields a larger number than x increased by y, w must be larger than y.

6. **65** Algebra: Solving Systems of Equations *Moderate*

In order to solve this problem, you need to write two equations. The phrase "Mary has 16 more marbles than John has" can be expressed algebraically as $M = J + 15$, where M represents the number of marbles Mary has and J represents the number of marbles John has. The phrase "If Mary buys an additional 35 marbles, she will have twice as many as John" can be expressed algebraically as $M + 35 = 2J$. Substitute $M - 15 = J$ into $M + 35 = 2J$ and solve for M:

$$M + 35 = 2(M - 15)$$

$$M + 35 = 2M - 30$$

$$35 = M - 30$$

$$65 = M$$

Solving Inequalities

An equation states that the values on either side of the = sign are of the same value. An inequality states that one side of the equation is greater than the other: $a < b$ states that a is less than b, while $a > b$ states that a is greater than b. $a \le b$ means that a is less than or equal to b, while $a \ge b$ means that a is greater than or equal to b.

Solving an inequality is basically the same as solving a normal equation: all the rules of simplification still apply, as does the rule stipulating that whatever you do to one side of the equation you must also do to the other side. The one rule that does differ for inequalities comes when you multiply both sides by a negative. If you do so, you must flip the greater than or less than sign: if $x > y$, then $-x < -y$.

Inequalities often appear in QC questions.

$2 \le 2y - 3 \le 4$

Column A	Column B
$y - 1$	$^7/_2$

The fastest way to answer this question is to substitute $7/2$ into the inequality $2 < 2y - 3 < 9$ to see if it is a possible value for y. If you did this, you'd see that $2(7/2) - 3 = 4$, making $7/2$ a possible value for y. Also, because when $7/2$ is plugged into the expression it gives you the value of 4, which is the highest possible allowed value of the expression as stated by $2y - 3 \leq 4$, you know that y can never be bigger than $7/2$. And since the expression in column A is $y - 1$, you know that Column B must be bigger than Column A.

Solving Inequalities

1. $1 < x < 8$ $5 < y < 22$ If $x + y$ is an integer, what is the smallest possible value of $x + y$?

   (A)   4
   (B)   5
   (C)   6
   (D)   7
   (E)   8

2.   If $x < 2x + 12$, which of the following could be a value for x?

   (A)   −15
   (B)   −14
   (C)   −13
   (D)   −12
   (E)   −11

3.

$$x < y$$

$$y < z$$

Column A	Column B
x	z

4.

$$j < k$$

$$k > m$$

Column A	Column B
j	m

5.

$$x - 3 < 0$$

$$y - 5 < 0$$

Column A	Column B
$x + y$	8

6.

$$2x + y > 20$$

$$y > 6$$

If x and y are positive integers, what is the smallest possible value of $x + 2y$?

Answers

1. **(D)**   Algebra: Solving Inequalities   *Easy*
Add the given inequalities in order to find the range of $x + y$.

$$\begin{aligned}1 < x < 8 \\ +5 < y < 22 \\ \hline 6 < x + y < 30\end{aligned}$$

Since $x + y$ is greater than but *not* equal to 6, the smallest possible integer value is 7.

2. **(E)**   Algebra: Solving Inequalities   *Difficult*
First solve the inequality for x:

$$x < 2x + 12$$

$$-x < 12$$

$$x > -12$$

Remember to reverse the direction of the inequality because the inequality is divided by a negative number. Of the answer choices, the only value greater than -12 is -11.

3. **(B)**   Algebra: Solving Inequalities   *Easy*
Since z is greater than y and since y is greater than x, z must also be greater than x.

4. **(D)**   Algebra: Solving Inequalities   *Moderate*
According to the given inequalities, k is greater than both j and m. However, these inequalitiesdo not tell you about the relationship between j and m, so the correct answer

to this question is choice (D) because the relationship between Columns A and B cannot be determined.

5. **(B)**   Algebra: Solving Inequalities   *Moderate*

You can find the range of $x + y$ by adding the two inequalities:

$$x - 3 < 0$$
$$\underline{+ \, y - 5 < 0}$$
$$x + y - 8 < 0$$

If you add 8 to each side of the inequality, you get: $x + y < 8$. Since 8 is greater than $x + y$, Column B is greater than Column A.

6. **21**   Algebra: Solving Inequalities   *Difficult*

To make $x + 2y$ as small as possible, you need to choose the smallest possible values for both x and y. Since y must be greater than 6, the smallest integer value of y is 7. Plug $y = 7$ into the first inequality:

$$2x + 7 > 20$$

$$2x > 13$$

$$x > 6.5$$

According to this inequality, the smallest integer value of x is 7. Plug $x = 7$ and $y = 7$ into $x + 2y$: $7 + 2(7) = 7 + 14 = 21$.

Multiplying Binomials and Polynomials

Multiplying binomials or polynomials can look like a daunting task, but it really isn't. It's actually pretty mindless. The most important thing is to be careful that you haven't forgotten a term somewhere.

Binomials

Problems that require you to multiply binomials are pretty common on the SAT. This is not a difficult task if you remember the acronym FOIL, which stands for First Outer Inner Last. For example, if you must multiply the binomials $(x + 1)(x + 3)$ you start by multiplying the first number in each polynomial $(x)(x)$, then the outer numbers $(x)(3)$, then the inner numbers $(1)(x)$, and finally the last numbers $(1)(3)$ and you get:

$$(x + 1)(x + 3)$$

$$x^2 + 3x + 1x + 3 = x^2 + 4x + 3$$

The only tricky part to following FOIL is remembering to pay attention to signs. For instance, if you have the polynomials $(x + 1)(x - 3)$, then the -3 comes to play an important role. You always add up the products of FOIL, but look what happens when there's a negative number involved:

$$(x + 1)(x - 3) = x^2 + 1x + (-3x) + (-3) = x^2 + 1x - 3x - 3 = x^2 - 2x - 3$$

There are a few standard binomials that ETS includes in almost every SAT. You should memorize how to multiply these binomials:

$$(x + y)(x - y) = x^2 - y^2$$
$$(x + y)(x + y) = x^2 + 2xy + y^2$$
$$(x - y)(x - y) = x^2 - 2xy + y^2$$

Polynomials

On extremely rare occasions, a question on the SAT might ask you to multiply polynomials. For example, you might be asked to multiply the polynomial $(a + b + c)$ by the binomial $(d + e)$. To carry out this multiplication, you should treat the larger polynomial as a single term and distribute the smaller one across it:

$$(d + e)(a + b + c) = d(a + b + c) + e(a + b + c) = da + db + dc + ea + eb + ec$$

To multiply $(2x + 3)(x^2 + 4x + 7)$:

$$2x(x^2 + 4x + 7) + 3(x^2 + 4x + 7) = 2x^3 + 8x^2 + 14x + 3x^2 + 12x + 21$$

Then combine like terms to get your final answer:

$$= 2x^3 + 11x^2 + 26x + 21$$

Multiplying Binomials and Polynomials

1.   If $(x + 1)(2x + 3) = ax^2 + bx + c$ for all values of x, what is the sum of b and c?

(A)   6
(B)   7
(C)   8
(D)   10
(E)   15

2.   For which of the following values of x does the expression $(x + 1)(x + 2)(x - 6)$ have a negative value?

(A)   –2
(B)   –1
(C)   0
(D)   6
(E)   12

3.   Solve for x in $\dfrac{(x^2 + 4)}{(x - 1)} = \dfrac{(2x + 1)}{2}$.

(A)   –9
(B)   –4
(C)   –2
(D)   1
(E)   2

4.   If $x + y = 6$ and $x - y = -2$, what is the value of $x^2 - y^2$?

(A)   –12
(B)   –4
(C)   4
(D) $4\sqrt{2}$
(E) $12\sqrt{2}$

5.

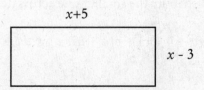

$x + 5$

$x - 3$

The area of the rectangle above is 48.

Column A	Column B
x	9

6.   What is the value of s if $(2x^2 + 6x + 1)(4x + 3) = qx^3 + rx^2 + sx + t$ for all values of x?

Answers

1.   **(C)**   Algebra: Multiplying Binomials and Polynomials   *Moderate*
First FOIL the factored polynomial: $(x + 1)(2x + 3) = 2x^2 + 5x + 3$. Since $2x^2 + 5x + 3 = ax^2 + bx + c$, you know that $a = 2$, $b = 5$, $c = 3$. The sum of b and c is $5 + 3 = 8$.

2.   **(C)**   Algebra: Multiplying Binomials and Polynomials   *Moderate*
An easy way to answer this problem is to plug each of the answer choices into the expression and see which one produces a negative value.

(A) $(-2+1)(-2+2)(-2-6) = (-1)(0)(-8) = 0$

(B) $(-1+1)(-1+2)(-1-6) = (0)(1)(-7) = 0$

(C) $(0+1)(0+2)(0-6) = (1)(2)(-6) = -12$

(D) $(6+1)(6+2)(6-6) = (7)(8)(0) = 0$

(E) $(12+1)(12+2)(12-6) = (13)(14)(6) = 1092$

Choice (C), $x = 0$, is the only answer that produces a negative value.

3.   **(A)**   Algebra: Multiplying Binomials and Polynomials   *Moderate*
First you need to cross-multiply the equation

$$\frac{x^2 + 4)}{(x-1)} = \frac{(2x+1)}{2}$$
$$2(x^2 + 4) = (2x+1)(x-1)$$

Now FOIL the right side of the equation:

$$2(x^2 + 4) = 2x^2 - 2x + 1x - 1$$

$$2x^2 + 8 = 2x^2 - 1x - 1$$

$$8 = -1x - 1$$

$$9 = -1x$$

$$-9 = x$$

4.   **(A)**   Algebra: Multiplying Binomials and Polynomials   *Difficult*
You should learn the following formula for binomial multiplication: $x^2 - y^2 = (x + y)(x - y)$. Since you know that $x + y = 6$ and that $x - y = -2$, you can plug those values into the formula above: $x^2 - y^2 = (x + y)(x - y) = (6)(-2) = -12$.

5.   **(B)**   Algebra: Multiplying Binomials and Polynomials   *Difficult*
The formula for the area of a rectangle is *Area = Length · Width*. Plug the area of the rectangle and the lengths of the two sides into this formula:

$$48 = (x + 5)(x - 3)$$

Now FOIL the right side of the equation:

$$48 = x^2 - 3x + 5x - 15$$

$$48 = x^2 + 2x - 15$$

$$0 = x^2 + 2x - 63$$

Factor the right side of the equation:

$$0 = (x - 7)(x + 9)$$

Therefore, $x = 7$ or $x = -9$. You can discard -9 because the length of a side of a rectangle cannot be negative. Since the value of Column A is $x = 7$, the correct answer to this question is Column B.

6. **22** Algebra: Multiplying Binomials and Polynomials   *Moderate*

If you multiply out the left side of the equation, you'll get an expression that resembles the right side of the equation:

$$(2x^2 + 6x + 1)(4x + 3) = 8x^3 + 6x^2 + 24x^2 + 18x + 4x + 3$$

$$(2x^2 + 6x + 1)(4x + 3) = 8x^3 + 30x^2 + 22x + 3$$

Since $8x^3 + 30x^2 + 22x + 3 = qx^3 + rx^2 + sx + t$, you know that the corresponding x terms on either side of the equation are equal. Since you want to find the value of s, you should set up the equation $22x = sx$, or $22 = s$.

SAT Unit Test–Algebra

1. If $x = 2y$ and $y = w + 3$, then what is the value of x when $w = 6$?

    (A) 4
    (B) 11
    (C) 15
    (D) 18
    (E) 36

2. Brendan has \$20 less than Robert. Robert has \$14 more than Craig. If Craig has \$10, how much money does Brendan have?

    (A) \$4
    (B) \$6
    (C) \$16
    (D) \$40
    (E) \$44

3. Simplify $\dfrac{a^5 b^4}{ab^3}$.

    (A) $(ab)^3$
    (B) $a^4 b$
    (C) $a^5 b^{\frac{4}{3}}$
    (D) $a^5 b^{12}$
    (E) $a^6 b^7$

4. If $3x + 7 = 5x + 1$, what is the value of x?

   (A) 1
   (B) 3
   (C) 5
   (D) 7
   (E) 9

5. If $x - y = 15$ and $x - 2y = 5$, what is the value of y?

   (A) 2
   (B) 5
   (C) 10
   (D) 15
   (E) 25

6.

   If $AC < CD$, $DB = 2$, and $AB = 12$, which of the following could be the value of CD?

   (A) 2
   (B) 3
   (C) 4
   (D) 5
   (E) 6

7. Nina has a number of identical boxes. Each box holds either 3 large cookies or 5 small cookies. If Nina's boxes are filled with a total of 27 large cookies and she wants to substitute small cookies for the large ones, how many small cookies can she fit into the same number of boxes?

   (A) 15
   (B) 18
   (C) 32
   (D) 45
   (E) 50

8. $$\frac{ax^2 - xy}{xy}$$

   Which of the following expressions is equivalent to the expression above?

   (A) ax

   (B) ax^2

   (C) $ax^2 - 1$

   (D) $\dfrac{ax - y}{y}$

   (E) $\dfrac{ax - y}{x}$

9.   If $a + b + c = 12$ and $a + b - c = 18$, what is the value of c?

   (A) -18
   (B) -3
   (C) 6
   (D) 12
   (E) 15

10.   If $\dfrac{x+1}{x+3} = \dfrac{x-5}{x-4}$, then what is the value of x?

   (A) 4
   (B) 7
   (C) 11
   (D) 13
   (E) 15

11.   What is the value of x in the following equation: $x - \dfrac{1}{2}(x+12) = 8$?

   (A) 4
   (B) 12
   (C) 14
   (D) 20
   (E) 28

12.   If $x < 5x + 12$, which of the following could be the value of x?

   (A) -6
   (B) -5
   (C) -4
   (D) -3
   (E) -2

13.   What is the product of the binomial $(x - y)$ and the trinomial $(x^2 + xy + y^2)$?

   (A) $x^3 - y^3$
   (B) $x^3 + y^3$
   (C) $x^3 + 4xy - y^3$
   (D) $x^3 + x^2y + y^2x - y^3$
   (E) $x^3 + 2x^2y + 2y^2x - y^3$

14. $a = 2b = 5c$

   If x is the sum of a, b, and c, which of the following expressions represents x in terms of a?

   (A) $\dfrac{3a}{7}$

   (B) $\dfrac{17a}{10}$

   (C) $3a$
   (D) $8a$
   (E) $11a$

15.   If $x = 2y^2$, then $(xy)^4 =$

    (A) $2y^7$

    (B) $2y^{12}$

    (C) $8y^7$

    (D) $16y^7$

    (E) $16y^{12}$

16. $Ax = B(x + y)$. Solve for x in terms of A, b, and y.

    (A) $\dfrac{By}{A - B}$

    (B) $\dfrac{A}{B} - y$

    (C) $\dfrac{y}{A - B}$

    (D) $\dfrac{By}{A + B}$

    (E) $\dfrac{A + B}{By}$

17.   If $\dfrac{x^2 - 100}{x + 10} = 17$, what is the value of $2x$?

    (A)   20

    (B)   27

    (C)   34

    (D)   54

    (E)   70

18.   If $\dfrac{x}{y} < -1$ and $y = -6$, which of the following must be true?

    (A) $x < 6$

    (B) $x + y > 0$

    (C) $x + y > 1$

    (D) $x + y < 0$

    (E) $x < -y$

19.   If $x^2 + y^2 = 14$ and $xy = -6$, what is the value of $(x + y)^2$?

    (A)   1

    (B)   2

    (C)   3

    (D)   8

    (E)   14

20.   What is the value of pq if $q > 0$ and $4x^2 + px + 9 = (2x + q)^2$ for all values of x?

    (A)   27

    (B)   36

    (C)   42

    (D)   48

    (E)   72

SAT Algebra

21.

$$3x + y = 12$$

$$y = 2x - 8$$

Column A	Column B
x	y

22.

$$y = 3x - 6$$

Column A	Column B
x	y

23.

9 less than twice n is equal to n increased by 6.

Column A	Column B
n	10

24.

$$2x^2 + 3y^2 = 35$$

$$x^2 - 3y^2 = 13$$

Column A	Column B
x	y

25.

$$w = \frac{m}{n}$$

Column A	Column B
w	$\dfrac{m+n}{n}$

26.   If $x + 2y = -2$, what is $3x + 6y + 50$?

27.   If $2x + 8 < 29 - x$, what is the largest possible integral value of x?

28.   If $3x + 5y = 18$ and $5x + 3y = 6$, what is the value of $x + y$?

29.   If $2x + 5y + 17 = 2y - x + 25$, what is the sum of x and y?

30.   If $x^4 - y^4 = 100$ and $x^2 + y^2 = 200$, what is the value of $x^2 - y^2$?

Answers

1. **(D)**   Algebra: Substitution   *Easy*
Plug $w = 6$ into $y = w + 3$: $y = 6 + 3 = 9$. Then plug $y = 9$ into $x = 2y$:

$$x = 2(9) = 18.$$

2. **(A)**   Algebra: Building Expressions and Equations   *Easy*
The phrase "Brendan has $20 less than Robert" can be expressed algebraically as $B = R - 20$, where B represents how much money Brendan has and R represents how much money Robert has. You can express "Robert has $14 more than Craig" algebraically as $R = 14 + C$, where C represents how much money Craig has. Since you know that Craig has $10, substitute 10 for C in the second equation: $R = 14 + 10 = 24$. Now, substitute 24 for R in the first equation: $B = 24 - 20 = 4$. Brendan has $4.

3. **(B)**   Algebra: Simplifying and Manipulating Expressions   *Easy*
Use the rules of exponents to simplify this expression. To divide exponential terms with the same bases, all you need to do is subtract the exponents. You can rewrite the expression as $(a^5 \div a^1)(b^4 \div b^3) = (a^{5-1})(b^{4-3}) = a^4 b$.

4. **(B)**   Algebra: Solving Linear Equations   *Easy*
To solve for x, you need to isolate x on one side of the equation. Start by subtracting $3x$ from both sides of the equation:

$$3x + 7 = 5x + 1$$
$$7 = 2x + 1$$
$$6 = 2x$$
$$3 = x$$

5. **(C)**   Algebra: Solving Systems of Equations   *Easy*
Since you're asked to find the value of y, you need to make y the only variable in an equation. You can eliminate x by subtracting the equations:

$$
\begin{aligned}
x - y &= 15 \\
-(x - 2y &= 5) \\
\hline
-y - (-2y) &= 15 - 5 \\
-y + 2y &= 10 \\
y &= 10
\end{aligned}
$$

6.   **(E)**   Algebra: Solving Inequalities   *Easy*

If $AB = 12$ and $DB = 2$, you can figure out the value of AD by subtracting DB from AB: $AD = 12 - 2 = 10$. $AC < CD$ means that AC is less than CD. Since you know that $AC + CD = 10$, try each of the answer choices to see which one fits the inequality $AC < CD$.

(A) If $CD = 2$, then $AC = 10 - 2 = 8$

(B) If $CD = 3$, then $AC = 10 - 3 = 7$

(C) If $CD = 4$, then $AC = 10 - 4 = 6$

(D) If $CD = 5$, then $AC = 10 - 5 = 5$

(E) If $CD = 6$, then $AC = 10 - 6 = 4$

Choice (E) is the only value of CD that makes CD greater in value than AC.

7.   **(D)**   Algebra: Substitution   *Moderate*

If Nina's boxes are filled with 27 large cookies and each box can hold 3 large cookies, you can divide the number of total cookies (27) by the number of cookies per box (3) to find the number of boxes she has: $27/3 = 9$ boxes. Since each box can hold 5 small cookies, you can multiply the number of boxes (9) by the number of small cookies per box (5) to determine the total number of small cookies that Nina can fit into her boxes: $9(5) = 45$ small cookies.

8.   **(D)**   Algebra: Simplifying and Manipulating Expressions   *Moderate*

You can simplify the numerator of the fraction by factoring: $ax^2 - xy = x(ax - y)$. Since x is common to both the numerator and the denominator, you can cancel it out:

$$\frac{x(ax - y)}{xy} = \frac{ax - y}{y}$$

9.   **(B)**   Algebra: Solving Systems of Equations   *Moderate*

In order to find the value of c, you first need to eliminate a and b. In this case, subtracting the two equations will eliminate a and b.

$$
\begin{array}{r}
a + b + c = 12 \\
-(a + b - c = 18) \\
\hline
c - (-c) = 12 - 18 \\
c + c = -6 \\
2c = -6 \\
c = -3
\end{array}
$$

10. **(C)**   Algebra: Solving Linear Equations   *Moderate*

To solve for x, you need to isolate the x terms on one side of the equation. Start by cross multiplying the equation:

$$\frac{(x+1)}{(x+3)} = \frac{(x-5)}{(x-4)}$$
$$(x+1)(x-4) = (x+3)(x-5)$$

Now FOIL each side of the equation:

$$x^2 - 4x + x - 4 = x^2 - 5x + 3x - 15$$

$$x^2 - 3x - 4 = x^2 - 2x - 15$$

$$-3x - 4 = -2x - 15$$

$$-4 = x - 15$$

$$11 = x$$

11. **(E)**   Algebra: Solving Linear Equations   *Moderate*

Your first step in simplifying this equation should be to distribute across the parentheses:

$$x - \frac{1}{2}(x+12) = 8$$

$$x - \frac{1}{2}x - \frac{1}{2}(12) = 8$$

$$x - \frac{1}{2}x - 6 = 8$$

$$\frac{1}{2}x - 6 = 8$$

$$\frac{1}{2}x = 14$$

Multiply both sides of the equation by 2:

$$x = 28$$

12. **(E)**   Algebra: Solving Inequalities   *Moderate*

In order to solve this problem, you need to isolate x on one side of the equation:

$$x < 5x + 12$$

$$-4x < 12$$

$$x > -3$$

You need to remember that dividing (or multiplying) an inequality by a negative number reverses the inequality sign. The only answer choice that fits this inequality is (E), –2.

13. **(A)** Algebra: Multiplying Binomials and Polynomials   *Moderate*

To find the product of the binomial and trinomial, simply multiply them together:

$$(x-y)(x^2+xy+y^2)=x(x^2+xy+y^2)-y(x^2+xy+y^2)$$
$$=x^3+x^2y+xy^2-x^2y-xy^2-y^3$$

If you combine like terms, you get the expression x^3-y^3.

14. **(B)** Algebra: Substitution   *Difficult*

You can express the phrase "x is the sum of a, b, and c" algebraically as $x=a+b+c$.

Because you want x in terms of a only, you need to substitute for both b and c. The

question tells you that $a=2b$; if you divide both sides of this equation by 2, you get

$\frac{a}{2}=b$. The question also says that $a=5c$, which you can rewrite as $\frac{a}{5}=c$. Plug these

expressions for b and c into $x=a+b+c$: $x=a+\frac{a}{2}+\frac{a}{5}$. You can add the fractions by

rewriting them in terms of a common denominator, 10: $x=\frac{10a}{10}+\frac{5a}{10}+\frac{2a}{10}=\frac{17}{10}$.

15. **(E)** Algebra: Substitution   *Difficult*

Since the answer choices include the variable y but not the variable x, you need to eliminate the x term through substitution. Substitute $x=2y^2$ into $(xy)^4$:

$$(xy)^4=[(2y^2)y]^4$$
$$=[2y^3]^4$$
$$=16y^{12}$$

16. **(A)** Algebra: Solving Linear Equations   *Difficult*

To solve for x in terms of A, B, and y, you need to isolate x. Start by distributing B on the right side of the equation.

$$Ax=B(x+y)$$
$$Ax=Bx+By$$
$$Ax-Bx=By$$
$$x(A-B)=By$$
$$x=\frac{By}{A-B}$$

17. **(D)** Algebra: Solving Linear Equations *Difficult*

Your first step should be to simplify the left side of the equation by factoring.

$$\frac{x^2 - 100}{x + 10} = \frac{(x - 10)(x + 10)}{(x + 10)}$$

By canceling like terms, you are left with $(x - 10)$. Now you have the equation $(x - 10) = 17$, and you can find x by adding 10 to both sides of the equation:

$$x - 10 = 17$$

$$x = 27$$

Remember that the question asks for the value of $2x$ not x: $2x = 54$.

18. **(B)** Algebra: Solving Inequalities *Difficult*

Substitute $y = -6$ for y into the inequality.

$$\frac{x}{y} < -1$$

$$\frac{x}{-6} < -1$$

Multiply both sides of the inequality by -6, remembering to reverse the direction of the inequality):

$$x > 6$$

If $y = -6$ and $x > 6$, the sum of x and y is greater than zero, so choice (B) must be true. You may be tempted to choose (C), but the inequality in (C) is not necessarily true, because x is not necessarily an integer, so the value of $x + y$ could be less than 1.

19. **(B)** Algebra: Multiplying Binomials and Polynomials *Difficult*

You should memorize how to multiply the binomial $(x + y)^2$: $(x + y)(x + y) = x^2 + 2xy + y^2$. Since $x^2 + y^2 = 14$, you can substitute 14 for $x^2 + y^2$ in $x^2 + 2xy + y^2$ to get: $14 + 2xy$. Since $xy = -6$, you can substitute -6 for xy: $14 + 2(-6) = 14 - 12 = 2$.

20. **(B)** Algebra: Multiplying Binomials and Polynomials *Difficult*

Your first step in solving this problem should be to multiply out the right side of the equation:

$$4x^2 + px + 9 = (2x + q)^2$$

$$4x^2 + px + 9 = 4x^2 + 4qx + q^2$$

Since this is an equation, the corresponding x terms in each quadratic must be equal: $4x^2 = 4x^2$, $px = 4qx$, and $9 = q^2$. You can find the values of p and q by setting these terms equal to each other. First solve for q:

$$9 = q^2$$

$$3 = q$$

Since the question says that $q > 0$, you know that q cannot equal -3. Now that you know q you can plug its value into $4qx$:

$$px = 4qx$$

$$px = 4(3)x$$

$$px = 12x$$

$$p = 12$$

The last step is to find the value of pq:

$$pq = 12(3)$$

$$pq = 36$$

21. **(A)** Algebra: Substitution   *Moderate*

You need to solve for x and y one variable at a time. First solve for x by substituting $y = 2x - 8$ into the first equation:

$$3x + y = 12$$

$$3x + 2x - 8 = 12$$

$$5x - 8 = 12$$

$$5x = 20$$

$$x = 4$$

Since you know $x = 4$, you can find the value of y. Plug $x = 4$ into $y = 2x - 8$: $y = 2(4) - 8$ $= 8 - 8 = 0$. Column (A), 4, is greater than Column B, 0.

22. **(D)** Algebra: Solving Linear Equations   *Easy*

You need two equations in order to solve for the two variables. Since the question gives only one equation, the relationship between x and y cannot be determined.

23. **(A)** Algebra: Building Expressions and Equations   *Moderate*

You need to write an equation to represent the situation given in the question. The phrase "9 less than twice n" can be expressed algebraically as $2n - 9$. The phrase "n increased by 6" can be expressed algebraically as $n + 6$. Set the two expressions equal to each other, and solve for n:

$$2n - 9 = n + 6$$

$$n - 9 = 6$$

$$n = 15$$

15 is greater than 10, so Column A is greater than Column B.

24. **(D)** Algebra: Solving Systems of Equations   *Moderate*

When you have two equations with two variables, you should solve for one variable and then use that value to find the other variable. First solve for x by adding the two equations together:

$$2x^2 + 3y^2 = 35$$

$$+ \ x^2 - 3y^2 = 13$$

_____

$$3x^2 = 48$$

If you divide both sides by 3, you get: $x^2 = 16$, or $x = \pm 4$. To find the y value, substitute $x = \pm 4$ into one of the equations:

$$x^2 - 3y^2 = 13$$

$$(\pm 4)^2 - 3y^2 = 13$$

$$16 - 3y^2 = 13$$

$$-3y^2 = -3$$

$$y^2 = 1$$

$$y = \pm 1$$

Because x and y can be either positive or negative, the relationship between the two columns cannot be determined.

25. **(B)** Algebra: Simplifying and Manipulating Expressions   *Difficult*

In order to compare Column A and Column B, you should make the expressions in the two columns as similar as possible. Replace the w in Column A with $\frac{m}{n}$. Now, compare to $\frac{m+n}{n}$. Rewrite as two fractions: $\frac{m+n}{n} = \frac{m}{n} + \frac{n}{n}$. Since $\frac{n}{n} = 1$, you can rewrite Column B as $\frac{m}{n} + 1$. is greater than $\frac{m}{n}$, so Column B is greater than Column A.

26. **44** Algebra: Simplifying and Manipulating Expressions   *Easy*

The key to solving this problem is realizing that $3x + 6y = 3(x + 2y)$. If you realize the relationship between these two expressions, you can find the value of $3x + 6y$ through substitution: $3x + 6y = 3(x + 2y) = 3(-2) = -6$. Now you can find $3x + 6y + 50 = -6 + 50 = 44$. While the algebra and math in this problem are pretty simple, recognizing the trick can be difficult. You should notice right away that you need two equations to solve a problem with two variables. Since you don't have two equations, you need to use a little creativity.

27.　**6**　Algebra: Solving Inequalities　　　　　　　　　　　　　　*Easy*
To find the range of x, isolate the variable on one side of the inequality:

$$2x + 8 < 29 - x$$

$$3x + 8 < 29$$

$$3x < 21$$

$$x < 7$$

Since x is an integer, the largest value that it can be is 6.

28.　**3**　Algebra: Solving Systems of Equations　　　　　　　　*Moderate*
A fast way of answering this question is not to solve for x and y individually but to solve for $x + y$ by adding the two equations together. If you add the two equations, you get:

$$3x + 5y = 18$$

$$\underline{+\ 5x + 3y = 6}$$

$$8x + 8y = 24$$

Now you can divide the equation by 8 to find $x + y = 3$.

29.　**8/3 or 2.66 or 2.67**　Algebra: Solving Linear Equations　　*Difficult*
Because the question gives you only one equation, you cannot find the values of x and y. Instead, you should try isolating the x and y terms on one side of the equation.

$$2x + 5y + 17 = 2y - x + 25$$

$$2x + 3y + 17 = -x + 25$$

$$3x + 3y + 17 = 25$$

$$3x + 3y = 8$$

If you divide both sides of the equation by 3, you can find $x + y = \frac{8}{3}$.

30.　**1/2**　Algebra: Multiplying Binomials and Polynomials　　*Difficult*
The trick to answering this question is using the difference of squares rule. According to this rule, $x^2 - y^2 = (x + y)(x - y)$. You need to recognize that x^4 is the square of x^2 and

that y^4 is the square of y^2, so the relationship among the expressions $x^4 - y^4$, $x^2 + y^2$, and $x^2 - y^2$ can be described as

$$x^4 - x^4 = (x^2 + y^2)(x^2 - y^2)$$

Since $x^4 - y^4 = 100$ and $x^2 + y^2 = 200$, you can rewrite the equation above as:

$$100 = 200(x^2 - y^2)$$
$$x^2 - y^2 = \frac{1}{2}$$

SAT Geometry

ABOUT A THIRD OF THE MATH questions on the SAT deal with topics of basic geometry. The geometry tested on the SAT is less complicated than the geometry taught in high school. For the test, you will have to know about lines, angles, triangles, circles, polygons and other shapes, but you will not have to write out a proof or prove a geometric theorem. The SAT contains no trigonometry.

There are seven main categories of geometry tested on the SAT, as you can see in the table of contents on this page. In addition to covering these seven topics, we also provide a brief run-through of the basics of geometry so that you're fresh on the concepts and terminology.

Geometry Basics

We've included this first little review of geometry basics because you need to understand certain terms and ideas before you can discuss the geometry topics tested on the SAT.

Points

A point is a way to describe a specific location in space. Below is pictured the point *B*.

B•

A point has no length or width. Though in the picture point *B* is a black dot, in real life, points take up no space and are not tangible. Points are useful for identifying specific locations but are not objects in themselves. They only appear so when drawn on a page.

Lines

A line is an infinite set of points arrayed in a straight formation, named by any two points in that set. A line has no thickness but is infinitely long in both directions. To form a line, take any two points, *A* and *B*, and draw a straight line through them. The resulting line is a called line *AB*.

A line can be drawn through any two points.

Line Segments

A line segment is the portion of a line that lies between two points on that line—in this example, points *A* and *B*. Whereas a line has infinite length, a line segment has a finite length. A line segment is named by the two points it lies between

A line segment can be drawn between any two points.

Rays

A ray is a cross between a line and a line segment. It extends without bound in one direction but not the other. Below is a figure of a ray:

A ray is named by its endpoint and another point that it passes through.

Okay, now we've covered the basics. All of the following topics are tested directly by the SAT.

Angles and Lines

An angle is a geometric figure consisting of two lines, rays, or line segments with a common endpoint:

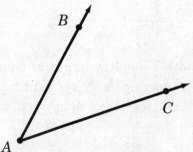

The endpoint of the angle is called the vertex. In the angle pictured above, the vertex is point *A*. The angle can be called either angle *CAB* or angle *BAC*. When naming an angle in this way, the only rule is that the vertex must be the middle "initial" of the angle. The SAT will also refer to angles using symbols: $\angle A$.

Measuring Angles

Angles are measured in degrees, sometimes denoted by the symbol °. There are 360° in a complete rotation around a point; a circle therefore has 360°. There are some other ways to measure angles, such as radians. You may not have learned about radians in high school. Well, don't worry about them. For the SAT, you only have to be familiar with degrees.

Take two intersecting lines. The intersection of these lines produces four angles.

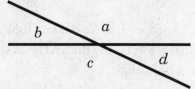

From the diagram below, you should see that the four angles together encompass one full revolution around the two lines' point of intersection. Therefore, the four angles produced by two intersection lines total 360°; angle $a + b + c + d = 360°$.

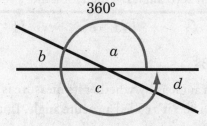

Types of Angles

There are different types of angles, categorized by the number of degrees they have.

Zero Angles

An angle with a measure of 0° is called a zero angle. If this is hard to visualize, consider two lines that form some angle greater than 0°. Then picture one of the lines rotating toward the other until they both fall on the same line. The angle they create has been shrunk from its original measure to 0°, forming a zero angle:

Right Angles

An angle with a measure of 90° is called a right angle. Notice that a right angle is symbolized with a square drawn in the corner of the angle. Whenever you see that little square, you know that you are dealing with a right angle.

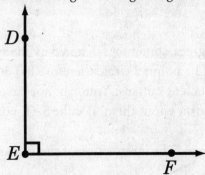

Right angles often have special properties. We'll take a look at these properties later on. For now, it's enough to say that while taking the SAT, you should be on the lookout for the little square that denotes a right angle.

Straight Angle

An angle with a measure of 180° is called a straight angle. It looks just like a line. Don't confuse straight angles with zero angles, which look like a single ray.

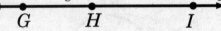

Acute and Obtuse Angles

Another way to classify an angle is by whether its measure is greater or less than 90°. If an angle measures less than 90°, it's called an acute angle. If it measures more than 90°, it's called an obtuse angle. Right angles are neither acute nor obtuse. They're just right.

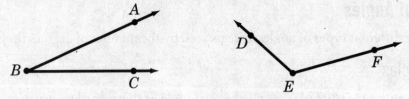

In the picture below, ∠ABC is acute while ∠DEF is obtuse.

Complementary and Supplementary Angles

Special names are given to pairs of angles whose sums equal either 90° or 180°. Angles whose sum is 90° are called complementary angles. If two angles sum to 180°, they're called supplementary angles.

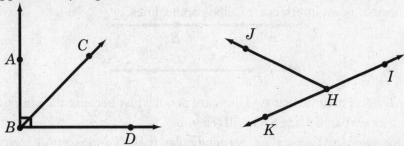

In the picture above ∠ABC and ∠CBD are complementary, since together they make up a right angle. Angle ∠JHK and ∠JHI are supplementary, since they make up a straight line.

On the SAT, you will often have to use the rules of complementary and supplementary angles to figure out the degree measure of an angle. For instance, let's say you are given the following diagram and are told that AC is a line:

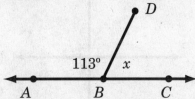

The picture tells you that ∠ABD is 113°, but how many degrees is ∠DBC? Well, since you know that AC is a line, you know that ∠ABC is a straight angle and equals 180°. You also know that ∠ABD and ∠DBC are supplementary angles that add up to 180°. Therefore, to find out the value of ∠DBC, you can simply take 180° and subtract 113°, which tells you that ∠DBC = 67°.

Vertical Angles

When two lines (or line segments) intersect, the angles that lie opposite each other, called vertical angles, are always equal.

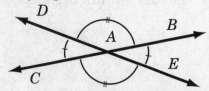

Angle ∠DAC and ∠BAE are vertical angles and are therefore equal to each other. Angle ∠DAB and ∠CAE are also vertical (and equal) angles. This is very important knowledge for the SAT. At some point during the test, you will likely be asked to figure out the degree of an angle, and knowing this rule will help you immensely.

Parallel and Perpendicular Lines

Pairs of lines that never intersect are called parallel lines.

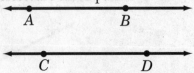

On the SAT, never assume that two lines are parallel just because they look as if they are. If the lines are parallel, the SAT will tell you.

Lines (or segments) are called perpendicular if their intersection forms a right angle. Notice that if one of the angles formed by the intersection of two lines or segments is a right angle, then all four angles created will also be right angles (incidentally illustrating our point that the four angles formed by two intersecting lines will equal 360°, since 90° + 90° + 90° + 90° = 360°).

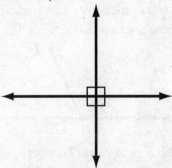

As with parallel lines, don't assume that lines on the SAT are perpendicular unless the SAT states that they are. The SAT will alert you to perpendicular lines either by stating that two lines are perpendicular or by using the little box to indicate that the angles are 90°.

Also, you should note that if you see two lines that intersect and you know that the two lines form one right angle, but you don't explicitly know the value of the other three angles, you still know that the two lines are perpendicular and that all four angles equal 90°. Think about it. If you know that one angle is equal to 90°, then you can use the rules of supplementary angles to prove that all angles are equal to 90°.

Parallel Lines Cut by a Transversal

When two parallel lines are cut by a third straight line, the third line, known as a transversal, will intersect with each of the parallel lines. The eight angles created by these two intersections have special relationships with one another.

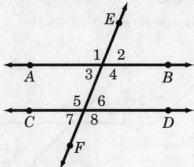

Angles 1, 4, 5, and 8 are all equal to each other. So are angles 2, 3, 6, and 7. Also, the sums of any two adjacent angles, such as 1 and 2 or 7 and 8 equal 180°. From these rules, you can make justified claims about seemingly unrelated angles. For example, since angles 1 and 2 sum to 180°—and since angle 2 and 7 are equal—the sum of angle 1 and 7 also equals 180°. The SAT likes to test this topic. When you see parallel lines cut by a transversal, you should immediately know how the angles are related. If you just know that angle 2 and angle 7 are equal, you will be able to answer the question a lot more quickly than if you have to work out the question by using the rules of supplementary and complementary angles.

Angles and Lines

Multiple Choice

1.   In the given figure, if line a is parallel to line b, $\angle y$ measures

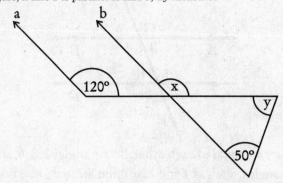

    (A)   50°
    (B)   10°
    (C)   120°
    (D)   70°
    (E)   60°

2.   If the measure of $\angle x$ is two-thirds the measure of its supplementary angle, $\angle y$, what is the measure of $\angle x$?

    (A)   54°
    (B)   108°
    (C)   60°
    (D)   120°
    (E)   72°

3.   Given that $\angle ABE$ is equal to x, $\overline{BE}$ is perpendicular to $\overline{AC}$, and $\angle ABF$ is equal to $5x-10$, what is the measure of $\angle FBD$?

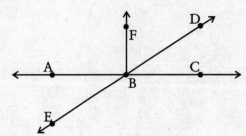

    (A)   52°
    (B)   20°
    (C)   90°
    (D)   70°
    (E)   110°

4. Given points A, B, and C on the number line below, on what position on the number line should point C be placed so that the distance between A and C is twice the distance between B and C?

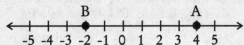

    (A) 2
    (B) −1
    (C) −2
    (D) 0
    (E) 3

5. If an angle measures 36°, its complementary angle measures

    (A) 144°
    (B) 36°
    (C) 54°
    (D) 90°
    (E) 126°

6. Suppose that the lines p and q are parallel and are cut by a transversal, r, as shown in the figure below. If the measure of $\angle 3$ is $x^2 - 3x$ and the measure of $\angle 6$ is $(x + 4)(x - 5)$, what is the measure of $\angle 4$?

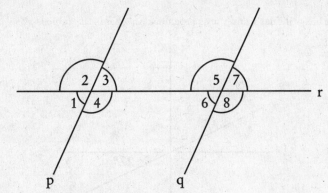

    (A) 110°
    (B) 50°
    (C) 70°
    (D) 10°
    (E) 90°

Quantitative Comparisons

7.

Given distinct points A, B, and C

Column A	Column B
The number of lines that pass through point A	The number of lines that pass through both point B and point C

8.

Suppose that points A, B, C, D, and E all lie on the
same line, and that $\overline{AB} \cong \overline{AE}$ and $\overline{BC} \cong \overline{DE}$.

Column A	Column B
The length of $\overline{AC}$	The length of $\overline{AD}$

Grid-ins

9.   Given the following figure, find the value of y.

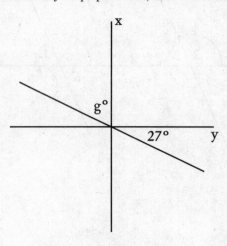

10.   In the figure below if lines x and y are perpendicular, what is the value of g?

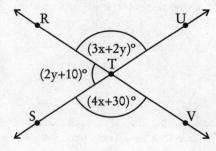

Angles and Lines—Answers

Multiple Choice

1. **(D)** Geometry: Angles and Lines *Easy*
Because the angle that corresponds to $\angle x$ measures 120°, $\angle x$ also measures 120°. Therefore, the supplementary angle to x in the triangle measures 60°. Knowing that the angles within a triangle total 180°, $y + 50° + 60° = 180°$, which yields $y = 70°$.

2. **(B)** Geometry: Angles and Lines *Easy*
If $\angle x$ and $\angle y$ are supplementary, $y + \frac{2}{3}y = 180°$, which simplifies to $\frac{5}{3}y = 180°$, and $y = 108°$. Thus, if $y = 108°$ and $x = \frac{2}{3}y$, $x = 72°$.

3. **(D)** Geometry: Angles and Lines *Easy*
Since $\overline{BF}$ is perpendicular to $\overline{AC}$, $\angle ABF$ measures 90°. By the information provided, $\angle ABF = 5x - 10 = 90°$. Solving for x yields $x = 20°$. Thus, $\angle FBD = 90° - \angle DBC = (90 - x)° = (90 - 20)° = 70°$.

4. **(D)** Geometry: Angles and Lines *Moderate*
The distance from A to B is 6. Let the distance from A to C be x, so $x + 2x = 6$, and hence, $x = 2$. Thus, the position on the number line that is 2 units away from B is 0.

5. **(C)** Geometry: Angles and Lines *Easy*
Complementary angles are two angles that sum to 90°, so the complement to a 36° angle is $90° - 36° = 54°$.

6. **(A)** Geometry: Angles and Lines *Moderate*
Alternate interior angles are equal, so $x^2 - 3x = (x + 4)(x - 5)$. Multiplying the right side out and simplifying yields $x = 10$. So, the measure of $\angle 4$ is $180° - [(10)^2 - 3(10)]° = 110°$.

Quantitative Comparisons

7. **(A)** Geometry: Angles and Lines *Easy*
There are infinitely many lines through a single point but only a single line through two distinct points. Therefore, only one line runs through both B and C, but an infinite number of lines runs through A.

8. **(D)** Geometry: Angles and Lines *Difficult*

Although the question specifies that *A*, *B*, *C*, *D*, and *E* are on the same line, it does not specify that the points are in any particular order. Therefore, although there are some scenarios under which $AC = AD$ (see below left), there are others in which $AC \neq AD$ (below right). Both diagrams fulfill the criteria $\overline{AB} \cong \overline{AE}$ and $\overline{BC} \cong \overline{DE}$, but the relationships between *AC* and *AD* are different.

Grid-ins

9. **(26)** Geometry: Angles and Lines *Difficult*

Set up two equations:

$$(4x + 30)° = (3x + 2y)° \text{ (vertical angles)}$$

$$(2y + 10)° + (4x + 30)° = 180° \text{ (supplementary angles)}$$

Simplify:

$$x - 2y = -30$$

$$\text{and } y + 2x = 70$$

Solve $y + 2x = 70$ for *y* to yield $y = 70 - 2x$. Then, substitute this expression into $x - 2y = -30$:

$$x - 2(70 - 2x) = -30$$

$$x - 140 + 4x = -30$$

$$5x = 110$$

$$x = 22$$

and therefore, $y = 70 - 2(22) = 26$.

10. **(63)** Geometry: Angles and Lines *Moderate*

Because *x* and *y* are perpendicular, the four angles formed by their intersection are right angles measuring 90°. *g* is equal to the angle directly across from it (which we will call *h*) because *g* and *h* are opposite angles. Because *h* and the 27° angle are complementary, $h + 27° = 90°$, so *h* is a 63° angle. Therefore, $g = 63$.

Triangles

Triangles are closed figures containing three angles and three sides. The sum of the three angles in a triangle will always equal 180°. This is a very important fact. You *must* know it. There are two other important rules of triangles that you should know for the SAT.

1. The longest side of a triangle is always opposite the largest angle; the second longest side is always opposite the second largest angle; and the shortest side of the triangle is opposite the smallest angle. The reverse is also true: the largest angle will stand opposite the longest side, etc.

2. No side of a triangle can be as large as the sum of the other two sides. If you know that a triangle has sides of length 4 and 6, you know the third side is smaller than 10 (6 + 4) and bigger than 2 (6 – 4). This can help you eliminate possible answer choices on MC questions.

There are a number of specialized types of triangles. Each of these types of triangles have special properties. The SAT will definitely test your understanding of these properties.

Scalene Triangles

A scalene triangle has no equal sides and, therefore, no equal angles.

The special property of this triangle is that it doesn't really have any special properties. SAT questions don't usually deal with scalenes.

Isosceles Triangles

Isosceles triangles have two equal sides, in this case sides *a* and *b* (the little marks in those two sides mark the sides as being congruent or equal in length). The angles opposite the congruent sides are also equal, in this case the angles marked by *x°* and *y°*.

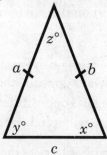

Because two of the angles of the isosceles triangle are equal and all triangles contain exactly 180°, if you know the value of one of the two equal angles, you can figure out the value of all the angles in the triangle. For example, if you know the value of ∠*x*, you know the value of ∠*y*, since ∠*x* and ∠*y* are equal. Angle *z* is equal to 180° – 2*x* (since *x* and *y* are equal, *x* + *y* = 2*x*). If you know the measure of ∠*z*, you can figure out the measures of ∠*x* and ∠*y*, since each equals $\frac{180-x}{2}$.

The SAT will test your knowledge of isosceles triangles. It might give you the length of a side and ask you the length of the other side to test your understanding of congruence. It might give you the value of an angle and ask you to figure out the value of another angle. It might ask you something else a little more indirect. But if you know these rules and remember them each time you see an isosceles triangle, you'll do fine.

Equilateral Triangles

An equilateral triangle is a triangle in which all the sides and all angles are equal. Since the angles of a triangle must total 180°, the measure of each angle of an equilateral triangle must be 60°.

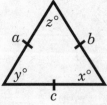

Right Triangles

A triangle with a right angle (90°) is called a right triangle. Because the angles of a triangle must total 180°, the non-right angles (∠*x* and ∠*y* in the diagram below) in a right triangle must add up to 90°. The side opposite the right angle (side c in the diagram below) is called the hypotenuse.

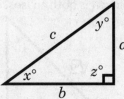

There are many different types of right triangles, but two are particularly important for the SAT.

30-60-90 Triangle

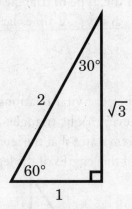

A 30-60-90 triangle is true to its name: it has angles of 30°, 60°, and 90°. A 30-60-90 triangle is actually half of an equilateral triangle. If you imagine an equilateral triangle and then cut it down the middle, you'll end up with a 30-60-90 (knowing this fact can often help you on SAT problems).

As the diagram shows, the ratio between the three sides of a 30-60-90 triangle is always the same. The side opposite the 90° angle is always twice as long as the side opposite the 30° angle. The side opposite the 60° angle is always $\sqrt{3}$ times as long as the side opposite the 30° angle. If you know these ratios and come across a 30-60-90 triangle during the SAT, you could spare yourself a lot of calculation. Note that these side lengths are *ratios*. A 30-60-90 triangle could have sides that measure 3, 6, and $3\sqrt{3}$ or 50, 100, and $50\sqrt{3}$.

SAT Geometry

45-45-90 Triangle

A 45-45-90 triangle lives a double life: it is both an isosceles triangle and a right triangle.

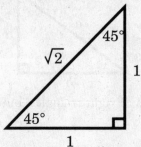

As the figure shows, the sides of this type of triangle always adhere to the same ratio. The side opposite the 90° angle is always $\sqrt{2}$ times larger than the two equal sides that sit opposite the 45° angles.

The Pythagorean Theorem

The Pythagorean theorem defines the vital relationship between the sides of every right triangle (and that means every right triangle, not just the special ones we've already talked about). The theorem states that the length of the hypotenuse squared is equal to the sum of the squares of the lengths of the legs.

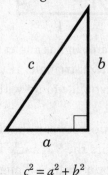

$$c^2 = a^2 + b^2$$

If a triangle is a right triangle, this formula will always hold. Conversely, if the formula holds for a particular triangle, you know that triangle is a right triangle. If you are given any two sides of a right triangle, you can use this formula to calculate the length of the third side.

Certain groups of three *integers* can be the lengths of a right triangle. Such groups of integers are called Pythagorean triples. Some common Pythagorean triples include {3, 4, 5}, {5, 12, 13}, {8, 15, 17}, {7, 24, 25}, and {9, 40, 41}. Any multiple of one of these groups of numbers also can be a Pythagorean triple. For example, {9, 12, 15} = 3{3, 4, 5}. If you know these basic Pythagorean triples, they might help you quickly determine, without calculation, the length of a side of a right triangle in a problem that gave you the length of the other two sides.

Similarity of Triangles

In reference to triangles, the word similar means "of the same shape." Two triangles are similar if their corresponding angles are equal. If this is the case, then the lengths of corresponding sides will be proportional to each other. For example, if ΔABC and ΔDEF are similar, then sides AB and DE correspond to each other, as do BC and EF, and CA and FE.

That corresponding sides are proportional means that $AB/DE = BC/EF = CA/FD$.

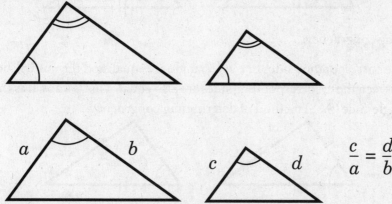

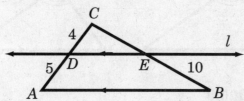

$$\frac{c}{a} = \frac{d}{b}$$

Similarity can be very helpful on the SAT. For example, let's say you come across the following question:

> Triangles ABC and DEC are similar, and line l is parallel to segment AB. What is the length of CE?

If you know the rule of similarity, then you can see that the ratio of $CD:CA$ is 4:9, and know that $CE:CB$ must obey the same ratio. Since EB is equal to 10, the only possible length of CE is 8, since 8:18 is equivalent to 4:9.

Trickier questions on the SAT might not tell you whether two triangles are similar. However, they will include information that will allow you to see that the two triangles are similar. If two pairs of corresponding angles are equal or if one pair of angles is equal and the two pairs of adjacent sides are proportional, then you know that two triangles are similar.

Congruence

Congruence is another helpful rule of triangles. Congruence means that two triangles are identical. Some questions or images may state directly that the two triangles pictured are congruent. Some questions may include congruent triangles without explicit mention, however. Two triangles are congruent if they meet any of the following criteria:

- All the corresponding sides of the two triangles are equal. This is known as the Side-Side-Side (SSS) method of determ

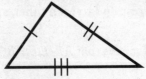 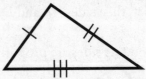

- ining congruency.

- The corresponding sides of each triangle are equal, and the mutual angles between those corresponding sides are also equal. This is known as the Side-Angle-Side (SAS) method of determining congruency.

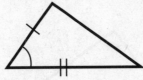 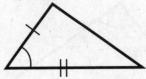

- The two triangles share two equal corresponding angles, and also share any pair of corresponding sides. This is known as the Angle-Side-Angle (ASA) method of determining congruency.

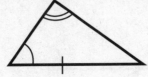 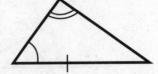

Perimeter of a Triangle

The perimeter of a triangle is equal to the sum of the lengths of the triangle's three sides. If a triangle has sides of lengths 4, 6, and 9, then its perimeter is $4 + 6 + 9 = 19$.

Area of a Triangle

The area of a triangle is equal to $\frac{1}{2}$ the base of the triangle times the height: $A = \frac{1}{2}bh$. For example, given the following triangle,

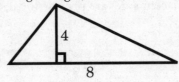

in which $b = 8$ and $h = 4$:

the area equals $\frac{1}{2}bh = \frac{1}{2}(8 \times 4) = 16$. The height of the triangle must be perpendicular to the base. You will almost definitely have to calculate the area of a triangle for the SAT. Know this formula.

Triangles

Multiple Choice

1.   In the figure below, the square in the center has an area of 9. What is the value of x? (Answers rounded to two decimal places)

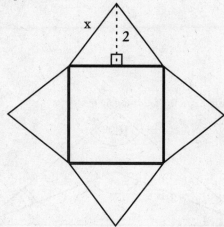

    (A)   3.00
    (B)   2.50
    (C)   3.61
    (D)   2.83
    (E)   1.32

2.   The area of a right triangle with sides of length 3, 4, and 5 is

    (A)   10
    (B)   6
    (C)   7.5
    (D)   15
    (E)   12

3. In the figure below, the area of △ABC is 8, and BC = CD. What is the area of △ACD?

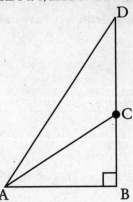

(A)   8
(B)   10
(C)   12
(D)   16
(E)   64

4. Determine the measure of ∠x in the following figure.

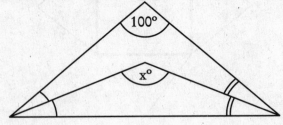

(A)   140°
(B)   120°
(C)   100°
(D)   70°
(E)   40°

5. If ∠ADC is a right angle in the following triangle, how long is AC?

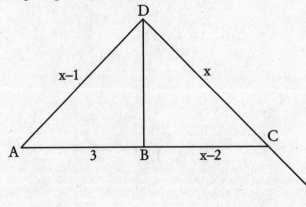

(A) 3
(B) 4
(C) 5
(D) 10
(E) 12

Quantitative Comparisons

6.

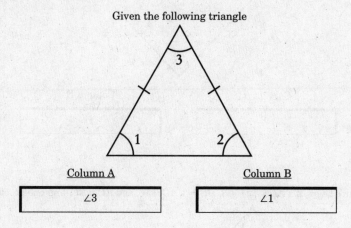

Given the following triangle

Column A	Column B
∠3	∠1

7.

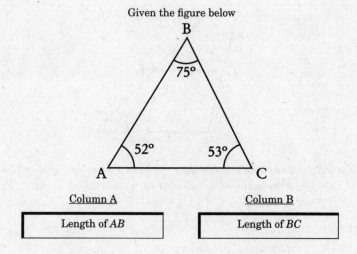

Given the figure below

Column A	Column B
Length of *AB*	Length of *BC*

8.

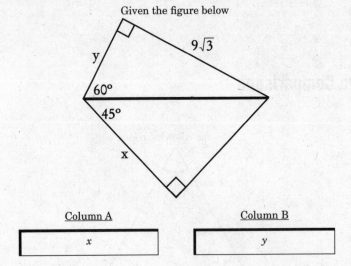

Given the figure below

Column A	Column B
x	y

Grid-ins

9.   In the figure below, if ∠*ADE* ≅ ∠*B*, *DE* = 3, *AC* = 16, and *EC* = *BC*, find one possible length of *BC*.

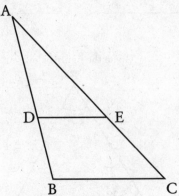

10.   A boy who is walking away from a 12-foot lamppost casts a 6-foot-long shadow. If the boy is at a distance of 12 feet from the lamppost at that moment, what is the boy's height?

Triangles–Answers

Multiple Choice

1. **(B)** Geometry: Triangles   *Moderate*
The area of the square is 9, so the length of each side of the square is 3. The two right triangles that make up the isosceles triangle on each side have sides of length 1.5, 2, and x. By the Pythagorean theorem, $(1.5)^2 + 2^2 = x^2$, so $x = \sqrt{(1.5)^2 + 2^2} = \sqrt{6.25} = 2.5$.

2. **(B)** Geometry: Triangles   *Easy*
The area of a triangle is equal to one-half of the base multiplied by the height. Knowing that the triangle in this question is a right triangle, the easiest way to proceed is to consider the sides of length 3 and 4 the base and height, respectively. Hence, the area is $\frac{1}{2}(3)(4) = 6$.

3. **(A)** Geometry: Triangles   *Moderate*
Label CB as y and AB as x so that the area of $\triangle ABC$ is $\frac{1}{2}xy = 8$. Knowing that $BC = CD$, the area of $\triangle ABD$ is $\frac{1}{2}x(2y) = xy = 16$. Therefore, the area of $\triangle ACD$ is $16 - 8 = 8$.

4. **(A)** Geometry: Triangles   *Difficult*
Look at the small triangle and label the unknown angles y and z to form the expression $x + y + z = 180°$. Then, looking at the large triangle, form the expression $2y + 2z + 100° = 180°$. Simplifying this expression yields $y + z = 40°$. Plugging this last equation into the first yields $x + 40° = 180°$, which simplifies to $x = 140°$.

5. **(C)** Geometry: Triangles   *Difficult*
Apply the Pythagorean theorem to get the following expression:

$$x^2 + (x-1)^2 = (x+1)^2$$

Simplify:

$$x^2 + x^2 - 2x + 1 = x^2 + 2x + 1$$

$$x^2 - 4x = 0$$

$$x(x-4) = 0$$

$$x = 0; x = 4$$

According to the diagram, $AC = 3 + (x - 2)$, so $AC = 3 + (4 - 2) = 5$.

Quantitative Comparisons

6. **(D)** Geometry: Triangles   *Moderate*
Since the triangle is an isosceles triangle, $\angle 1 \cong \angle 2$. That is all we know. Therefore, the answer cannot be determined from the information given.

7. **(A)** Geometry: Triangles   *Easy*
Since the smallest angle is 52°, then the shortest side has to be BC, the side opposite that smallest angle. Therefore, the length of AB is greater than the length of BC.

8. **(A)** Geometry: Triangles   *Difficult*
The top triangle is a 30°–60°–90° right triangle, so if the length of the side across from the 60° angle is $9\sqrt{3}$, then y must equal 9. The side across from the 90° (the other side of the top triangle) can be found by using the Pythagorean theorem: $\sqrt{9^2 + (9\sqrt{3})^2} = \sqrt{81 + 243} = \sqrt{324} = 18$. The bottom triangle is a 45°–45°–90° right triangle, so if its hypotenuse is 18, $x = 9\sqrt{2}$. Therefore, x is greater than y.

Grid-ins

9. **(4 or 12)** Geometry: Triangles   *Difficult*
$\triangle ABC$ and $\triangle ADE$ are similar triangles, so set up the proportion $\dfrac{DE}{BC} = \dfrac{AE}{AC}$. Let the length of $EC = BC = x$. Therefore, the proportion becomes $\dfrac{3}{x} = \dfrac{16-x}{16}$. This simplifies to $48 = 16x - x^2$. Rearranging this equation yields $x^2 - 16x + 48 = 0$. This quadratic equation can be factored to $(x-4)(x-12) = 0$. Therefore, x (the length of BC) can equal either 4 or 12.

10. **(4 ft)** Geometry: Triangles   *Moderate*
Draw a diagram (see figure below) and set up common ratios. $\dfrac{12}{x} = \dfrac{18}{6}$ indicates that $3x = 12$ or $x = 4$. The boy is 4 feet tall.

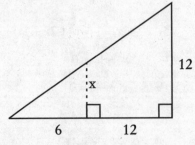

Polygons

By definition, a polygon is a two-dimensional figure with three or more straight sides. Under that definition, triangles are a type of polygon. However, since triangles are such an important part of the SAT, we gave them their own section. This section will deal with polygons of four sides or more.

There are a number of properties common to all polygons.

Perimeter of Polygons

As with triangles, the perimeter of a polygon is equal to the sum of the length of its sides. The SAT occasionally makes up fancy perimeter questions in which they create diagrams such as the following:

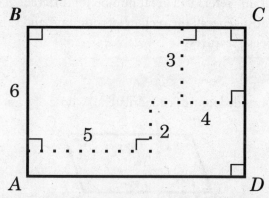

Such a figure looks more complicated than it is. It's actually just a little puzzle where all the information is given to you. You can figure out that the lengths of AD and BC are 9 since the dotted lines of 4 and 5 span the same distance as AD and BC.

Another good rule to remember for perimeter problems on the SAT is that a straight line will always be shorter than a curved or otherwise non-straight line.

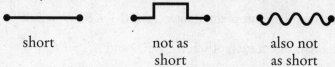

| short | not as short | also not as short |

Polygons and the Number of Degrees They Hold

Just as the angles of triangles always add up to 180 degrees, the angles in various polygons will also add up to the same number. The formula that defines the sum of the angles of all polygons is $180° \times (n - 2)$, where n equals the number of sides of the polygon. Take a look at the table below.

| Triangle | 3 | $180° \times (1)$ | $180°$ |

Rectangle	4	180° × (2)	360°
Pentagon	5	180° × (3)	540°
Hexagon	6	180° × (4)	720°
Septagon	7	180° × (5)	900°

If you come upon any questions on the SAT in which you are shown a polygon and the angle values of all of the vertices but one are given, you can always find the lone missing value by using this formula to calculate the total angle value and subtracting the value of each angle you know.

Parallelograms

The word "parallelogram" refers to a great number of different geometric figures. The parallelogram is the most general; the rectangle, rhombus, and square are all parallelograms with certain special features.

Parallelogram

A parallelogram is a four sided figure (a quadrilateral) whose opposite sides are parallel.

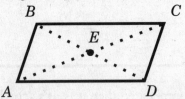

In a parallelogram:

- Opposite sides are equal in length: $BC = AD$ and $AB = DC$

- Opposite angles are equal: $\angle ABC = \angle ADC$ and $\angle BAD = \angle BCD$

- Adjacent angles are supplementary: $\angle ABC + \angle BCD = 180°$

- The diagonals bisect each other: $BE = ED$ and $AE = EC$

- One diagonal splits a parallelogram into two congruent triangles: $\triangle ABD = \triangle BCD$

- Two diagonals split a parallelogram into two pairs of congruent triangles: $\triangle AEB = \triangle DEC$ and $\triangle BEC = \triangle AED$.

Rectangle

A rectangle is a parallelogram whose angles all equal 90°. All of the rules that hold for a parallelogram also hold for a rectangle. A rectangle has further properties, however, that you should also know.

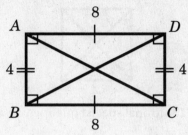

In a rectangle:

- The angles are all equal to 90°.

- The diagonals are equal in length: $BD = AC$

- A diagonal splits a rectangle into two 30-60-90 triangles: triangle BAD and BCD are 30-60-90 triangles.

- The area of a triangle is equal to length multiplied by width: $A = lw$. In the case of the rectangle pictured above, the area equals $8 \times 4 = 32$ square units.

Rhombus

A rhombus is a specialized parallelogram in which all four sides are of equal length.

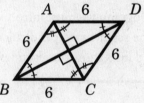

In a rhombus:

- All four sides are equal: $AD = DC = CB = BA$

- The diagonals bisect each other and form perpendicular lines (but note that the diagonals are not equal in length).

- The diagonals bisect the vertex angles ($\angle ADB = \angle CDB$, $\angle DCA = \angle BCA$)

Square

A square combines the special features of the rectangle and rhombus: all its angles are 90°, and all four sides are equal in length.

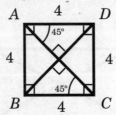

The square has many, many additional special qualities. In a square:

- All sides are of equal length: $AD = DC = CB = BA$

- All angles = 90°

- Diagonals bisect each other at right angles.

- Diagonals bisect the vertex angles to create 45° angles. (This means that the two diagonals break the square into four 45-45-90 triangles.)

- Diagonals are equal in length.

- Area equals one side times another. Since any two sides are equal, $A = s^2$. In the case of the square above, the area is $A = 4^2 = 16$.

Area of a Parallelogram

To calculate the area of a parallelogram, we must introduce a new term: altitude. The altitude of a parallelogram is the line segment perpendicular to a pair of opposite sides with one endpoint on each. The dotted lines show the altitudes of various parallelograms.

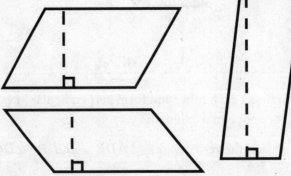

The area of a parallelogram is the product of the length of its altitude and the length of a side that contains an endpoint of the altitude. This side is called the base of the parallelogram. Any side can become a base of a given parallelogram: all you need to do is draw an altitude from it to the opposite side. A common way to describe the area of a parallelogram is the base times the height (base × height), where the height is the altitude.

The formulas for the area of various special parallelograms are even simpler.

For a rectangle, the area is the product of the lengths of any two adjacent sides. Because the sides of a square are equal, the area of a square is the length of any one side squared. The area of a rhombus is equal to one-half the product of its diagonals.

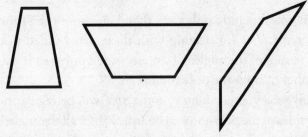

Trapezoid

Trapezoids are four-sided figures but not parallelograms. In a trapezoid, one pair of sides is parallel while the other is not.

Area of a Trapezoid

The area of a trapezoid equals the product of half the sum of the length of its bases and the height of the altitude: $A = \frac{1}{2}(b_1 + b_2) \times h$. The altitude of a trapezoid is a segment perpendicular to the bases (the pair of parallel lines) with one endpoint on each base. In the images, below, the lines marked by an a are the altitudes of the trapezoids:

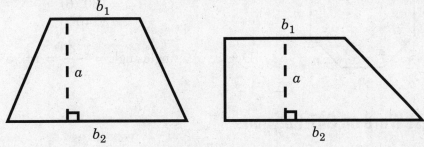

SAT Geometry

If you were presented with the trapezoid pictured below, you can just plug the numbers from the trapezoid into the trapezoid area formula.

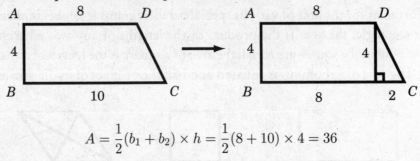

$$A = \frac{1}{2}(b_1 + b_2) \times h = \frac{1}{2}(8 + 10) \times 4 = 36$$

It is also sometimes possible to solve for the area of a trapezoid by transforming the trapezoid into a rectangle and a triangle. In the picture above, the area of the trapezoid *ABCD* is equal to the area of the rectangle (4×8) plus the area of the triangle $(\frac{1}{2} \times 4 \times 2)$, which means the total area is $32 + 4 = 36$.

Polygons with More than Four Sides

The SAT will sometimes include polygons that have more than four sides. The most important rule to remember for dealing with these many-sided polygons is one we already covered: the sum of the angles of a many-sided polygon is equal to $180° (n-2)$, where *n* is the number of sides the polygon has.

Many of the polygons you encounter on the SAT will be regular polygons, meaning that the angles and sides of the polygon will be equal. Since all the angles of a regular polygon are equal, you can easily calculate the value of every angle within that polygon. All you have to do is calculate the sum of the angles and divide by the number of angles.

Therefore, the value of an angle in a regular polygon is $\frac{180°(n-2)}{n}$.

$$\text{Sum of angles} = 180°(n - 2)$$
$$= 180°(8 - 2)$$
$$= 180°(6)$$
$$= 1140°$$

$$\text{Degree of a single angle} = \frac{1140°}{8} = 142.5°$$

The Last Word on SAT Polygons

If you are working with polygons, especially if you are trying to find the area of an irregular polygon, it is often a good idea to try to cut the polygon down into more manageable parts. For example, you might be able to cut a trapezoid into two triangles and a square rather than have to deal with it as a trapezoid at all.

The ability to see simpler shapes within more complicated ones can be a powerful tool on the SAT. A part of this skill rests on being able to deal with shapes in reference to each other. For example, let's say you are shown the following diagram:

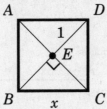

This figure asks you to determine the value of x based only on the information that DE equals 1. The question might seem impossible, but if you have some knowledge of squares and triangles, it's extremely easy. If you remember, the diagonals of a square bisect each other, so just as $ED = 1$, so too do EB and EC.

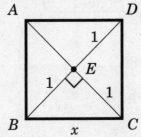

You should also know that two diagonals cut a square into four 45-45-90 triangles. DC is the hypotenuse of one of these triangles, since it is opposite the right angle. And, as you should know from the section on triangles, the ratio of sides to hypotenuse in a 45-45-90 triangle is always $1 : \sqrt{2}$.

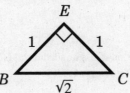

$$x = \sqrt{2}$$

We solved this problem simply by knowing about the attributes of squares and 45-45-90 triangles and without having to do any time-consuming math.

Polygons

Multiple Choice

1. Given parallelogram *ABCD* below, find *x*.

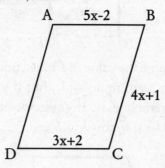

    (A) $\frac{1}{2}$

    (B) 3
    (C) 2
    (D) 0
    (E) 9

2. A rhombus has diagonals measuring 6 and 8. Each congruent side of the rhombus has a length of

    (A) 10
    (B) 6
    (C) 8
    (D) 5
    (E) 5.29

3. The ratio of the measures of the sides of a quadrilateral is 2:4:5:9, and the perimeter of the quadrilateral is 60. The length of its largest side is

    (A) 3
    (B) 15
    (C) 18
    (D) 27
    (E) 36

4.   Find the area of the quadrilateral below.

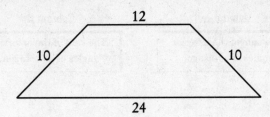

(A)   168
(B)   144
(C)   120
(D)   100
(E)   288

5.   Which of the following regular polygons has an interior angle of 144°?

(A)   hexagon
(B)   pentagon
(C)   decagon
(D)   octagon
(E)   heptagon

Quantitative Comparisons

6.

Column A	Column B
The measure of the central angle of a regular pentagon	The measure of the central angle of a regular hexagon

7.

Given that quadrilateral *ABCD* is
circumscribed about the circle *O*

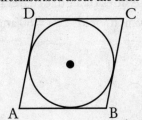

Column A	Column B
The length of (*AB* + *CD*)	The length of (*DA* + *BC*)

8.

Column A	Column B
The sum of the exterior angles of a hexagon	The sum of the exterior angles of an octagon

Grid-ins

9. Polygon *ABCDE* is similar to polygon *PQRST*. What is the measure of ∠A if ∠P measures 120°?

10. A circle is inscribed inside a square. A second square is then inscribed inside the circle. What is the value of the area of the square that is circumscribed outside the circle divided by the area of the square that is inscribed inside the circle?

Polygons–Answers

Multiple Choice

1. **(C)** Geometry: Polygons   *Moderate*
Since *ABCD* is a parallelogram, *AB* must be the same length as *DC*. Set up the equation $5x - 2 = 3x + 2$, which yields $x = 2$.

2. **(D)** Geometry: Polygons   *Moderate*
Since the diagonals intersect at a right angle, the rhombus is broken into 4 right triangles with sides of length 3 and 4. Thus, the third side of each triangle (which is also a side of the rhombus) has a length of 5.

3. **(D)** Geometry: Polygons   *Moderate*
If the ratio of the measures of the sides of a quadrilateral is 2:4:5:9, and the perimeter is 60, then $2a + 4a + 5a + 9a = 60$, which yields $20a = 60$ and thus $a = 3$. Thus, the length of the longest side is $9(3) = 27$.

4. **(B)** Geometry: Polygons   *Difficult*

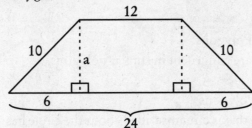

The area of a trapezoid is $\frac{1}{2}(b_1 + b_2) \cdot h = \frac{1}{2}24 + 12 \cdot h = 18h$. Find h by dropping a perpendicular down from the end of the side of length 12 to get a right triangle with sides 6, 10, and h. By the Pythagorean theorem, $h = 8$, so the area of the trapezoid is $18(8) = 144$.

5. **(C)** Geometry: Polygons   *Moderate*

Using the standard formula to find the number of sides in a regular polygon, $144° = \frac{180°(n-2)}{n}$, yields $144°n = 180°n - 360°$, which simplifies to $36°n = 360°$. So, $n = 10$, and the regular polygon is a decagon.

Quantitative Comparisons

6. **(A)** Geometry: Polygons   *Easy*

The central angle of a regular pentagon is $\frac{360∫}{5} = 72°$, and the central angle of a regular hexagon is $\frac{360∫}{6} = 60°$.

7. **(C)** Geometry: Polygons   *Difficult*

Since BC and BA are tangent to circle O at points E and F, respectively, they have point B in common. Thus, $BE = BF$. Similarly, DC and DA are tangent to circle O at points G and H, respectively, and have point D in common. Therefore, $DG = DH$. Similar reasoning shows that $AH = AF$ and $CG = CE$. Thus, $AF + BF + DG + CG = AH + BE + DH + CE = AH + DH + BE + CE = AD + BC$. They are equal.

8. **(C)** Geometry: Polygons   *Moderate*

The sum of the exterior angles of any regular polygon is 360°.

Grid-ins

9. **(120)** Geometry: Polygons *Moderate*
Corresponding angles are congruent in similar polygons.

10. **(2)** Geometry: Polygons *Difficult*
Each side of the square that is circumscribed about the circle has a length $2r$, since each side of the square is equal to the diameter of the circle. Thus, the area of this outside square is $(2r)(2r) = 4r^2$. Then, find the lengths of the sides of the square inscribed in the circle by using the Pythagorean Theorem. Noting that the distance from the center of the square to one of its corners is r, the sides of the square must each have length $r\sqrt{2}$, so the area of the square is thus $2r^2$. Thus, the area of the larger square divided by the area of the smaller square is 2.

Circles

A circle is the set of all points equidistant from a given point. The point from which all the points on a circle are equidistant is called the center, and the distance from that point to the circle is called the radius.

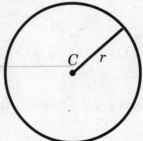

The circle above has its center at point C and a radius of length r. All circles also have a diameter. The diameter of a circle is a segment that contains the center and whose endpoints are both on the circle. The length of the diameter is twice that of the radius.

Circumference of a Circle

It is almost certain that you will encounter an SAT question or two that will in some way test your ability to find the circumference of a circle. The formula to find the circumference of a circle is $2\pi r$, where r stands for the length of the radius. Because two times the radius is also equal to a circle's diameter, the formula for the circumference of a circle can also be written as πd.

This is one of the equations found in the reference section of every math SAT section. You should memorize it, but if you do forget it, you've got back up.

Area of a Circle

The area of a circle is the square of the radius multiplied by π: πr^2. Again, this formula can be found in the reference bar at the top of each SAT math section, but you should memorize it for the sake of efficiency, and because we told you to.

Arcs

An arc of a circle consists of two points on the circle and of the points on the circle that lie between those two points. It's like a line segment that has been wrapped partway around a circle. An arc is measured not by its length (although it can be, of course) but most often by the measure of the angle whose vertex is the center of the circle and whose rays intercept the endpoints of the arc. Hence, an arc can be anywhere from 0 to 360 degrees.

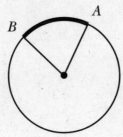

Chords

A chord is a line segment whose endpoints are on a circle. A diameter is a special chord that includes the center, but note that a chord does not have to include the center.

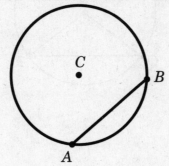

A chord and two radii, each extending from one endpoint of the chord to the center of the circle, form an isosceles triangle.

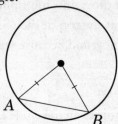

Circles

Multiple Choice

1. If a circle has an area of 2.25π, what is its radius?

    (A) 15
    (B) 3.0
    (C) 30
    (D) 1.5
    (E) 1.25

2. In the circle below, the measure of arc QR is equal to 100°. Find the measure of ∠PQR.

    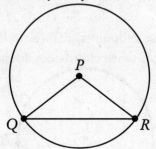

    (A) 40°
    (B) 45°
    (C) 60°
    (D) 80°
    (E) 100°

3.   In the figure below, the measure of arc *AB* is 86° and the measure of arc *AC* is 94°. What is the
      measure of ∠*BAC*?

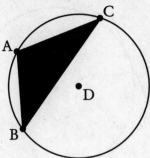

      (A)   94°
      (B)   90°
      (C)   86°
      (D)   47°
      (E)   43°

4.   In the figure below, the circumference of each of the three identical circles is 8π. What is the
      perimeter of the rectangle?

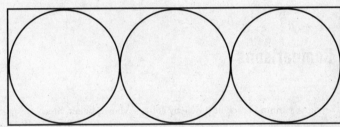

      (A)   24
      (B)   32
      (C)   64
      (D)   72
      (E)   80

5.   In the figure below, two tangents drawn to a circle from the same external point *I* form an angle measuring 100°. The measure of the minor intercepted arc is

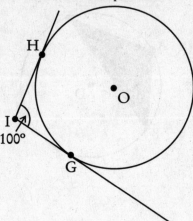

(A)   50°
(B)   80°
(C)   100°
(D)   130°
(E)   280°

Quantitative Comparisons

6.

A running track at a nearby college, shown below, has straightaways of 100 meters and turns with radii of 50 meters.

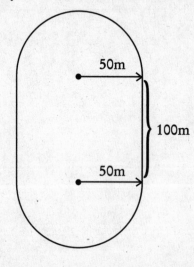

Column A	Column B
The length of one lap around the track	500m

7.

Square *ABCD* is circumscribed about a circle. Square *EFGH* is inscribed within that same circle.

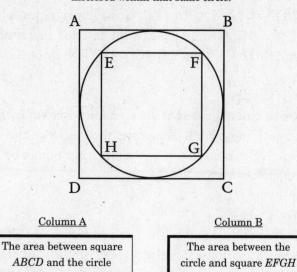

Column A	Column B
The area between square *ABCD* and the circle	The area between the circle and square *EFGH*

Grid-ins

8.   The ratio of the circumferences of two circles is 2:1. Calculate the area of the larger circle divided by the area of the smaller circle.

9.   A circle has a diameter of $\dfrac{10}{\sqrt{\pi}}$. If a sector of this circle has a central angle of 72°, what is the area of this sector?

Circles–Answers

Multiple Choice

1.   **(D)**   Geometry: Circles   *Easy*

The area of a circle is πr^2. Set up the equation $\pi r^2 = 2.25\pi$ to yield $r = 1.5$.

2.   **(A)**   Geometry: Circles   *Difficult*

Because *PQ* and *PR* are both radii of the circle, they are of the same length, so ΔPQR is an isosceles triangle. Knowing that measure of $\angle QPR$ is 100° and that the sum of the interior angles in a triangle is 180°, set up the equation $\angle QPR + 2(\angle PQR) = 180°$. This yields a measure of 40° for $\angle PQR$.

3. **(B)** Geometry: Circles   *Moderate*

Knowing the measures of the two arcs, it follows that $\angle BDA$ measures 86° and $\angle ADC$ measures 84°. Because *BD*, *AD*, and *CD* are all radii of the circle, they are the same length, and thus $\triangle BDA$ and $\triangle ADC$ are both isosceles triangles. Therefore, $\angle ABD = \angle BAD$ and $\angle DAC = \angle ACD$. Knowing that the interior angles of a triangle sum to 180°, it follows that $\angle BAD = 47°$ and $\angle DAC = 43°$. Therefore, $\angle BAC = 90°$.

4. **(C)** Geometry: Circles   *Difficult*

The circumference of a circle is πd, so if the circumferences of each of these circles is 8π, the diameter of each must be 8. Therefore, the height of the rectangle is 8, and because the rectangle is three diameters across, its length must be 24. Therefore, the perimeter of the rectangle is $8 + 8 + 24 + 24 = 64$.

5. **(D)** Geometry: Circles   *Difficult*

Because *IH* and *IG* are both tangent to the circle, $\angle IHO = \angle IGO = 90°$. The sum of the interior angles in a quadrilateral is always 360°, so the sum of the interior angles in quadrilateral *IGOH* must be 360°. Knowing that $\angle GIH = 100°$, it follows that $\angle GOH = 360° - [100° + 2(90°)] = 80°$. Therefore, the measure of minor arc *HG* is 80°.

Quantitative Comparisons

6. **(A)** Geometry: Circles   *Moderate*

To find the length of one lap around the track, add the length of the straightaways, which is 2(100m) = 200m, to the length of the curves. The length of the curves is the circumference of two half-circles with radius 50, or the circumference of one full circle with radius 50. The lengths of the curves is thus $2\pi r = 100\pi \approx 314$m. Therefore, the total length of the track is approximately 200m + 314m = 514m.

7. **(B)** Geometry: Circles   *Difficult*

First, find the area of *ABCD*, the area of *EFGH*, and the area of the circle. Let the radius of the circle be *x*. Each side of *ABCD*, therefore, is length 2*x*, so the area of *ABCD* is $(2x)^2 = 4x^2$. Because the distance from the center of *EFGH* to each of its corners is *x*, each side of *EFGH* is length $x\sqrt{2}$ (based on the properties of 45°–45°–90° triangles). Therefore, the area of *EFGH* is $(x)^2 = 2x^2$. Finally, the area of the circle is πx^2. With the areas of the three figures now known, determining the areas between the three figures requires simple subtraction. The quantity in Column A, the area between *ABCD* and the circle, is $A_{ABCD} - A_{circle} = 4x^2 - \pi x^2 = (4 - \pi)x^2 \approx 0.86x^2$. The quantity in Column B, the area between the circle and *EFGH*, is $A_{circle} - A_{EFGH} = \pi x^2 - 2x^2 = (\pi - 2)x^2 \approx 1.14x^2$. Therefore, the quantity in Column B is greater.

Grid-ins

1. **(4)** Geometry: Circles *Moderate*

The ratio of the circumferences of the two circles is $\dfrac{2\pi r_1}{2\pi r_2} = \dfrac{2}{1}$, which says that $\dfrac{r_1}{r_2} = \dfrac{2}{1}$.

Thus, the ratio of areas of the circles is $\dfrac{\pi(r_1)^2}{\pi(r_2)^2} = \left(\dfrac{r_1}{r_2}\right)^2 = \left(\dfrac{2}{1}\right)^2 = \dfrac{4}{1}$, or 4:1.

2. **(5)** Geometry: Circles *Moderate*

Because the diameter of the circle is , the radius of the circle is $\dfrac{5}{\sqrt{\pi}}$. The area of the circle is $\pi r^2 = \pi\left(\dfrac{5}{\sqrt{\pi}}\right)^2 = 25$. Because 72° is one-fifth of 360°, the area of the sector in question is one-fifth of the area of the circle. Therefore, the area of the sector is 5.

Solids

Solids refer to three-dimensional shapes. On the SAT, the only solids you will have to deal with are cubes, rectangular solids, and right cylinders. For these shapes, you will have to know how to calculate surface area and volume.

Cubes and Rectangular Solids

A rectangular solid is a six-sided shape in which all angles are 90°. It has length, depth, and height.

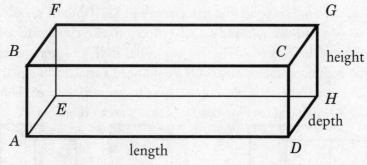

SAT Geometry

Just as squares are specialized rectangles, so are cubes specialized rectangular solids. For a cube, the length, depth, and height are all equal.

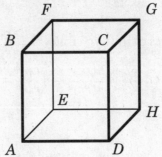

Surface Area of a Rectangular Solid

The surface area of a solid is the area of its outermost skin. A cardboard box, for example, is made up of a bunch of rectangles fastened together. The sum of the areas of those rectangles is the surface area of the cardboard box.

To calculate the surface area of a rectangular solid, all you have to do is find the area of each of the sides and add them together. In fact, your job is even easier than that. The six sides of a rectangular solid can be divided into three pairs of two. If you look at the rectangular solid diagramed above, you should see that panel *ABFE* = *DCGH*, *BCDA* = *FGHE*, and *BCGF* = *ADHE*. Therefore, you only have to calculate the areas of one of each of the three pairs, sum those areas, and multiply that answer by 2.

With a cube, finding the surface area is even easier. By definition, each side of a cube will always be the same, so to calculate the surface area, find the area of one side, and multiply it by 6.

Finally, there is one property of surface area of which you should be aware. Pictured below is a rectangular solid that has a length of 8, a depth of 4, and a height of 4. Then a giant cleaver comes down and cuts the solid into two cubes, each of which have lengths, widths, and heights of 4. Do the two cubes have a bigger combined surface area? A smaller combined surface area? Or a combined surface area equal to the original solid? The answer is that the two cubes have a bigger surface area. Think about the cleaver coming down: it creates two new faces that weren't there before.

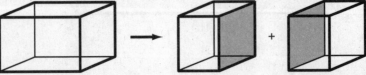

Whenever something is cut into smaller pieces, its surface area increases (although its volume is unchanged). The SAT loves to test this fact.

Volume of a Rectangular Solid

The volume of a rectangular solid can be found by multiplying the length × width × height ($V = lwh$; this formula can be found in the reference area at the beginning of each math SAT section).

Because all the dimensions of the cube are equal, the volume of a cube is even easier to calculate: just raise the length of one edge to the third power. If a cube has a length, width, and height of 3, the volume is $3^3 = 27$.

Right Circular Cylinders

You probably know what a cube or rectangular solid looks like, but you might not know what a right circular cylinder looks like. Here's a picture of one:

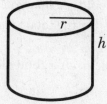

Surface Area of a Right Circular Cylinder

You will never have to calculate the surface area of a right circular cylinder on the SAT.

Volume of a Right Circular Cylinder

It's perfectly likely that you will have to calculate the volume of a right circular cylinder. Luckily, the formula isn't so hard, and it's available in the reference bar at the beginning of every SAT math section. Of course, as we say every time, you should still memorize the formula. The formula is: Volume $= \pi r^2 h$. Like all other volumes, to get the volume of a right cylinder, you have to find the area of a base (in this case a circle) and then multiply it by the height.

Solids and Word Problems

Often, the SAT will pose its problems on solids as word problems. It will say something like: what is the total surface area of two boxes, each with dimensions of $3 \times 4 \times 5$? Often, the best approach to these word problems is to draw a sketch:

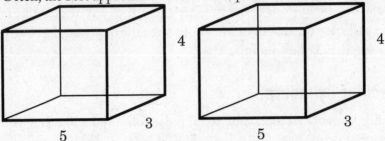

Once you see the drawing, you should see that you have four panels of 3×5, four of 4×5, and four of 3×4, meaning that the total area is $4(15) + 4(20) + 4(12) = 60 + 80 + 48 = 188$.

Whenever you see a word problem, it's a good idea to draw a sketch.

Solids

Multiple Choice

1. If the total surface area of a cube is 216 square feet, find the length of an edge of the cube.

    (A)   3 feet
    (B) $6\sqrt{6}$ feet
    (C) $3\sqrt{6}$ feet
    (D)   6 feet
    (E)   12 feet

2. The total surface area of two rectangular solids, each with dimensions of 2 x 5 x 7, is

    (A)   70
    (B)   118
    (C)   140
    (D)   236
    (E)   472

3. The volume of a right circular cylinder with a height of 5 feet and a radius of 10 feet is

    (A) 50π ft^3
    (B) 500π ft^3
    (C) 250π ft^3
    (D) 100π ft^3
    (E) 200π ft^3

Quantitative Comparisons

4.

Column A	Column B
The volume of a right circular cylinder with a height of 3 feet and radius of 3 feet	The volume of a rectangular solid that measures 3 feet by 4 feet by 7 feet

5.

Column A	Column B
The radius of a right cylinder with height 8 and volume 200π	The height of a right cylinder with radius 6 and volume 216π

Grid-ins

6.   What is the volume of the figure shown below?

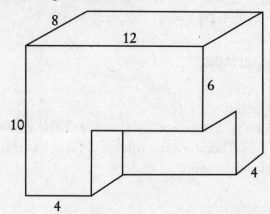

7.   What is the volume of the solid below if the radius of the hole is $\frac{2}{\sqrt{\pi}}$?

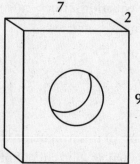

Answers–Solids

Multiple Choice

1. **(D)** Geometry: Solids *Moderate*

Let e be the length of one side of the cube. There are six sides, so total surface area is given by $6e^2$. If $6e^2 = 216$, $e^2 = 36$, so $e = 6$.

2. **(D)** Geometry: Solids *Moderate*

Drawing the two solids of dimensions 2 x 5 x 7, we see that the total surface area consists of four panels of 2 x 5, four of 2 x 7, and four of 5 x 7. The total surface area is thus $4(10) + 4(14) + 4(35) =$

3. **(B)** Geometry: Solids *Easy*

The formula for the volume of a right circular cylinder is $V = \pi r^2 h$. Therefore, the volume of this particular cylinder is $V = \pi(10^2)(5) = 500\pi$ ft^3.

Quantitative Comparisons

4. **(A)** Geometry: Solids *Moderate*

The volume of the cylinder is $\pi r^2 h = \pi(3^2)(3) \approx 84.8$. The volume of the rectangular solid is $lwh = 3(4)(7) = 84$. Therefore, the volume of the cylinder is slightly greater than the volume of the rectangular solid.

5. **(B)** Geometry: Solids *Moderate*

The formula for the volume of a right cylinder is $V = \pi r^2 h$. Therefore, for the cylinder in Column A, set up the equation $200\pi = \pi r^2(8)$, which simplifies to $r = 5$. For the cylinder in Column B, set up the equation $216\pi = \pi(6^2)(h)$, which simplifies to $h = 6$. Therefore, the quantity in Column B is greater.

Grid-ins

6. **6.832** Geometry: Solids *Difficult*

The easiest way to find the volume of this irregular solid is to imagine it as a large rectangular solid with a smaller rectangular solid cut out of one Finding the volume of this larger solid and subtracting the volume of the smaller solid will yield the answer. The volume of the large rectangular solid is $lwh = 8(12)(10) = 960$. The volume of the missing corner is $lwh = (8-4)(12-4)(10-6) = 128$. Therefore, the volume of the irregular solid is $960 - 128 = 832$.

7.   **(118)** Geometry: Solids   *Difficult*

To find the volume of the solid, find the volume of the rectangular solid and subtract the volume of the cylindrical hole. The volume of the rectangular solid is $lwh = 7(2)(9) = 126$. The volume of the hole is $\pi r^2 h = \pi\left(\dfrac{2}{\sqrt{\pi}}\right)^2(2) = \pi\left(\dfrac{4}{\pi}\right)(2) = 8$. Therefore, the final volume of the solid is $126 - 8 = 118$.

Coordinate Geometry

Coordinate geometry questions test your ability to interpret and deal with geometric figures on an *xy*-graph.

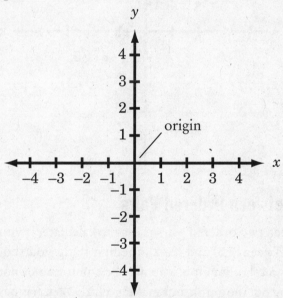

The point at which the *x* and *y* axes meet is called the origin. As you go to the right on the *x*-axis, you move into positive numbers, and as you go to the left, you move into negative numbers. Likewise, as you go up on the *y*-axis, you move into positive numbers, while moving down brings you into negative numbers (*xy*-graphs on the SAT will not have their intervals as clearly marked as this diagram does).

To specify a particular point on any *xy*-graph, you must use ordered pairs. Ordered pairs are two numbers put in parentheses and separated by commas: (*x,y*). The first number represents a position on the *x*-axis and the second a position on the *y*-axis. To think of it another way, the first number tells you how far the point is to the left or right of the origin, and the second number tells you how far up or down the point is.

For example, to graph (2, 3), you should move two spaces to the right (since 2 is positive) and three spaces up (since 3 is positive). To graph (–2, 1), move two spaces to the left (since –2 is negative) and one space up (since 1 is positive). To graph (1.5, –1), move 1.5 spaces to the right, and 1 space down (since –1 is negative).

By the time the SAT rolls around, you should be able to graph or interpret any ordered pairs that you might see. You should know how to calculate the distance between two pairs and be able to state what the mirror of an ordered pair might be.

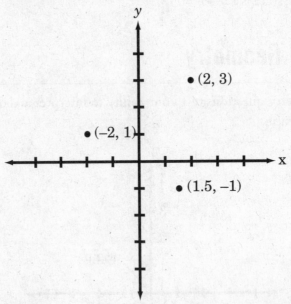

The Distance Between Ordered Pairs

The distance between two ordered pairs is easy to calculate. If you are asked to calculate the distance between (2,3) and (2,–2), the first thing you should do is figure out where each appears on the *xy*-graph. You may be comfortable enough to do this without actually drawing out the graph, but making a little sketch is never a bad idea.

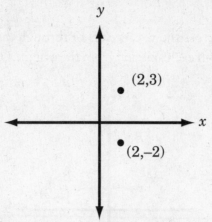

As the ordered pairs indicate, there is no difference between the two pairs in reference to the x-axis: both points are the same number of spaces to the right. But the points are not equal in reference to the y-axis. One is positive 3, and so it is three spaces up, while the other is –2, meaning it is two spaces down. Therefore, to get from one to the other, you would have to move a total of five spaces, mathematically $(3 - (-2)) = 5$.

In working out this example we've come to a rule about finding the distance between two ordered pairs: if the pairs have one coordinate in common, then the distance between the two pairs is the absolute value or difference between the dissimilar coordinates. For example, the distance between: $(4,6)$ and $(2,6)$ is $4–2 = 2$. The distance between the points $(-2, 7)$ and $(-2, -1)$ is $7 - (-1) = 8$.

For the SAT, you will not have to calculate the length between two ordered pairs with different coordinates in each place. You will not, for instance, have to calculate the distance between $(1,6)$ and $(-4,2)$.

Reflected Points

Points can be reflected across the *x*- or *y*-axis or through the origin. Pairs of reflected points are equidistant from each axis and from the origin. Take a look at the following problem:

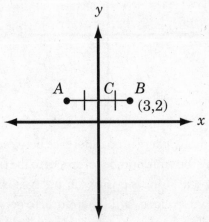

Because AC = BC, this drawing tells you that point A is the same distance to the left of the *y*-axis as B is to the right of it. It also tells you that line AB is parallel to the *x*-axis, which means that the *y* coordinate for each ordered pair will be the same. Immediately we know that the coordinates of A are (*x*,2). To find *x*, all we need is a little common sense. If the coordinates of point B are (3,2) and A is just as far from the *y*-axis but on the opposite side, then the size of the *x* coordinate of point A must be the same as the *x*-coordinate for point B. Only the sign must be different. Therefore, the coordinates of A must be (–3,2).

Points that reflect through the origin are only slightly more difficult to deal with:

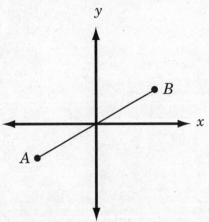

Here, the signs of the coordinates will be opposite, but their values will be the same. For example, in the diagram above, if point A were (–4,–1), point B would have to be (4,1).

Slope

In addition to its familiar meaning, the word "slope" has a precise mathematical definition. The slope of a line is known as the "rise over run," or the change in y divided by the change in x. To find the slope of a line, pick any two points on that line. Then subtract their y-coordinates and their x-coordinates, in the same order, and divide the difference of the y-coordinates by the difference of the x-coordinates. For example, to find the slope of the line which passes through the points (2, 5) and (0, 1):

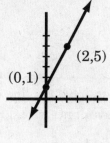

$$m = \frac{5-1}{2-0} = \frac{4}{2} = 2$$

A slope of 2 means that for each unit x increases anywhere on the line, y increases by 2 units; whenever x decreases by 1, y decreases by 2.

Positive and Negative Slope

The sign, positive or negative, of a slope indicates how the line moves away from the origin. Since slope is the measure of "rise over run"—the change in y divided by the change in x—the slope of a line will be positive when the change in y is positive and the change in x is positive, or when both are negative. This is true because of the division rules we covered earlier: both a positive number divided by a positive number and a negative number divided by a negative number will result in positive quotients.

$$\frac{+ \text{ change in } y}{+ \text{ change in } x} = + \text{ slope} \qquad \frac{- \text{ change in } y}{- \text{ change in } x} = + \text{ slope}$$

Alternatively, if the change in y and the change in x have different signs, meaning one is positive and one is negative, the slope of the line will be negative.

$$\frac{- \text{ change in } y}{+ \text{ change in } x} = - \text{ slope} \qquad \frac{+ \text{ change in } y}{- \text{ change in } x} = - \text{ slope}$$

For the SAT, you should be able to look at two sets of coordinate points located on a line, such as (2, 3) and (4, 1), and be able to tell if the slope of that line is positive or negative. In the case of these two points, you can see that the x-coordinate is increasing from 2 to 4 while the y-coordinate is decreasing from 3 to 1, meaning that the slope must be negative.

A line with positive slope on a graph will rise moving from left to right. A line with negative slope will lower moving from left to right.

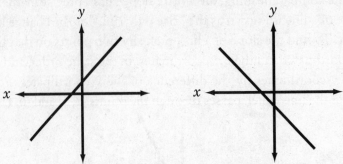

positive slope   negative slope

For the SAT, you should be able to look at a line on a coordinate graph and know immediately whether it has a positive or negative slope.

Slopes of Horizontal and Vertical Lines

Horizontal and vertical lines have special slope values. Horizontal lines always have the same y-coordinate. There is no rise over run.

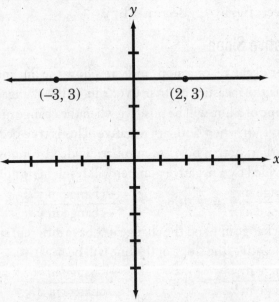

The slope of this line is: $m = \frac{3-3}{2-(-3)} = \frac{0}{5} = 0$. The slope of any horizontal line is 0, indicating that as x increases or decreases, y does not change.

For vertical lines, x remains constant as y increases or decreases:

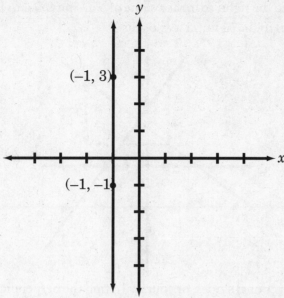

Vertical lines have no "run," so the change in x is 0. Yet the slope equation demands that you divide by the change in x. Division by 0 is impossible and makes the slope undefined: $m = {}^{3-(-1)}/_{-1-(-1)} = {}^{4}/_{0} =$ undefined. Since it is impossible to divide a number by zero, the slope of any vertical line is undefined.

Slope and Parallel and Perpendicular Lines

Two lines are parallel if they have the same slope. Parallel lines, when extended, do not intersect at any point because they have the exact same rise over run, so one line can never get closer to another. In the image below, lines AB and CD have the same slope, so they are parallel.

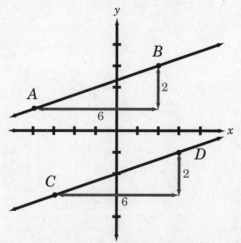

Perpendicular lines intersect each other at right angles. Two lines are perpendicular if their slopes are negative reciprocals of each other. Perpendicular lines have exact opposite rise over runs. For example, in the image below, line *AB* rises three units for every four units it moves to the right, so it has a slope of ³/₄. Line *CD falls* four spaces for each three spaces it moves to the right, so its slope is –⁴/₃.

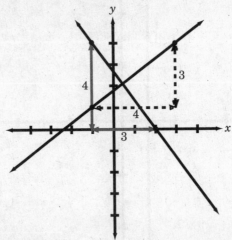

Not all lines have fractional slopes, of course. To find the perpendicular slope for a line with a whole number slope, for example a line with a slope of 2, just think of the whole number as if it was a fraction ²/₁ and take the negative reciprocal: –¹/₂

Coordinate Geometry

Multiple Choice

1. The distance between points (3, 2) and (–1, –1) is

    (A) $2\sqrt{2}$
    (B) $\sqrt{7}$
    (C) 5
    (D) $\sqrt{5}$
    (E) 3

2. The slope of the line through points (1, a) and (4, –2) is $\frac{2}{3}$. Find a.

    (A) –4
    (B) –2
    (C) 0
    (D) 2
    (E) 4

3. The lines $2x + 3y = 6$ and $2x - 3y = 12$ are

    (A) parallel
    (B) perpendicular
    (C) neither parallel nor perpendicular
    (D) of indeterminable slope
    (E) the same line

4. The slope of the line through points $(-5, 3)$ and $(-3, 3)$ is

    (A) 1
    (B) −1
    (C) 2
    (D) 0
    (E) undefined

5. The equation of the line through point $(1, 2)$ with slope 6 is

    (A) $y = 6x - 4$
    (B) $y = 6x - 11$
    (C) $y = 6x - 8$
    (D) $y = 6x + 4$
    (E) $y = 6x + 2$

Quantitative Comparisons

6.

Column A	Column B
The slope of the line through points $(-2, 3)$ and $(3, -2)$	The slope of the line through points $(-3, 2)$ and $(2, -3)$

Grid-ins

7. What is the area of a rectangle with vertices at $(-1, 4)$, $(2, 4)$, $(2, -1)$, and $(-1, -1)$?

Answers–Coordinate Geometry

Multiple Choice

1. **(C)** Geometry: Coordinate Geometry   *Easy*
By the Pythagorean Theorem, the distance between the points $(3, 2)$ and $(-1, -1)$ is $\sqrt{(3 - (-1))^2 + (2 - (-1))^2} = \sqrt{4^2 + 3^2} = 5$.

SAT Geometry

2. **(A)** Geometry: Coordinate Geometry *Easy*

The slope between $(1, a)$ and $(4, -2)$ is $\dfrac{a - (-2)}{1 - 4} = \dfrac{a + 2}{3}$. So $-\left(\dfrac{a + 2}{3}\right) = \dfrac{2}{3}$, which

yields $a + 2 = -2$, or $a = -4$.

3. **(C)** Geometry: Coordinate Geometry *Moderate*

The slope of $2x + 3y = 6$ is $-\dfrac{2}{3}$, and the slope of $2x - 3y = 12$ is $\dfrac{2}{3}$. Therefore, the lines are

neither parallel nor perpendicular.

4. **(D)** Geometry: Coordinate Geometry *Easy*

The line through points $(-5, 3)$ and $(-3, 3)$ is a horizontal line, so there is never any change in the y-coordinate no matter how much the x-coordinate changes. The slope of any horizontal line is 0.

5. **(A)** Geometry: Coordinate Geometry *Easy*

The slope is $m = 6$, and the point is $(1, 2)$. So, the equation can be found by solving $y - 2 = 6(x - 1)$ to get $y = 6x - 4$.

Quantitative Comparisons

6. **(C)** Geometry: Coordinate Geometry *Moderate*

The slope of a line between two points is found by dividing the difference between the y-coordinates of the two points by the difference between the x-coordinates of the two points (the "rise" over the "run"). For the line in Column A, the slope is thus $\dfrac{((-2) - 3)}{(3 - (-2))} = \dfrac{-5}{5} = -1$. Similarly, the slope of the line in Column B is $\dfrac{((-3) - 2)}{(2 - (-3))} = \dfrac{-5}{5} = -1$. The slopes of the two lines are equal.

Grid-ins

7. **(15)** Geometry: Coordinate Geometry *Moderate*

Plotting the points on a graph, we see that the rectangle is 3 units wide (from -1 to 2 on the x-axis) and 5 units tall (from -1 to 4 on the y-axis). Therefore, the area of the rectangle is 15 square units.

Geometric Visualizations

Geometric-visualization questions test your ability to twist and flip in your mind an image presented to you on paper. For example, look at the problem below:

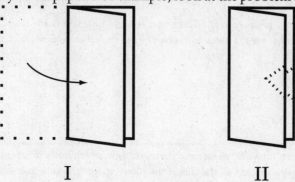

I   II

If a square piece of paper were folded into a rectangle as seen in Fig. I and then cut, as seen in Fig. II, what would the paper look like when it was unfolded again?

There isn't any good way for us to teach you how to do this problem other than to tell you that you should always draw a sketch before looking at the answers on this type of problem. The only thing that can make you better on geometric visualizations is practice, so pay attention when you see them in practice tests.

The answer, incidentally, is:

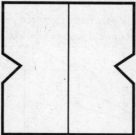

So there you have it. That's SAT geometry.

Geometric Visualization

Multiple Choice

1. Given eight points, no three of which are on a straight line, how many line segments total are required to connect every of point with every one of the other points?

    (A)   7
    (B)   8
    (C)   21
    (D)   28
    (E)   56

2. The picture below shows three views of the same cube, which has a different figure on each of its faces. Which figure appears on the side of the cube opposite the side that contains the dotted triangle?

    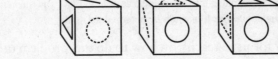

    (A)   The dotted line
    (B)   The solid line
    (C)   The dotted circle
    (D)   The solid circle
    (E)   The solid triangle

3. Given the box shown below, if cuts were made down the vertical and slanted edges so that the box could be laid flat on the floor, what would the box look like?

    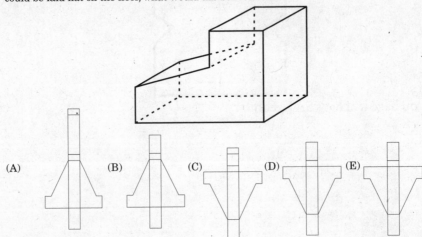

    (A)   (B)   (C)   (D)   (E)

4.   How many blocks need to be added so that the figure below is symmetric about the vertical axis? No blocks already in the figure may be moved or repositioned.

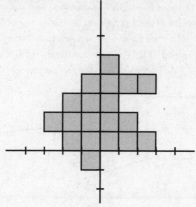

   (A)   16
   (B)   6
   (C)   7
   (D)   8
   (E)   17

5.   In the figure below, a rectangular piece of paper, *ABCD,* is folded along dotted line *UX* so that *A* is on top of *B, D* is on top of *C, T* is on top of *V,* and *W* is on top of *Y.* A second fold is achieved by folding along dotted line *TW* (or *VY*) so that *U* is on top of *B* and *X* is on top of *C.* A small rectangle, *S,* is cut out of the folded paper.

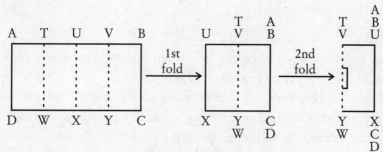

If the paper were unfolded, which of the following would it look like?

   (A)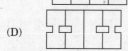

   (B)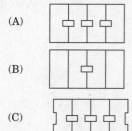

   (C)

   (D)

   (E)

Grid-ins

6. An equilateral triangle with sides of length 1 is adjoined to a square along one side with sides of a length equal to that of the sides of the equilateral triangle. A pentagon is then joined along one side of the square, opposite the side used to join the square to the triangle. A hexagon is similarly adjoined to the square, and so on. If this process continues until a 14-sided polygon has been joined to one of the sides of the 13-sided polygon, what is the perimeter of the resulting object?

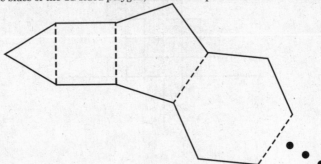

Geometric Visualization–Answers

Multiple Choice

1. **(D)** Geometry: Geometric Visualization   *Moderate*
Each of the 8 points can be connected to 7 other points. Therefore, multiply 7 x 8, which yields 56 line segments. However, this total counts each connection between two points twice: e.g., for points *A* and *B*, it counts *AB* and *BA* as two different line segments. To eliminate this double counting, divide 56 by 2, which yields 28 unique line segments connecting the 8 different points.

2. **(C)** Geometry: Geometric Visualization   *Moderate*
The cube should look like

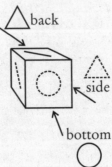

The dotted circle is opposite the dotted triangle.

3.   **(A)**   Geometry: Geometric Visualization   *Easy*

If you cut all the vertical and slanted sides and laid the pattern flat, you would get answer (A).

4.   **(C)**   Geometry: Geometric Visualization   *Easy*

For the figure to be symmetrical about the vertical axis, the number of blocks to the right of the vertical axis must be the same as the number to the left of the axis. A total of 7 extra blocks must be added to accomplish this.

5.   **(E)**   Geometry: Geometric Visualization   *Moderate*

Take a piece a paper and try it. You will get the pattern in (E).

Grid-ins

6.   **(80)**   Geometry: Geometric Visualization   *Difficult*

The perimeter of the equilateral triangle is 3 because each side has length 1. Adjoining a square to the triangle, the perimeter becomes 5, because there are now 5 sides of length 1 facing out (one side is shared between the triangle and square and therefore does not count toward the perimeter). Adjoining a pentagon to the square, the perimeter of the resulting object is 8, and so on. Every time a new polygon is added, add to the perimeter the number of sides in the new polygon but subtract 2 in order to account for the shared sides. This pattern yields $3 + (4-2) + (5-2) + (6-2) + (7-2) + (8-2) + (9-2) + (10-2) + (11-2) + (12-2) + (13-2) + (14-2) = 80$.

SAT Unit Test–Geometry

Multiple Choice

1.   Given that the measure of $\angle A$ is $2x+1$ and the measure of $\angle C$ is $3x - 37$ in the parallelogram ABCD, find the measure of $\angle B$.

    (A)   20°
    (B)   38°
    (C)   77°
    (D)   103°
    (E)   206°

2. Each side of a rhombus measures 13 inches, and one diagonal is 24 inches long. The other diagonal is how many inches long?

    (A)   5
    (B)   10
    (C)   11
    (D)   37
    (E) $\sqrt{407}$

3. The volume of the right circular cylinder below is

    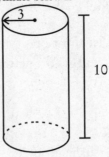

    (A) 9π
    (B) 30π
    (C) 45π
    (D) 90π
    (E) 180π

4. The radius of a circle with an area of 64π is

    (A)   2
    (B)   4
    (C)   8
    (D)   16
    (E)   32

5. Given the points $(1, a)$ and $(4, 2)$, and the distance between the points is 5 units, the value(s) of a is (are)

    (A)   no value of a exists
    (B)   6
    (C)   −2 and 6
    (D)   −2
    (E) $\pm 2\sqrt{3}$

6. The slope of the line perpendicular to the line containing the points $(a, 0)$ and $(0, b)$ is

    (A) $\dfrac{b}{a}$

    (B) $\dfrac{a}{b}$

    (C) $-\dfrac{a}{b}$

    (D) $-\dfrac{b}{a}$

    (E)   0

7.   The volume of a rectangular solid of 4 feet by 5 feet by 10 feet is

    (A)   200 cubic feet

    (B)   400 cubic feet

    (C)   450 cubic feet

    (D)   800 cubic feet

    (E)   2000 cubic feet

8.   The slope of a vertical line is

    (A)   0

    (B)   1

    (C)   −1

    (D)   an imaginary number

    (E)   undefined

9.   What is the measure of arc BC in the following figure if the measure of $\angle ACB$ is 68° and rays AB and AC are tangent to circle O?

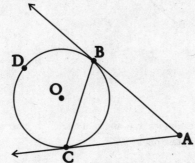

    (A)   22°

    (B)   88°

    (C)   136°

    (D)   144°

    (E)   224°

10.   In regular hexagon $QRSTUV$, the distance from the center to the midpoint of a side is 1, and the distance from the center to a vertex is 2. The perimeter of hexagon $QRSTUV$ is

    (A)   6

    (B) $6\sqrt{3}$

    (C)   12

    (D) $12\sqrt{3}$

    (E)   36

11.   The central angle of a regular octagon is

    (A)   45°

    (B)   60°

    (C)   135°

    (D)   150°

    (E)   180°

12.   The supplementary angle to an angle of 88° measures

    (A)   2°
    (B)   12°
    (C)   82°
    (D)   92°
    (E)   272°

13.   Find the value of x in the following figure is p and q are parallel:

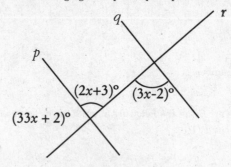

    (A)   –5
    (B)   –4
    (C)   0
    (D)   4
    (E)   5

14.   Suppose that you have three angles, $x, y,$ and z, of a triangle, and you know that $\frac{y}{x} = 2$ and $\frac{z}{x} = 6$. What is the value of the greatest angle, z?

    (A)   150°
    (B)   120°
    (C)   100°
    (D)   40°
    (E)   20°

15.   Find x in the following triangle:

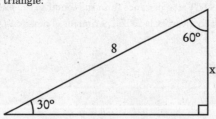

    (A) 2
    (B) 4
    (C) $4\sqrt{2}$
    (D) $4\sqrt{3}$
    (E) 8

16.   The area of ∆*ABC* shown below is

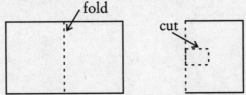

(A) 12

(B) 15

(C) 18

(D) 24

(E) 36

17.   A piece of paper is folded in half and then cut as shown in the figure below.

fold

cut

Which of the following best describes the appearance of the piece of paper after the cut?

(A)   (B)   (C)   (D)   (E)

18.   Given the top, front, and side views of a three-dimensional object, determine which of the drawings below illustrate(s) the appearance of the three-dimensional object.

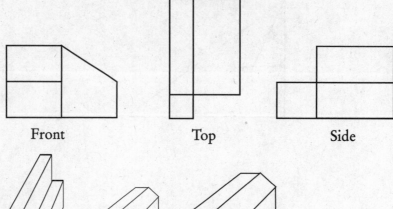

Front   Top   Side

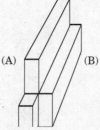 (A)   (B) 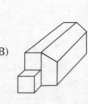   (C)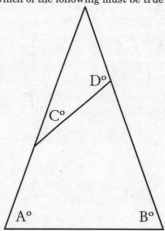

(D) Both B & C are correct

(E) None of the above

19.   Based on the figure below, which of the following must be true?

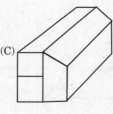

(A) $A + B = C + D$
(B) $A + C = B + D$
(C) $A = D$
(D) $B = C$
(E) $C = A$

20.   In the figure below, there is a total of n rectangular solids, each with a width of 1 inch, length of 2 inches, and height of 1 inch. If $n > 1$, what is the total surface area, in square inches, of the resulting solid?

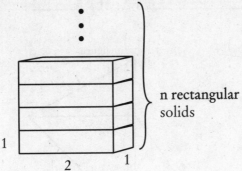

(A) $2n^2 + 2n$
(B) $4n + 8$
(C) $6n + 4$
(D) $4n + 6$
(E) n

Quantitative Comparisons

21.

Column A	Column B
The slope of the line through points (1, –1) and (5, 7)	The slope of the line through points (0, 0) and (1, 2)

22.

Column A	Column B
The volume of a cube with sides of 3.5 feet	The volume of a right circular cylinder with radius 1.5 and height 6.5

23.

Column A	Column B
Area of a circle with radius 2	Area of a washer with inner radius 2 and outer radius 3

24.

Ray ST bisects $\angle RSV$, the measure of $\angle RST$ is $-5x + y$, the measure of $\angle TSV$ is $4x - 3y + 1$, and the measure of $\angle RSV$ is $14x - 8y$.

Column A	Column B
x	y

25.

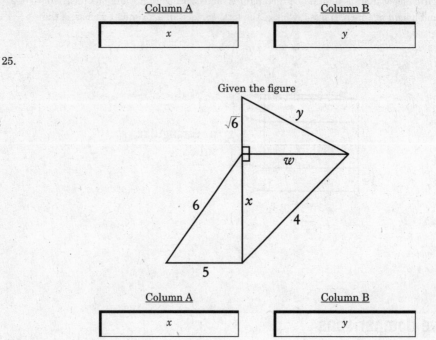

Given the figure

Column A	Column B
x	y

Grid-ins

26. What is the greatest number of sides that a regular polygon can have and still have interior angles whose degree measure is an integer?

27. What is the area of a square with a perimeter of 100?

28. Find the value of b so that the graphs of $ax + by = 7$ and $ax - by = 13$ intersect at $(5, -1)$.

29. Let M be the midpoint of AB, the distance from A to M be $2(x-1)$, and the distance from M to B be $3(x-2)$. What is the length of AB?

30. In the figure below, the measure of $\angle DCA$ is 130°, the measure of $\angle BAC$ is $2x + y$, the measure of $\angle BCE$ is 150°, and the measure of $\angle DEC$ is $2x - y$. Find y.

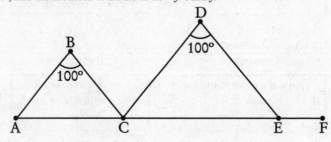

Geometry Unit Test–Answers

Multiple Choice

1. **(D)**   Geometry: Polygons   *Moderate*
Because opposite angles are equal in a parallelogram, $\angle A = \angle C$, so $2x + 1 = 3x - 37$, or $x = 38$. Therefore, angles A and C are both equal to $(2(38) + 1)° = 77°$. Because the interior angles of a quadrilateral must sum to $360°$, $\angle B$ and $\angle D$ must sum to $360° - 2(77°) = 360° - 154° = 206°$. For the same reason that $\angle A = \angle C$, $\angle B = \angle D$, so the measure of $\angle B$ is half of $206°$, thus $103°$.

2. **(B)**   Geometry: Polygons   *Moderate*
The diagonals of the rhombus divide the rhombus into four right triangles with sides of length x, 12, and 13, where x is the half the length of the other diagonal. Solving for x using the Pythagorean Theorem yields $x = 5$. Therefore, the second diagonal measures 10.

3. **(D)**   Geometry: Solids   *Easy*
The volume of a right circular cylinder is $\pi r^2 h$. Therefore, the volume of this cylinder is $\pi(3^2)(10) = 90\pi$.

4. **(C)**   Geometry: Circles   *Easy*
The formula for the area of a circle is $A = \pi r^2$. Because the question asks for r, rearrange the equation to form $r = \sqrt{\dfrac{A}{\pi}}$. For this particular circle, $r = \sqrt{\dfrac{64\pi}{\pi}} = \sqrt{64} = 8$.

5. **(C)**   Geometry: Coordinate Geometry   *Moderate*
By the Pythagorean Theorem, the distance between the two points is $\sqrt{3^2 + (2 - a)^2} = 5$. Squaring both sides and simplifying yields $(2 - a)^2 = 16$. Therefore, $-a = \pm 4 - 2$. Therefore, $a = -2$ and 6.

6. **(B)**   Geometry: Coordinate Geometry   *Moderate*
The slope of the line that passes through the two points is $-\dfrac{b}{a}$, so the slope of the line perpendicular to the line passing through the two points is $-\dfrac{1}{-\dfrac{b}{a}} = \dfrac{a}{b}$.

7.   **(A)**   Geometry: Solids   *Easy*
The volume of a rectangular solid is given by $V = lwh$. For this particular solid, $V = 4(5)(10) = 200$ cubic feet.

8.   **(E)**   Geometry: Coordinate Geometry   *Easy*
Because the change in the x-coordinate between any two points on a vertical line is always zero, the slope between two such points would always be some number over zero, which is undefined.

9.   **(C)**   Geometry: Circles   *Difficult*
The measure of $\angle A$ is equal to $\frac{1}{2}$ (measure of major arc BC – measure of minor arc BC). Let the measure of minor arc BC be x and the measure of major arc BC be $360° - x$. Therefore, the measure of angle A is $\frac{1}{2}(360° - 2x)$. On the other hand, the measure of $\angle A$ is $180°$ – measure of $\angle B$ – measure of $\angle C = 180° - 68° - 68° = 44°$. Solving $\frac{1}{2}(360° - 2x) = 44°$ yields $x = 136°$.

10.   **(D)**   Geometry: Polygons   *Difficult*
Connecting the center of the hexagon to one vertex of the hexagon and connecting the center of the hexagon to the midpoint of one of the sides forms a 30°–60°–90° right triangle with sides 1, 2, and x. By the properties of 30°–60°–90° right triangles, the third side (which is the segment from the midpoint of a side to a vertex) has a length of $\sqrt{3}$. Therefore, the length of one side of the hexagon is $2\sqrt{3}$, and the perimeter is $6(2\sqrt{3}) = 12\sqrt{3}$.

11.   **(A)**   Geometry: Polygons   *Easy*
The central angle of a regular octagon measures $\frac{360°}{8} = 45°$.

12.   **(D)**   Geometry: Angles and Lines   *Easy*
The supplementary angle to 88° is $180° - 88° = 92°$.

13.   **(E)**   Geometry: Angles and Lines   *Easy*
Because p and q are parallel, the alternate interior angles are equal. Therefore, $2x + 3 = 3x - 2$. Simplifying this yields $x = 5$.

14. **(B)** Geometry: Triangles *Difficult*

The measures of angles x, y, and z have to add up to 180°. Knowing that $y = 2x$ and $z = 6x$, set up the equation $x + 2x + 6x = 180°$. This simplifies to $9x = 180°$ or $x = 20°$. Therefore, the largest angle is z, which measures $6x$ or 120°.

15. **(B)** Geometry: Triangles *Easy*

In a 30°–60°–90° right triangle, the length of the hypotenuse is always twice the length of the side opposite the 30° angle. Therefore, x is half the length of the hypotenuse, which is length 8. It follows that $2x = 8$, or $x = 4$.

16. **(A)** Geometry: Triangles *Easy*

By the Pythagorean Theorem, the length of the third side $\triangle ABD$ measures 4. Therefore, the height of both $\triangle ABD$ and $\triangle ABC$ is 4. The area of $\triangle ABC$ is $\frac{1}{2}bh = \frac{1}{2}(6)4 = 12$.

17. **(D)** Geometry: Geometric Visualization *Easy*

Try this by folding a piece of paper and cutting it as shown.

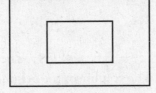

18. **(B)** Geometry: Geometric Visualization *Moderate*

The figure must have a slanted top and a cube protruding from the front.

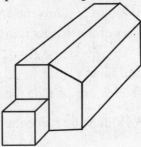

19. **(A)** Geometry: Geometric Visualization *Difficult*

The interior angles of a triangle must sum to 180°. The large triangle (with A and B as angles) and the small one (with C and D as angles) share a common angle—the angle at the top, which we can call E. Therefore, $A + B + E = 180° = C + D + E$. Subtracting E from both sides yields $A + B = C + D$.

20. **(C)** Geometry: Geometric Visualization   *Difficult*
Every time a new solid is added to the stack, the surface area increases by 6 (two panels of 2 by 1, and two panels of 1 by 1). In addition, we must count the bottom and top surfaces of the solid, which are both panels of 2 by 1. Therefore, the top and bottom of the stack always have a surface area of 4, regardless of how many blocks there are in the stack. This pattern results in a formula of $6n + 4$ for the total surface area of n rectangular solids.

Quantitative Comparisons

21. **(C)** Geometry: Coordinate Geometry   *Easy*
Using the standard "rise over run" formula of the change in the y-coordinate over the change in the x-coordinate, the slope between the points in column A is $\frac{7-(-1)}{5-1} = 2$, while the slope between the points in column B is $\frac{2-0}{1-0} = 2$. The quantities in the two columns are equal.

22. **(B)** Geometry: Solids   *Moderate*
The volume of the cube is $s^3 = 3.5^3 \approx 42.88$. The volume of the cylinder is $\pi r^2 h = \pi(1.5^2)(6.5) \approx 45.92$. The volume of the cylinder is greater.

23. **(B)** Geometry: Circles   Moderate
The area of the circle of radius 2 is $\pi r^2 = 4\pi$. The area of the washer is effectively equal to the area of the outer circle of radius 3 minus the area of the inner circle of radius 2: $9\pi - 4\pi = 5\pi$. Therefore, the area of the washer is greater than the area of the circle.

24. **(B)** Geometry: Angles and Lines   *Difficult*
Since ray ST bisects $\angle RSV$, the measure of $\angle RST$ has to be equal to the measure of $\angle TSV$ and the measure of $\angle RSV$ must be twice the measure of $\angle RST$. Thus, we can set up the equations $-5x + y = 4x - 3y + 1$ ($\angle RST = \angle TSV$) and $-10x + 2y = 14x - 8y$ (($\angle RST \times 2 = \angle RSV$). Simplifying these two equations yields $-9x + 4y = 1$ and $24x - 10y = 0$. The second of these equations can easily be solved for y to yield $y = 2.4x$, and this can be substituted into the first equation to get $-9x + 4(2.4x) = 1$, or $-9x + 9.6x = 1$. That is, $x = \frac{5}{3}$. Substituting this into the first equation yields $-9\left(\frac{5}{3}\right) + 4y = 1$, or $4y = 16$. Therefore, $y = 4$, and $y > x$.

25. **(C)** Geometry: Triangles   *Moderate*

First, use the Pythagorean Theorem to find the value of x: $x^2 + 5^2 + 6^2$, so $x = \sqrt{36-25} = \sqrt{11}$. Now, use the Pythagorean Theorem again to find w: $\sqrt{11}^2 + w^2 = 4^2$, so $w = \sqrt{16-11} = \sqrt{5}$. Applying the Pythagorean Theorem a third time to find y yields $y = \sqrt{5+6} = \sqrt{11}$. Therefore, x and y are equal.

Grid-ins

26. **(360)** Geometry: Polygons   *Difficult*

The formula for the interior angle of a polygon is $180° - \dfrac{360°}{n}$, where n is the number of sides. Once n is more than 360, then $\dfrac{360°}{n}$ is less than 1, which would make the measure of the interior angles a non-integer number between 179° and 180°. If n is less than 360, then the interior angle will be smaller than 179°. However, when $n = 360$, the interior angles measure exactly 179°, which is the largest integer angle measure possible less than 180°.

27. **(625)** Geometry: Solids   *Easy*

In order to have a perimeter of 100, each side of the square must measure 25. The area of that square is 25^2 or 625.

28. **(3)** Geometry: Coordinate Geometry   *Difficult*

Substitute the point $(5,-1)$ into both equations to get $5a - b = 7$ and $5a + b = 13$. Add the two equations and solve for a to get $a = 2$. Substitute $a = 2$ into either of the above equations and solve for b to get $b = 3$.

29. **(12)** Geometry: Angles and Lines   *Moderate*

If M is the midpoint of AB, then $AM = BM$, or $2(x-1) = 3(x-2)$, which yields $x = 4$. Therefore, the length of AM is $2(4-1) = 6$, and the length of AB is $2(6) = 12$.

30. **(10)** Geometry: Triangles   *Moderate*

Because $\angle DCA$ measures 130°, its supplementary angle $\angle DCE$ must measure 50°. Similarly, because $\angle BCE$ measures 150°, $\angle BCA$ must measure 30°. Then, knowing that the sum of the angles in a triangle is 180°, set up the equations $(2x + y) + 100° + 30° = 180°$ (for $\triangle ABC$) and $2x - y + 100° + 50° = 180°$ (for $\triangle CDE$). These equations yield $2x + y = 50°$ and $2x - y = 30°$. So, $4x = 80$, $x = 20$, and therefore $y = 10$.

Special SAT Math: Charts, Logic, Symbols

I<small>N THE SECTIONS ON ARITHMETIC, GEOMETRY, AND ALGEBRA WE COVERED</small> the vast majority of the math topics tested by the SAT. But there are three math topics that often pop up in the SAT that do not fit into any of those standard math categories. These three topics are charts and graphs, logical reasoning, and weird symbols questions. As in the arithmetic, geometry, and algebra sections, we will go through each topic, break it down, and explain the best ways to approach each type of question.

Charts and Graphs

There are two varieties of SAT questions on charts and graphs. The first type asks you to look at data organized in a chart or graph and interpret it. The second type asks you to perform some type of operation on data found in a chart or graph, such as calculating a mean or a percent.

Reading Charts and Graphs

Reading charts and graphs questions are pretty simple: the question will show you a chart or graph and then ask you about the data presented.

In the following bar graph, between what two months was the greatest change in the net income of Joe's Lemonade Stand?

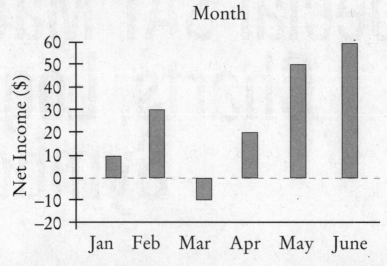

It may be that you look at this question and realize that you don't know what the term "net income" means. *That doesn't matter.* The graph tells you that the bars represent net income, so all you have to do is interpret the bars to figure out between which months the net income differed most. This is a key fact about SAT charts: you don't have to completely understand the terms that describe the data in the chart, you just have to be able to figure out how the data is related. In the case of this chart describing net income, it is only important that you see that the net income changes from month to month.

To figure out the two months between which Joe's net income changed most, you need to determine which two bars on the graph represent the two numbers that are most different in size. For this graph, the two biggest differences in terms of net income per month are obviously between April and May, and between February and March. The net income in April was $20 and the net income in May was $50, making the April-May difference $30. The net income in February was $30 and the net income in March was –$10, so the February-March difference was $40. The answer, therefore, is February to March. This question throws a tiny trick at you by including negative numbers as net income. If you don't realize that March is negative, then you might choose the April–May difference. When dealing with graphs and charts, be sure to pay attention to negative and positive values.

Performing Operations on Charts and Graphs

This second type of charts and graphs question asks you to do more than just interpret a graph or chart. You must also use the data and perform some operation on it in order to get the right answer. For instance, you may be asked to figure out the mean of the data shown in a graph. You might also be asked to look at a bar graph like the one shown previously and then to calculate the percentage change in net income between two of the months. Here's a question involving that same graph from before:

What was the percent increase in the net income from April to May?

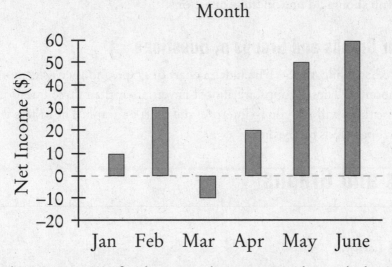

To answer this question, you first have to make sure you understand what it is asking. First, the question mentions percent increase. This means that the question is asking you to find out how much the net income increased between April and May and then to compare that increase to the original net income in April. The difference between the net incomes from April to May is the increase in income. The percent increase of net income can only be found if you look at that increase in relation to the original income. (You should know what percent increase means from our discussion of percents starting on page 54.)

Once you've figured out what the question is asking for, working out the math is easy. The difference in net income between April and May is:

May net income ($50) − April net income ($20) = $30

Now, to calculate the percent increase, you have to divide the change in net income by the original income in April:

$$\frac{30}{20} = 1.5$$

Here's the final trick in the question. The answer is *not* 1.5% change. Remember, to get percents, you must multiply by a hundred. The answer is therefore $1.5 \times 100 = 150\%$. But you can be sure that in this sort of question the SAT will include 1.5% as one of its answer choices to try to fool you.

This example is just one of the ways that the SAT might test your ability to work with graphs. There's no way for us to prepare you for all the different varieties of hybrid charts and graphs questions that might appear. However, the majority of these questions deal with means, medians, modes, or percentages. So if you are comfortable interpreting graphs and charts, and you understand means, medians, modes, and percentages, you should do fine on these questions.

Charts or Graphs and Groups of Questions

Every once in a while, the SAT includes a chart or graph and then asks more than one question about it. These groups are almost never larger than three questions. One or two of those three will ask you to interpret the chart or graph. The others will ask you to perform operations on the data.

Charts and Graphs

Multiple Choice

1.   The pie chart below is divided into five sectors labeled A, B, C, D, and E. Which sector has the greatest area?

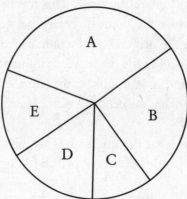

(A)   A
(B)   B
(C)   C
(D)   D
(E)   E

2.   Seventy-five people were asked how many holiday cards they send in a typical year. The results are shown in the following chart.

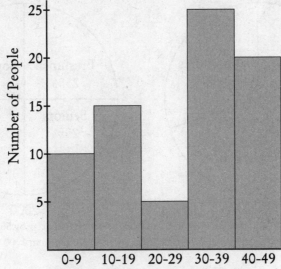

How many people sent fewer than 20 cards?

(A)   3
(B)   5
(C)   15
(D)   25
(E)   45

3.   The following pie charts show the breakdown of the student population at Centennial High School in 1990 and 2000.

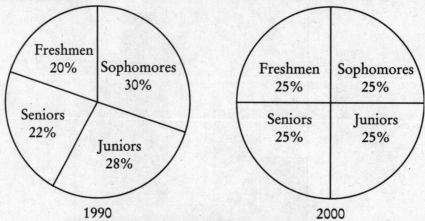

1990   2000

If there were 4,200 students in 1990, and the student population grew by 560 students from 1990 to 2000, what was the percent increase in the number of freshmen from 1990 to 2000?

(A)   5%

(B) $13\frac{1}{3}$ %

(C) $29\frac{1}{4}$ %

(D) $41\frac{2}{3}$ %

(E)   50%

4.   Four roommates pool their monthly income to share expenses for their living arrangements. In the following chart, each "$" represents $100 of monthly income.

Lauren	$$
Erika	$$$$$$
Barbara	$$$
Giselle	$$$$

If a pie chart were drawn to represent the above information, how many degrees would be in the central angle of the sector representing Barbara's income?

(A)   20°
(B)   30°
(C)   36°
(D)   72°
(E)   300°

Quantitative Comparisons

5.

Jim	***
Ella	* (1/2 star)
Dan	* * (1/2 star)
Lynn	* * * * * *

In the chart above, each star represents one dozen cupcakes
baked for the school bake sale.

Column A	Column B
The number of cupcakes Lynn baked	The number of cupcakes Jim, Ella, and Dan baked

Grid-ins

6 The pie chart below shows the distribution of shoe styles produced by the Walters Factory. If the
factory makes 5,000 shoes per month, and half of the sport shoes produced are running shoes, how
many running shoes does the Walters Factory make each year?

Charts and Graphs—Answers

Multiple Choice

1.   **(A)**   Special Math: Charts and Graphs   *Easy*
The question asks us to look at the pie chart and decide which sector is greatest. The
angle for sector A is clearly obtuse, whereas none of the other angles appears to be
greater than 90°.

2.   **(D)**   Special Math: Charts and Graphs   *Moderate*
The bar graph shows that 10 people send between 0 and 9 cards in a typical season, 15 people send between 10 and 19 cards, and so on. Only the first two bars would be included in "fewer than 20," for the last three bars indicate only people who send 20 or more cards. Therefore, 10 + 15 = 25 people who send fewer than 20 cards.

3.   **(D)**   Special Math: Charts and Graphs   *Difficult*
To calculate the percent increase, determine the number of freshmen in 1990 and 2000. There were 4,200 students in 1990, and 20% of them were freshmen. To calculate 20% of 4,200, multiply 4,200 by 0.20 to yield 20(4,200) = 840 freshmen in 1990. Then, calculate how many students there were in 2000. To do so, add 4,200 + 560 = 4,760. Next, calculate the number of freshmen in 2000, the same way that the number of freshmen in 1990 was calculated: .25(4,760) = 1190 freshmen in 2000.

The formula for percent of increase is $\dfrac{\text{final number} - \text{original number}}{\text{original number}} \times 100$.

Applying this formula to calculate the percent change in number of freshmen from 1990 to 2000 yields $\dfrac{1190 - 840}{840} \times 100 = \dfrac{350}{840} \times 100 = 41\frac{2}{3}\%$ % increase.

4.   **(D)**   Special Math: Charts and Graphs   *Difficult*
The pie chart would have four sectors—one for each roommate. The size of the sector would depend upon each roommate's percentage of the four roommates' total monthly income. First, find the four roommates' total income: $200 + $600 + $300 + $400 = $1,500.

Lauren $\dfrac{\$200}{\$1,500}(100) = 13\frac{1}{3}\%$

Erika $\dfrac{\$600}{\$1,500}(100) = 40\%$

Barbara $\dfrac{\$300}{\$1,500}(100) = 20\%$

Giselle $\dfrac{\$400}{\$1,500}(100) = 26\frac{2}{3}\%$

The central angle of the sector representing Barbara's income would be 20% of the circle in the pie chart. Since a circle contains 360°, 20% of 360° = .20(360) = 72°.

Quantitative Comparisons

5.   **(C)**   Special Math: Charts and Graphs   *Easy*
In the chart, we see that Jim made 3 dozen cupcakes, Ella made $1\frac{1}{2}$ dozen, Dan made $2\frac{1}{2}$ dozen, and Lynn made 7 dozen. The value in Column A is 7 dozen. To determine the value in Column B, we need to add $3 + 1\frac{1}{2} + 2\frac{1}{2} = 7$ dozen. The quantities in Column A and Column B are equal.

Grid-ins

6.   **7,500** Special Math: Charts and Graphs   *Moderate*
If the factory produces 5,000 pairs of shoes each month and 25% are sport shoes, the quantity of sport shoes produced per month is 0.25(5,000) = 1,250. If half of the sports shoes are running shoes, we must divide 1,250 by 2 to yield $\frac{1250}{2} = 625$. Therefore, the Walters Factory makes 625 running shoes per month. We now multiply by 12 to determine the number running shoes made per year: 625(12) = 7,500.

Logical Reasoning

As you would expect from the name, logical reasoning questions test your ability to reason logically. There probably won't be more than two logic problems on any SAT test you take. There are two types of logic problems you might encounter: chart problems and word problems.

Chart Logic Problems

Chart logic problems present you with a partially filled in chart or table and ask you to fill it in completely given either the information in the chart, or some information given by the question. For example,

8		y
x		
4	9	2

In the figure above, each of the nine boxes must be filled by an integer from 1 to 9, so that each row and diagonal is equal. No integer may be repeated. What is the value of $x + y$?

To answer these problems, you need only rely on your common sense. For this problem, you should see that the bottom row is equal to 15. Since the question states that each row is of equal value, you should see that:

$$8 + x + 4 = 15$$
$$x = 15 - 8 - 4$$
$$x = 3$$

The question also states that each box must be filled with a number from 1 and 9 and that each number can only be used once. The numbers 2, 3, 4, 8, and 9 have already been used, leaving you with 1, 5, 6, and 7 to fill in the remaining boxes. You should see immediately that the 7 can't go in the same row or diagonal with the 8, because that would add up to 15 for just two boxes in a row, and the *entire* row must add up to fifteen. The seven therefore must go here:

8		y
x		7
4	9	2

Now you can see that:

$$y + 7 + 2 = 15$$
$$y = 15 - 7 - 2$$
$$y = 6$$

Since the problem asks you for the value of $x + y$, add $3 + 6 = 9$.

Word Logic Problems

Word logic problems are less common than chart logic problems. A word logic problem on the SAT will involve some initial statements of fact and will ask you to determine which statement logically follows from the initial facts. For example:

Carlos traveled to City X, which is accessible only by sea or air. Which of the following must be true?

(A)   Carlos traveled by boat.
(B)   Carlos traveled by airplane.
(C)   Carlos did not travel by bus.
(D)   Carlos did not travel to City X.
(E)   Carlos did not fly first class.

To answer questions of this kind, you have to understand the conditions set up by the initial statement and the question asked about the initial statement. In regard to this specific question, the conditions are as follows: 1) the city can be reached only through the air or by sea (implicitly this means City X *cannot* be reached by land); and 2) the answer you choose *must* be true. In other words, there must not be any situation within the given conditions in which the statement could be untrue. Now let's go through the answer choices and see how they fit within these conditions:

Carlos traveled by boat.

The city is accessible by boat, so Carlos could have traveled there by boat. Therefore this could be the correct answer, right? Well, actually this choice is a bit of a trick. Carlos could have traveled to the city by boat, but he didn't *have to* travel there by boat. He could have flown. This statement therefore doesn't fulfill the condition set up by the question when it said the answer must be true.

Carlos traveled by plane.

This statement does not fit the given conditions for the same reasons we just covered above. Carlos might have traveled to City X by plane, but he might also have traveled by boat.

Carlos did not travel by bus.

Given the conditions stated by the question, is there any way Carlos could have traveled to City X by bus? Well, the city is accessible only by sea or air. Can buses float or fly? No. So Carlos *must* not have traveled to the city by bus. This statement must be true.

Carlos did not travel to City X.

The question clearly stated that Carlos did go to City X. This statement is definitely false.

Carlos did not fly first class.

We know that Carlos might have taken a plane to City X, and if he took a plane, there's certainly the possibility that he flew first class. This statement will not *always* be true, so it can't be the answer.

The answer is **(C)**. Carlos did not travel by bus. See, just a little logic bit of logic lets you figure out this question pretty easily.

Logical Reasoning

Multiple Choice

1. If the first day of a 30–day month is a Thursday, what is the last day of that month?

    (A) A Monday
    (B) A Tuesday
    (C) A Wednesday
    (D) A Thursday
    (E) A Friday

2. In a certain class, 25 students study Spanish and 20 study French. If 8 students in the class study both languages and 3 students in the class study neither language, how many students are in the class?

    (A) 28
    (B) 31
    (C) 36
    (D) 40
    (E) 48

3. A nurse needs to give her patient one pill every 30 minutes. If she is careful to give her patient a pill as soon as she arrives on duty and another one just as she leaves at the end of the day, how many pills will the patient get if the nurse starts work at 11:00am and leaves at 5:00pm?

    (A) 10
    (B) 11
    (C) 12
    (D) 13
    (E) 14

4. "If I cook dinner, then I get dessert." Which of the following statements is logically equivalent to the statement above?

    (A) If I get dessert, then I cooked dinner.
    (B) If I don't get dessert, then I didn't cook dinner.
    (C) I cook dinner and I get dessert.
    (D) I cook dinner or I get dessert.
    (E) If I don't cook dinner, then I don't get dessert.

Grid-ins

5.   There are four rules pertaining to the house number of each house in the town of Richardsville:

1.   If the house number is even, then the house cannot be red.

2.   If the house number is greater than 30, then the house must be taller than two stories.

3.   If the house number is less than 16, then the house cannot have a large backyard.

4.   None of the house numbers Richardsville may be divisible by 3 or 5.

What is one possible number for a red, two-story house in Richardsville that has a large back yard?

Logical Reasoning—Answers

Multiple Choice

1.   **(E)**   Special Math: Logical Reasoning   *Easy*
Since each week has 7 days, if the first day of the month is a Thursday, we add $1 + 7 = 8$ to determine the next Thursday. Following through the whole month, we find that the Thursdays will be numbered 1, 8, 15, 22, and 29. If the 29th is a Thursday, then the 30th (the last day of the month) will be a Friday.

2.   **(D)**   Special Math: Logical Reasoning   *Moderate*
Based on the information given, 25 students study Spanish. If 8 students study both languages, then $25 - 8 = 17$ study Spanish only. Similarly, $20 - 8 = 12$ study French only. Now, we can add the total number of students: 3 (who study no language) + 17 (who study Spanish only) + 12 (who study French only) + 8 (who study both) = 40 students total in the class.

3.   **(D)**   Special Math: Logical Reasoning   *Moderate*
If the nurse is at work from 11:00 am to 5:00pm, she works for 6 hours. One pill every 30 minutes means 2 pills per hour. Since 6 2 = 12, it seems intuitive that the patient should receive 12 pills during the nurse's shift. However, recall that the nurse gives one pill to the patient as soon as she arrives. Counting that pill, the patient would get 3 during the first hour, even though he would only get 2 during every successive hour. Therefore, the correct answer is 13.

4.   **(B)**   Special Math: Logical Reasoning   *Difficult*
The statement "If I cook dinner, then I get dessert," means that if I do cook dinner, I am assured of getting dessert, but it does *not* say that cooking dinner is the only way to

be assured of getting dessert. Hence, Choice A is not correct, because something else I did might have entitled me to a dessert. And, the same is true for Choice E. Choices C and D do not indicate an "if: then" relationship, as the original statement does, so they are therefore incorrect. Choice B is the only correct answer.

Grid-ins

1. **17 or 19 or 23 or 29** Special Math: Logical Reasoning   *Difficult*
First of all, the house in question is red. Rule 1 says that if the house is red, the house number is not even. Thus, we know that the number is odd. Rule 2 states that if the house number is greater than 30, the house must be taller than two stories. Given that the house in question is only two stories tall, its number must be less than or equal to 30. Rule 3 states that if the house number is less than 16, the house cannot have a large backyard. Given that the house in question has a large backyard, its number must be greater than or equal to 16. Finally, Rule 4 says that no house numbers in Richardsville may be divisible by 3 or 5.

Summarizing all of the requirements for the number of the house in question:

1. The number must be odd

2. The number must be less than or equal to 30

3. The number must be greater than or equal to 16.

4. The number must not be divisible by 3 or 5.

The only odd numbers between 16 and 30 that are not divisible by 3 or 5 are 17, 19, 23, and 29. Therefore, these are the only four possibilities.

Weird Symbols Questions (Algebra in Disguise)

The writers of the SAT seem to get a wacky thrill from creating odd symbols and then defining those symbols as mathematical functions. For example, a typical easy symbol SAT question might say:

Let a @ b be defined as a^2/b, where $b \neq 0$. What is the value of 4 @ 2?

To answer this question, simply take the given numbers and plug them into the appropriate parts of the function assigned to a @ b. In other words, symbol questions are often just a glorified type of algebraic substitution question: you look at the formula with its variables and plug in the given numbers. In this specific problem,

$$4 @ 2 = \frac{4^2}{2} = \frac{16}{2} = 8$$

Some students get frazzled when they see the odd symbols in their test booklet, which is exactly what the SAT wants. The test-makers figure that if you get nervous and can't get the answer right, then you can't be all that good or comfortable with math. But if you know that you shouldn't be frightened of these problems, you can answer them easily because they really aren't all that hard.

More Difficult Symbol Questions

Having said that symbol questions aren't all that hard, we must admit that the SAT does throw out some more difficult variations. For example, the SAT might "stack" a symbol question, asking you to perform the operation defined by the symbol twice.

Let $a\#b\#c\#d$ be defined for all numbers by $a\#b\#c\#d = ab - cd$. If $x = 6\#3\#5\#4$, then what is the value of $7\#x\#3\#11$?

Here you have a question with strange symbols all over the place, and, furthermore, the question is asking you to calculate the value of a strange symbol with a variable in it! Again, many students will see this question and be overwhelmed. But you shouldn't be. To answer this question, you have to do two things:

1. Calculate the value of x.

2. Calculate the value of $7\#x\#3\#11$ (which won't be very hard, since by that time you'll know exactly what x equals).

Since

$$a\#b\#c\#d = ab - cd$$
$$x = 6\#3\#5\#4 = (6)(3) - (5)(4) = 18 - 20 = -2$$
$$x = -2$$

Now that it is clear that $x = -2$, you can easily calculate the value of $7\#x\#3\#11$:

$$7\#x\#3\#11 = 7\# - 2\#3\#11 = (7)(-2) - (3)(11) = -14 - 33 = -47$$

You should see from this example that the difficult symbol questions are simply more intricate versions of the simpler symbol questions. In both cases, you have to substitute numbers into the function with which the symbol is associated. It's just that in the difficult questions, you have to substitute into the function more than once.

Special SAT Math

The key to answering symbol questions is to avoid getting bogged down in the symbol at all. Whenever you see the symbol, you should immediately think of the associated function. To make sure you don't get confused by symbols, it is always a good idea to write in the function above the symbol each time it appears in the question.

Strange Symbols

Multiple Choice

1. If $\textcircled{n}$ is defined as $2n + 2$, what is the value of $\textcircled{5} + \textcircled{5}$?

    (A) 10
    (B) 11
    (C) 21
    (D) 22
    (E) 25

2. Let $\boxed{x}$ be defined as $x^2 - x$. For example, $\boxed{3} = 3^2 - 3 = 9 - 3 = 6$. Which of the following is true?

    (A) $\boxed{\tfrac{1}{2}} < \boxed{1} < \boxed{-1}$

    (B) $\boxed{1} < \boxed{-1} < \boxed{\tfrac{1}{2}}$

    (C) $\boxed{-1} < \boxed{\tfrac{1}{2}} < \boxed{1}$

    (D) $\boxed{\tfrac{1}{2}} < \boxed{-1} < \boxed{1}$

    (E) $\boxed{-1} < \boxed{1} < \boxed{\tfrac{1}{2}}$

3. If $\triangle{m} = m^2 - 2m + 3$ and $\triangle{x} = 2$, what is the value of x?

    (A) 0
    (B) 1
    (C) 2
    (D) 3
    (E) 4

Grid-ins

4. If A @ B is defined as $3A + 2B$, what is value of 5 @ 2?

5. If $m \# n = \dfrac{m}{n}$, what is the value of $(4 \# 3) / (12 \# 6)$?

Strange Symbols–Answers

Multiple Choice

1.   **(D)**   Special Math: Strange Symbols   *Moderate*
(n) is defined as $2n + 1$ means $(n) = 2n + 1$. Therefore, (5) means $2(5) + 1 = 11$. Therefore, $(5) + (5)$ yields $11 + 11 = 22$.

2.   **(A)**   Special Math: Strange Symbols   *Difficult*
All of the choices in this problem involve values of $\boxed{\tfrac{1}{2}}$, $\boxed{1}$ and $\boxed{-1}$. To begin, calculate each of these.

$$\boxed{x} = x^2 - x$$
$$\boxed{\tfrac{1}{2}} = \left(\tfrac{1}{2}\right)^2 - \tfrac{1}{2} = \tfrac{1}{4} - \tfrac{1}{2} = -\tfrac{1}{4}$$
$$\boxed{1} = (1)^2 - 1 = 1 - 1 = 0$$
$$\boxed{-1} = (-1)^2 - (-1) = 1 + 1 = 2$$

Since is the smallest value and 2 is the largest value, Choice A has the three items in the correct order.

3.   **(B)**   Special Math: Strange Symbols   *Difficult*
Since $\triangle{m} = m^2 - 2m + 3$, but the answer involves $\triangle{x}$, substitute x for m: $\triangle{x} = x^2 - 2x + 3$. Since $\triangle{x} = 2$, we have:

$$2 = x^2 - 2x + 3$$

Subtract:

$$20 = x^2 - 2x + 1$$

Factor:

$$0 = (x - 1)(x - 1)$$

Therefore, $x = 1$.

Grid-ins

4. **19** Special Math: Strange Symbols *Easy*

Knowing that A @ B = 3A + 2B, substitute 5 for A and 2 for B to determine 5 @ 2. Therefore, 5 @ 2 = 3(5) + 2(2) = 15 + 4 = 19.

5. **2/3 or .666 or .667** Special Math: Strange Symbols *Moderate*

We are told that $m \# n = \dfrac{m}{n}$. To determine the value of (4 # 3)/(12 # 6), we need to evaluate the numerator and denominator separately. The numerator is $4 \# 3 = \dfrac{4}{3}$, while the denominator is $12 \# 6 = \dfrac{12}{6} = 2$. This yields $\dfrac{\frac{4}{3}}{2}$, which is equivalent to $\dfrac{4}{3} \div 2 = \dfrac{2}{3}$.

SAT Unit Test–Special Math

Multiple Choice

1. The following table shows the number of miles driven by each of 5 company cars on January 10th.

Car	Miles
I	40
II	50
III	17
IV	21
V	42

What is the average number of miles driven per car?

(A) 32
(B) 34
(C) 36
(D) 38
(E) 40

2. One of the jobs at Stuart Steel Mill involves packing steel balls into cartons. If a steel ball weighs between 6 and 10 pounds and one carton holds 12 steel balls, what is the maximum weight of the contents of one carton?

(A) 72 lbs.
(B) 80 lbs.
(C) 96 lbs.
(D) 120 lbs.
(E) 192 lbs.

3.

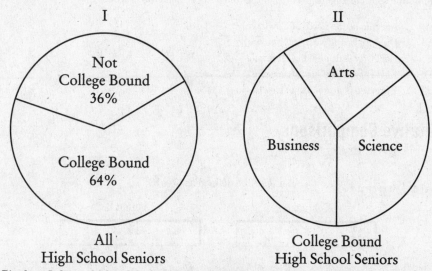

I

Not
College Bound
36%

College Bound
64%

All
High School Seniors

II

Arts

Business   Science

College Bound
High School Seniors

Pie chart I shows the breakdown of college and non-college-bound students among a group of high school seniors. The college-bound seniors were asked to indicate a preference for their college major. The results were tabulated and displayed in pie chart II. Of the college-bound seniors, 26% planned to major in the arts, with the remainder split equally between business and science. If pie chart I covers 1,250 high school seniors, how many students planned to major in science in college?

(A) 208
(B) 296
(C) 460
(D) 576
(E) 800

4. Four lines, l, m, p, and q, are drawn in a plane. If $l \mid \mid m$ and $p \mid \mid q$, what is the minimum number of points of intersection among the four lines?

(A) 0
(B) 1
(C) 2
(D) 3
(E) 4

5. Let A @ B = A + 2B and A # B = A – 2B. What is the value of $(x\ y)\ \#\ (y\ @\ x)$ when $x = 4$ and $y = 3$?

    (A)   –12
    (B)   –1
    (C)   0
    (D)   21
    (E)   110

6. Blueville is 6 miles due south of Arcville. To travel from Blueville to Cowtown, one must head 4 miles west and then 3 miles north. Digburg is 12 miles due east of Cowtown, and Earl City is 3 miles due south of Digburg. Which of the following statements is true?

    (A)   Arcville is due north of Cowtown.
    (B)   Digburg is due west of Cowtown.
    (C)   Earl City is due east of Blueville
    (D)   Earl City is due east of Arcville.
    (E)   Blueville is due south of Cowtown.

Quantitative Comparisons

7.

Let $J \$ K$ be defined as $(J + K)^2$.

Column A	Column B
3 $ 4	–3 $ –4

8.

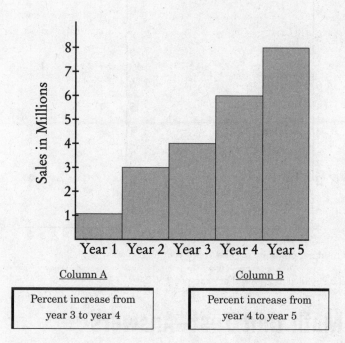

**The New Company
Sales Chart**

Column A

| Percent increase from year 3 to year 4 |

Column B

| Percent increase from year 4 to year 5 |

Grid–ins

9.   The following scatter plots detail the income and expenses of Mary's new business during first 4 years of operation.

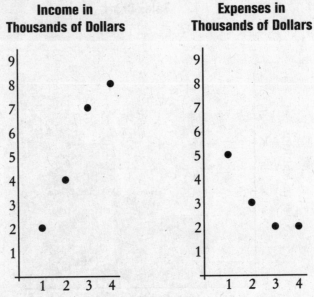

What was Mary's total net profit during the first 4 years?

10.   Let $A \% B$ be defined as $A^2 + B$. For example, $1 \% 2 = 1^2 + 2 = 1 + 2 = 3$. If $A \% 36 = 12A$, what is A?

Special Math Unit Test–Answers

Multiple Choice

1.   **(B)**   Special Math: Charts and Graphs   *Easy*
The chart tells us that car I drove 40 miles, car II drove 50 miles, car III drove 17 miles, and so on. To calculate the average number of miles, we need to add the five mileage numbers and then divide by 5: $\frac{40 + 50 + 17 + 21 + 42}{5} = \frac{170}{5} = 34$ miles.

2.   **(D)**   Special Math: Logical Reasoning   *Easy*
If a steel ball weighs between 6 and 10 pounds and we need to maximize the weight in one carton, we must choose the highest weight available for each ball. That value is 10 pounds. Since one carton holds 12 balls, $12(10) = 120$.

3.   **(B)**   Special Math: Charts and Graphs   *Moderate*
Pie chart I covers a group of 1,250 high school seniors, so we need to calculate 64% of 1,250 to determine the number of students incorporated into pie chart II: 64% of 1,250 yields 0.64(1250) = 800. Therefore, 800 seniors are college bound. Of these, 26% are planning an arts major: 0.26(800) = 208. This means that 800 − 208 = 592 are either business or science majors. Since those majors are split evenly, the number of science majors is $\frac{1}{2}$(592) = 296 .

4.   **(A)**   Special Math: Logical Reasoning   *Moderate*
The four lines are drawn in a plane, which means that they all lie on the same flat surface. We can use our paper to simulate the plane. We need to make the four lines cross as few times as possible. Remember that lines continue forever, so we cannot draw our lines like this and consider them two separate lines: − − − − − − − −. Lines will never intersect if they are parallel. Nowhere does the problem say that the four lines may not all be parallel to one another. Therefore, draw the following arrangement:

_____ *l*
_____ *m*
_____ *p*
_____ *q*

If all the lines are parallel, then there are no points of intersection among them.

5.   **(A)**   Special Math: Strange Symbols   *Difficult*
We are told that *A* @ *B* = *A* + 2*B*, and we are asked to find *x* @ *y* when *x* = 4 and *y* = 3. *x* is the value before the symbol @, and *y* is the value after the symbol ≅. In other words, *x* = *A* and *y* = *B*. Our numbers, therefore, are *A* = 4 and *B* = 3.

$$4 @ 3 = 4 + 2(3) = 4 + 6 = 10.$$

That is the value of the first parentheses in the problem. For the second parentheses, the values are reversed – namely, *A* = 3 and *B* = 4.

$$3 @ 4 = 3 + 2(4) = 3 + 8 = 11$$

Now the problem has been simplified to 10 # 11. Use the other given information in the problem, which tells us about the symbol #: *A* # *B* = *A* − 2*B*. Using this formula for the values in question yields 10 # 11 = 10 − 2(11) = 10 − 22 = −12.

6. **(C)** Special math: Logical Reasoning *Difficult*

The best way to approach the problem is to draw a picture to represent the locations of the five towns described in the problem.

Blueville (B) is 6 miles due south of Arcville (A).

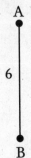

To travel from Blueville (B) to Cowtown (C), one must head 4 miles west and then 3 miles north.

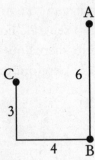

Diburg (D) is 12 miles due east of Cowtown (C).

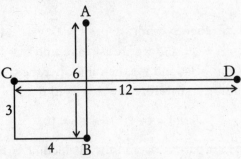

Earl City (E) is 3 miles due south of Digburg (D).

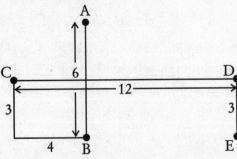

Now that the picture is finished, check the five answer choices:

(A) Arcville (A) is due north of Cowtown (C)NO

(B) Digburg (D) is due west of Cowtown (C)NO

(C) Earl City (E) is due east of Blueville (B)YES

(D) Earl City (E) is due east of Arcville (A)NO

(E) Blueville (B) is due south of Cowtown (C)NO

Quantitative Comparisons

7. **(C)** Special Math: Strange Symbols   *Easy*

Let $J \$ K$ be defined as $(J + K)^2$ means that $J \$ K = (J + K)^2$.

Column A: If $J = 3$ and $K = 4$, then $3 \$ 4 = (3 + 4)^2 = (7)^2 = 49$

Column B: If $J = -3$ and $K = -4$, then $-3 \$ -4 = (-3 + -4)^2 = (-7)^2 = 49$

The quantities in the two columns are equal.

8. **(A)** Special Math: Charts and Graphs   *Moderate*

The bar graph shows the sales, in millions, for the new company over five different years. Both Column A and Column B are concerned with percent increase. The formula for percent increase is $\dfrac{\text{final value} - \text{original value}}{\text{original value}} \times 100\%$. Therefore, the quantity in Column A $= \dfrac{\text{year 4} - \text{year 3}}{\text{year 3}} \times 100 = \dfrac{6 - 4}{4} \times 100 = \dfrac{2}{4} \times 100 = 50\%$, while the quantity in Column B $= \dfrac{\text{year 5} - \text{year 4}}{\text{year 4}} \times 100 = \dfrac{8 - 6}{6} \times 100 = \dfrac{2}{6} \times 100 = 33\dfrac{1}{3}\%$. The quantity in Column A is greater.

Grid-ins

9. **9,000** Special Math: Charts and Graphs   *Moderate*

The scatter plot displaying income shows that the income from Mary's business was $2,000 in year 1, $4,000 in year 2, and so on. The scatter plot displaying expenses shows that the expenses for Mary's business were $5,000 in year 1, $3,000 in year 2, and so on.

We need to calculate the total net profit over the 4 years. Net profit equals income minus expenses.

Total income = $2,000 + $4,000 + $7,000 + $8,000 = $21,000

Total expenses = $5,000 + $3,000 + $2,000 + $2,000 = $12,000

Net profit: $21,000 − $12,000 = $9,000

10. **6**   Special Math: Strange Symbols   *Difficult*

We are told that $A \% B = A^2 + B$ and that $A \% 36 = 12A$. The second equation tells us that $B = 36$. Knowing that $A \% 36 = A^2 + 36$ and that $A \% 36 = 12A$, we can set up the equation $A^2 + 36 = 12A$. This equation can be rearranged to $A^2 - 12A + 36 = 0$ and then factored to $(A - 6)(A - 6) = 0$. Therefore, $A = 6$.

Practice Test 1

SAT PRACTICE TEST 1 ANSWER SHEET

MATH SECTION 1	MATH SECTION 2	MATH SECTION 3
1. Ⓐ Ⓑ Ⓒ Ⓓ Ⓔ	1. Ⓐ Ⓑ Ⓒ Ⓓ Ⓔ	1. Ⓐ Ⓑ Ⓒ Ⓓ Ⓔ
2. Ⓐ Ⓑ Ⓒ Ⓓ Ⓔ	2. Ⓐ Ⓑ Ⓒ Ⓓ Ⓔ	2. Ⓐ Ⓑ Ⓒ Ⓓ Ⓔ
3. Ⓐ Ⓑ Ⓒ Ⓓ Ⓔ	3. Ⓐ Ⓑ Ⓒ Ⓓ Ⓔ	3. Ⓐ Ⓑ Ⓒ Ⓓ Ⓔ
4. Ⓐ Ⓑ Ⓒ Ⓓ Ⓔ	4. Ⓐ Ⓑ Ⓒ Ⓓ Ⓔ	4. Ⓐ Ⓑ Ⓒ Ⓓ Ⓔ
5. Ⓐ Ⓑ Ⓒ Ⓓ Ⓔ	5. Ⓐ Ⓑ Ⓒ Ⓓ Ⓔ	5. Ⓐ Ⓑ Ⓒ Ⓓ Ⓔ
6. Ⓐ Ⓑ Ⓒ Ⓓ Ⓔ	6. Ⓐ Ⓑ Ⓒ Ⓓ Ⓔ	6. Ⓐ Ⓑ Ⓒ Ⓓ Ⓔ
7. Ⓐ Ⓑ Ⓒ Ⓓ Ⓔ	7. Ⓐ Ⓑ Ⓒ Ⓓ Ⓔ	7. Ⓐ Ⓑ Ⓒ Ⓓ Ⓔ
8. Ⓐ Ⓑ Ⓒ Ⓓ Ⓔ	8. Ⓐ Ⓑ Ⓒ Ⓓ Ⓔ	8. Ⓐ Ⓑ Ⓒ Ⓓ Ⓔ
9. Ⓐ Ⓑ Ⓒ Ⓓ Ⓔ	9. Ⓐ Ⓑ Ⓒ Ⓓ Ⓔ	9. Ⓐ Ⓑ Ⓒ Ⓓ Ⓔ
10. Ⓐ Ⓑ Ⓒ Ⓓ Ⓔ	10. Ⓐ Ⓑ Ⓒ Ⓓ Ⓔ	10. Ⓐ Ⓑ Ⓒ Ⓓ Ⓔ
11. Ⓐ Ⓑ Ⓒ Ⓓ Ⓔ	11. Ⓐ Ⓑ Ⓒ Ⓓ Ⓔ	
12. Ⓐ Ⓑ Ⓒ Ⓓ Ⓔ	12. Ⓐ Ⓑ Ⓒ Ⓓ Ⓔ	
13. Ⓐ Ⓑ Ⓒ Ⓓ Ⓔ	13. Ⓐ Ⓑ Ⓒ Ⓓ Ⓔ	
14. Ⓐ Ⓑ Ⓒ Ⓓ Ⓔ	14. Ⓐ Ⓑ Ⓒ Ⓓ Ⓔ	
15. Ⓐ Ⓑ Ⓒ Ⓓ Ⓔ	15. Ⓐ Ⓑ Ⓒ Ⓓ Ⓔ	
16. Ⓐ Ⓑ Ⓒ Ⓓ Ⓔ	16. Ⓐ Ⓑ Ⓒ Ⓓ Ⓔ	
17. Ⓐ Ⓑ Ⓒ Ⓓ Ⓔ	17. Ⓐ Ⓑ Ⓒ Ⓓ Ⓔ	
18. Ⓐ Ⓑ Ⓒ Ⓓ Ⓔ	18. Ⓐ Ⓑ Ⓒ Ⓓ Ⓔ	
19. Ⓐ Ⓑ Ⓒ Ⓓ Ⓔ	19. Ⓐ Ⓑ Ⓒ Ⓓ Ⓔ	
20. Ⓐ Ⓑ Ⓒ Ⓓ Ⓔ	20. Ⓐ Ⓑ Ⓒ Ⓓ Ⓔ	
21. Ⓐ Ⓑ Ⓒ Ⓓ Ⓔ	21. Ⓐ Ⓑ Ⓒ Ⓓ Ⓔ	
22. Ⓐ Ⓑ Ⓒ Ⓓ Ⓔ	22. Ⓐ Ⓑ Ⓒ Ⓓ Ⓔ	
23. Ⓐ Ⓑ Ⓒ Ⓓ Ⓔ	23. Ⓐ Ⓑ Ⓒ Ⓓ Ⓔ	
24. Ⓐ Ⓑ Ⓒ Ⓓ Ⓔ	24. Ⓐ Ⓑ Ⓒ Ⓓ Ⓔ	
25. Ⓐ Ⓑ Ⓒ Ⓓ Ⓔ	25. Ⓐ Ⓑ Ⓒ Ⓓ Ⓔ	
26. Ⓐ Ⓑ Ⓒ Ⓓ Ⓔ		
27. Ⓐ Ⓑ Ⓒ Ⓓ Ⓔ		
28. Ⓐ Ⓑ Ⓒ Ⓓ Ⓔ		
29. Ⓐ Ⓑ Ⓒ Ⓓ Ⓔ		
30. Ⓐ Ⓑ Ⓒ Ⓓ Ⓔ		

SAT TEST

In this section solve each problem, using any available space on the page for scratchwork. Then decide which is the best of the choices given and fill in the corresponding oval on the answer sheet.

Notes:
1. The use of a calculator is permitted. All numbers used are real numbers.

2. Figures that accompany problems in this test are intended to provide information useful in solving the problems. They are drawn as accurately as possible EXCEPT when it is stated in a specific problem that the figure is not drawn to scale. All figures lie in a plane unless otherwise indicated.

Reference Information

$A = \pi r^2$
$C = 2\pi r$

$A = \ell w$

$A = \frac{1}{2}bh$

$V = \ell w h$

$V = \pi r^2 h$

$c^2 = a^2 + b^2$

Special Right Triangles

The number of degrees of arc in a circle is 360.
The measure in degrees of a straight angle is 180.
The sum of the measures in degrees of the angles of a triangle is 180.

---

1. What is $\frac{1}{3}$ of $6 + 3^2$?

    (A) 5
    (B) 6
    (C) 11
    (D) 18
    (E) 54

2. What is the area of a circle whose diameter is d centimeters?

    (A) $\pi d \ \text{cm}^2$
    (B) $\pi d^2 \ \text{cm}^2$
    (C) $\frac{\pi d}{2} \ \text{cm}^2$
    (D) $\frac{\pi d^2}{2} \ \text{cm}^2$
    (E) $\frac{\pi d^2}{4} \ \text{cm}^2$

3. If $6x - 12 = 18$, then $3x =$

    (A) 5
    (B) 6
    (C) 9
    (D) 15
    (E) 30

4. Kayla reads 30 pages of a book in 45 minutes. At this rate, how many pages will she read in 60 minutes?

    (A) 40
    (B) 45
    (C) 60
    (D) 75
    (E) 90

5. If $x = -2$, $y = 2$, and $z = 4$, which of the following must be true?

    I. $xy - z = 0$
    II. $x^y = z$
    III. $\frac{z}{y} - x = 0$

    (A) I only
    (B) II only
    (C) I and III only
    (D) II and III only
    (E) I, II, and III

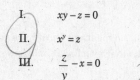
GO ON TO THE NEXT PAGE

6.

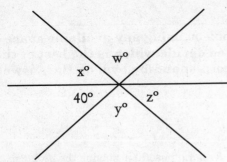

In the figure above, what is the measure of $w + z$?

(A) 50°
(B) 120°
(C) 140°
(D) 220°
(E) It cannot be determined.

7. If $b < -1 < a < 0$, which of the following has the greatest value?

(A) $a + b$
(B) $a - b$
(C) ab
(D) $\dfrac{a}{b}$
(E) $\dfrac{ab}{2}$

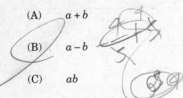

8. Jeannine has no more than $250 to spend on holiday gifts for her three friends. She wants to get each of them an equal number of CDs. If each CD costs $15.99, how many CDs can Jeannine get for each of her friends?

(A) 5
(B) 6
(C) 9
(D) 15
(E) 16

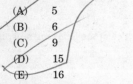

9. A local chess club has 8 members. During the year, if each member plays each other member 4 times, how many total games are played?

(A) 16
(B) 32
(C) 64
(D) 112
(E) 224

10. If $4^{3x-2} = 256$, what is the value of 3^{1-x}?

(A) 27
(B) 3
(C) $\dfrac{1}{3}$
(D) $\dfrac{1}{9}$
(E) 3

11. If lines l and m are parallel, and if line n intersects both l and m, which of the following must be true?

   I.   Line n is perpendicular to both line l and line m.
   II.   If the slopes of l and m are positive, the slope of n is negative.
   III. The sum of the angles formed by the intersection of lines l and m is 360°.

(A) None
(B) II only
(C) III only
(D) I and II only
(E) II and III only

12. If $rst \neq 0$, then $\dfrac{r^3 st + rs^3 t + rst^3}{rst} =$

(A) rst
(B) $r^2 s^2 t^2$
(C) $r + s + t$
(D) $r^2 + s^2 + t^2$
(E) $r^3 + s^3 + t^3$

13. Jerome can paint a 12-foot by 15-foot room in p hours. Denise can paint the same-size room in q hours. If they work together, how long will it take both Jerome and Denise to paint the room?

(A) pq
(B) $\dfrac{p}{q}$
(C) $p + q$
(D) $\dfrac{pq}{p+q}$
(E) $\dfrac{p+q}{pq}$

GO ON TO THE NEXT PAGE

14.

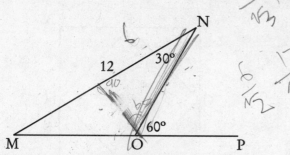

In the figure above ∠MNO measures 30°, ∠NOP measures 60°, and $\overline{MN}$ = 12 inches. What is the length of $\overline{MO}$?

(A) $2\sqrt{3}$
(B) $3\sqrt{3}$
(C) $4\sqrt{3}$
(D) 6
(E) $6\sqrt{3}$

15. If $a = 2b$, $b = 5c$, and $c = \dfrac{d}{10}$, then what is the value of a?

(A) d
(B) $10d$
(C) $25d$
(D) $50d$
(E) $100d$

16. If x is an even number and y is an odd number, which of the following must be even?

    I. $x + y$
    II. $x - y$
    III. xy

(A) I only
(B) III only
(C) I and II only
(D) II and III only
(E) I, II, and III

17.

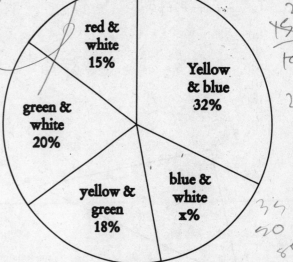

Eastview High School is changing its school colors. A vote was taken to determine the new colors. The percentage breakdown is displayed in the pie chart above. Of the 1,200 students who voted, how many chose blue as one of the colors?

(A) 120
(B) 180
(C) 216
(D) 384
(E) 564

18. In a bowling match, players must bowl 5 games. Tyler bowled a 156, 193, 163, and 188 in his first 4 games. The top scorer's average is 185. What score must Tyler get in his last game in order to have the same average as the top scorer?

(A) 175
(B) 185
(C) 200
(D) 210
(E) 225

19. If w and z are real numbers, what is the value of $(w + z)^2 + (w - z)^2$?

(A) $w + z$
(B) $2w + 2z$
(C) $2w^2$
(D) $w^2 + z^2$
(E) $2w^2 + 2z^2$

GO ON TO THE NEXT PAGE

20. On a coordinate system, point P has coordinates $(-1, -1)$ and point Q has coordinates $(-5, -4)$. What is the distance between points P and Q?

(A) 3
(B) 4
(C) 5
(D) 6
(E) 7

21.

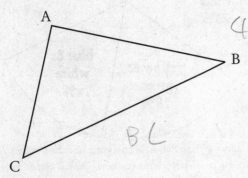

Note: Figure not drawn to scale.

In $\triangle ABC$, $\angle A > \angle B$ and $\angle B > \angle C$. Which of the following must be true?

(A) $AB > BC > AC$
(B) $AB > CB > BC$
(C) $BC > AC > AB$
(D) $BC > AB > AC$
(E) $AC > AB > BC$

22. In the span of an hour, a television show runs for a total of 44 minutes. An additional 4 minutes are used to run credits, and the remainder of the time is used to air commercials. If the television is turned on sometime during that hour, what is the probability that a commercial will NOT be airing at that moment?

(A) $\frac{1}{5}$
(B) $\frac{4}{15}$
(C) $\frac{1}{3}$
(D) $\frac{11}{15}$
(E) $\frac{4}{5}$

23.

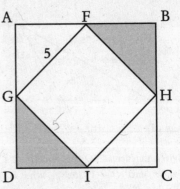

In the diagram above, if figures $ABCD$ and $FGHI$ are squares, and the length of is 5 units, what is the area of the shaded region?

(A) $\frac{5\sqrt{2}}{2}$
(B) $5\sqrt{2}$
(C) $\frac{25}{2}$
(D) $\frac{25\sqrt{2}}{2}$
(E) 25

24. Which of the following equations is perpendicular to $3x - 2y = 5$?

(A) $y = -\frac{2}{3}x + 4$
(B) $y = -\frac{3}{2}x + 1$
(C) $y = \frac{2}{3}x + 3$
(D) $y = \frac{3}{2}x + 6$
(E) $y = -x + 2$

25. If a number n is evenly divisible by 6, then which of the following must always be evenly divisible by 8?

(A) $\frac{2}{3}n$
(B) $\frac{3}{4}n$
(C) $\frac{4}{3}n$
(D) $3n$
(E) n^2

GO ON TO THE NEXT PAGE

SAT TEST

Time—30 Minutes **25 Questions**	In this section solve each problem, using any available space on the page for scratchwork. Then decide which is the best of the choices given and fill in the corresponding oval on the answer sheet.

Notes:

1.   The use of a calculator is permitted. All numbers used are real numbers.

2.   Figures that accompany problems in this test are intended to provide information useful in solving the problems. They are drawn as accurately as possible EXCEPT when it is stated in a specific problem that the figure is not drawn to scale. All figures lie in a plane unless otherwise indicated.

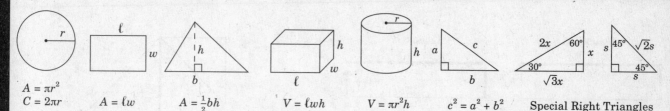
Directions for Quantitative Comparison Questions

Questions 1–15 each consist of two quantities in boxes, one in Column A and one in Column B.
You are to compare the two quantities and on the answer sheet fill in oval

A   if the quantity in Column A is greater;
B   if the quantity in Column B is greater;
C   if the two quantities are equal;
D   if the relationship cannot be determined from the information given.

AN E RESPONSE WILL NOT BE SCORED.

Notes:

1. In some questions, information is given about one or both of the quantities to be compared. In such cases, the given information is centered above the two columns and is not boxed.
2. In a given question, a symbol that appears in both columns represents the same thing in Column A as it does in Column B.
3. Letters such as x, n, and k stand for real numbers.

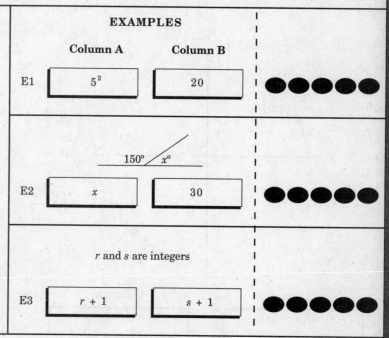

EXAMPLES

	Column A	Column B	
E1	5^2	20	●●●●●
E2	x	30	●●●●●
E3	$r + 1$	$s + 1$	●●●●●

(r and s are integers)

1.

$S = \{4.5, 7.9, 3.3, 8.1, 4.5, 6.2, 8.0, 5.9, 7.4, 6.4\}$

Column A	Column B
The mean of set S	The median of set S

2.

Column A	Column B
The radius of a circle whose circumference is 4π	The radius of a circle whose area is 4π

3.

$m < n < 0$

Column A	Column B
$\dfrac{1}{m}$	$\dfrac{1}{n}$

4.

$r < t + 5$

Column A	Column B
r	t

5.

Column A	Column B
The slope of the line parallel to MN	The slope of the line perpendicular to MN

6.

q is a prime number

Column A	Column B
The number of distinct prime factors in $5q$	2

7.

Column A	Column B
$x^2 + y^2$	$x^2 - y^2$

8.

Column A	Column B
$2a$	b

9.

Two 6-sided dice, each numbered 1 through 6, are rolled.

Column A	Column B
The probability that the sum of the numbers on the dice will be a prime number	The probability that the sum of the numbers on the dice will be divisible by 3

GO ON TO THE NEXT PAGE

10.

$$x + 2y = 0$$

$$2x - y = 10$$

Column A	Column B
$x - y$	$x + y$

11.

Three cans of soup cost $5.00 and two boxes of crackers cost $3.50.

Column A	Column B
The cost of 2 cans of soup and 1 box of crackers	The cost of 1 can of soup and 2 boxes of crackers

12.

$$\Theta x \Theta \ = x^2 - 2x \text{ when } x \text{ is even.}$$

$$= x^3 + x^2 \text{ when } x \text{ is odd.}$$

Column A	Column B
$\Theta{-}1\Theta$	$\Theta 2\Theta$

13.

$$ab = 0$$

Column A	Column B
$(a + b)^2$	$(a - b)^2$

14.

When n is divided by 5, the remainder is 2.

Column A	Column B
The remainder when $8n$ is divided by 5	The remainder when $n + 8$ is divided by 5

15.

Column A	Column B
The area of a rectangle whose perimeter is 12	The area of a rectangle whose perimeter is 16

GO ON TO THE NEXT PAGE

SAT TEST

Directions for Student-Produced Response Questions

Each of the remaining 10 questions (16–25) requires you to solve the problem and enter your answer by marking the ovals in the special grid, as shown in the examples below.

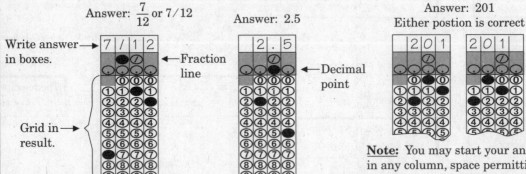

Answer: $\frac{7}{12}$ or 7/12

Answer: 2.5

Answer: 201
Either postion is correct

Write answer in boxes. → ←Fraction line

←Decimal point

Grid in result. →

Note: You may start your answers in any column, space permitting. Columns not needed should be left blank.

- Mark no more than one oval in any column.

- Because the answer sheet will be machine-scored, **you will receive credit only if the ovals are filled in correctly.**

- Although not required, it is suggested that you write your answer in the boxes at the top of the columns to help you fill in the ovals accurately.

- Some problems may have more than one correct answer. In such cases, grid only one answer.

- No question has a negative answer.

- **Mixed numbers** such as $2\frac{1}{2}$ must be gridded as 2.5 or 5/2. If | 2 | 1 | / | 2 | is gridded, it will be interpreted as $\frac{21}{2}$, not $2\frac{1}{2}$.)

- **Decimal Accuracy:** If you obtain a decimal answer, **enter the most accurate value the grid will accommodate.** For example, if you obtain an answer such as 0.6666 . . . , you should record the result as .666 or .667. **Less accurate values such as .66 or .67 are not acceptable.** Acceptable ways to grid $\frac{2}{3}$ = .6666 . . .

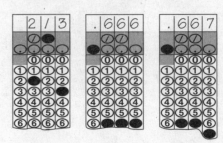

16.

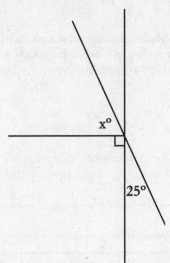

In the figure above, what is the measure of angle x in degrees?

17. If $8(r + s) - 3(r + s) = 105$, what is the value of $r + s$?

18. The number of bacteria in a petri dish doubles every half hour. If the petri dish currently contains 10 bacteria, how many bacteria will there be in 3 hours?

19. It takes Mr. Jenkins $\frac{3}{4}$ of an hour to travel 30 miles. At this rate, how many minutes will it take him to travel 60 miles?

20. If the height of a right circular cylinder remains the same but its diameter is cut in half, by what percentage does the volume of the cylinder decrease?

21. Twenty-five students are on the soccer team, and 17 students are on the football team. If 9 students play on both teams, how many students play these sports?

22.

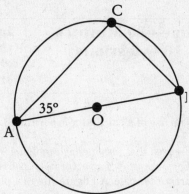

Triangle ABC is inscribed inside circle O, as shown above. Given that AB is the diameter of circle O and that $\angle CAB = 35°$, what is the measure of arc AC?

23.

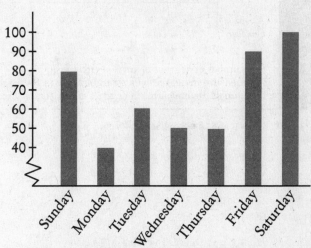

The chart above shows the number of ice cream cones that were sold during one week at the Tasty Ice Cream Shoppe. If cones cost $1.25 each, how much more money was earned on the day with the highest sales compared to the day with the lowest sales?

24. 4 CDs and 2 DVDs cost $92. 3 CDs and 4 DVDs cost $114. How much do 1 CD and 1 DVD cost?

25. A jacket is on sale for 25% off. Three days later, the jacket is reduced an additional 20%. If the new sale price is $120, what was the total amount saved on the price of the jacket?

GO ON TO THE NEXT PAGE

SAT TEST

Time—30 Minutes
10 Questions

In this section solve each problem, using any available space on the page for scratchwork. Then decide which is the best of the choices given and fill in the corresponding oval on the answer sheet.

Notes:

1. The use of a calculator is permitted. All numbers used are real numbers.

2. Figures that accompany problems in this test are intended to provide information useful in solvin gthe problems. They are drawn as accurately as possible EXCEPT when it is stated in a specific problem that the figure is not drawn to scale. All figures lie in a plane unless otherwise indicated.

Reference Information

       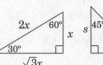

$A = \pi r^2$
$C = 2\pi r$ $A = \ell w$ $A = \frac{1}{2}bh$ $V = \ell wh$ $V = \pi r^2 h$ $c^2 = a^2 + b^2$ Special Right Triangles

The number of degrees of arc in a circle is 360.
The measure in degrees of a straight angle is 180.
The sum of the measures in degrees of the angles of a triangle is 180.

---

1. If $p > 0$ and $p^2 = 8$, what is the value of p^3?

   (A) $2\sqrt{2}$
   (B) 8
   (C) 16
   (D) 16
   (E) 32

2. If $x \approx y = y^x$, what is the value of $7 \approx 3$?

   (A) 4
   (B) 10
   (C) 21
   (D) 343
   (E) 2,187

3. If $2c + 3d = -6$ and $3c - 2d = 4$, which of the following CANNOT be true?

   (A) $c > d$
   (B) $c - d > 0$
   (C) $c + d < 0$
   (D) $c > 4d$
   (E) $cd < 0$

4. If the radius of a circle increases by 100%, by what percentage does the circumference increase?

   (A) 50%
   (B) 100%
   (C) 200%
   (D) 300%
   (E) 400%

5. The second and fourth numbers in a geometric series are $\frac{1}{3}$ and $\frac{3}{4}$, respectively. What is the fifth term in the series?

   (A) $\frac{4}{9}$
   (B) $\frac{3}{5}$
   (C) $\frac{3}{2}$
   (D) $\frac{5}{3}$
   (E) $\frac{9}{8}$

GO ON TO THE NEXT PAGE

6.

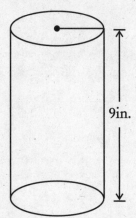

9in.

In the figure above, the cylinder has a height of 9 inches and a volume of 81π cubic inches. What is the cylinder's diameter?

(A)   3 inches
(B)   6 inches
(C)   9 inches
(D)   12 inches
(E)   18 inches

7.   A rectangular garden is 8 feet long by 6 feet wide. If the width is increased such that the area of the garden is doubled, what is the perimeter of the enlarged garden?

(A)   34 feet
(B)   40 feet
(C)   46 feet
(D)   48 feet
(E)   96 feet

8.   If a and b are consecutive prime integers and $ab = 221$, what is the value of $a + b$?

(A)   23
(B)   25
(C)   28
(D)   30
(E)   33

9.   If $(x + y)^2 = 50$ and $xy = 10$, what is $2x^2 + 2y^2$?

(A)   30
(B)   40
(C)   60
(D)   80
(E)   120

10.   Last week, a stereo was marked down 25%. This week, it is not on sale. By what percentage was the stereo marked up to raise it to its original price?

(A)   20%

(B)   25%

(C)   30%

(D) $33\frac{1}{3}$ %

(E)   50%

S T O P

IF YOU FINISH BEFORE TIME IS CALLED, YOU MAY CHECK YOUR WORK IN THIS SECTION ONLY.
DO NOT TURN TO ANY OTHER SECTION IN THE TEST.

SAT Math
Workbook
Practice Test I
Explanations

Answers to SAT Math Workbook Practice Test I

Question Number	Correct Answer	Right	Wrong	Question Number	Correct Answer	Right	Wrong	Question Number	Correct Answer	Right	Wrong
				Section I: Multiple Choice Answers (25)							
1.	A			10.	C			19.	E		
2.	E			11.	A			20.	C		
3.	D			12.	D			21.	C		
4.	A			13.	D			22.	E		
5.	B			14.	C			23.	C		
6.	C			15.	A			24.	A		
7.	B			16.	B			25.	C		
8.	A			17.	E						
9.	D			18.	E						
				Section II: Quantitative Comparisons Answers (15)							
1.	B			6.	D			11.	B		
2.	C			7.	D			12.	C		
3.	A			8.	B			13.	C		
4.	D			9.	A			14.	A		
5.	B			10.	A			15.	D		
				Section II: Grid-In Answers (10)							
1.	65			5.	75			9.	32		
2.	21			6.	33			10.	80		
3.	640			7.	110						
4.	90			8.	75						
				Section III: Multiple Choice Answers (10)							
1.	D			5.	E			9.	C		
2.	E			6.	B			10.	D		
3.	E			7.	B						
4.	B			8.	D						

Multiple Choice Explanations (25)

1. **(A)** Arithmetic: Fractions   *Easy*

A careless test-taker might fly through this question, taking the value of $\frac{1}{3}$ of 6 and then adding that to 3^2, but that is incorrect. The question asks for $\frac{1}{3}$ of the *total* value of $6 + 3^2$. $6 + 3^2 = 6 + 9 = 15$. Then multiply the result by: $\frac{1}{3} : \frac{1}{3} \times 15 = 5$.

2. **(E)** Geometry: Circles   *Easy*

The area of a circle is πr^2, where r is the radius of the circle. The trick here is to recognize that the problem gives a value for the diameter, not the radius. The radius has to be written in terms of the diameter, d. The radius is equal to half the diameter, so $r = \frac{d}{2}$. Plugging this value in for r, the area of the circle is $\pi \frac{d}{2} r^2 = \frac{\pi d^2}{2} = \frac{\pi d^2}{4}$.

3. **(D)** Algebra: Manipulating Equations   *Easy*

Remember that the question asks for the value of $3x$, not the value of x. Make sure to avoid giving a partial answer. Your first step should be to solve for x:

$$6x - 12 = 18$$

$$6x = 30$$

$$x = 5$$

Therefore, $3x = 3(5) = 15$.

4. **(A)** Arithmetic: Ratios and Proportions   *Easy*

The question asks you to set up a ratio between the number of pages that Kayla reads in 45 minutes and the number of pages that she reads in 60 minutes. If x represents the unknown number of pages read, then the proportion is:

$$\frac{30 \text{ pages read}}{45 \text{ minutes}} = \frac{x \text{ pages read}}{60 \text{ minutes}}$$

Using cross-multiplication, find x: $30 \cdot 60 = 45x$. $1800 = 45x$. $\frac{1800}{45} = 40 = x$.

5. **(B)** Algebra: Substitution   *Easy*

Plug the given values for x, y, and z into each option:

I. $xy - z = 0(-2)(2) - 4 = -4 - 4 = -8$

II. $xy = z(-2)2 = 4$

III. $\frac{z}{y} - x = 0 \, \frac{4}{2} - (-2) = 2 + 2 = 4$

Option II is the only situation that is true.

6. **(C)** Geometry: Angles and Lines   *Moderate*

In the given figure, the 40° angle and the unmarked angle are vertical angles, so the unmarked angle must also be 40°. Angles w, z, and the unmarked angle form a straight line, so the sum of their measures is 180°. Therefore, $w + 40 + z = 180°$, and $w + z = 180° - 40° = 140°$.

7. **(B)** Arithmetic: Signed Numbers   *Moderate*

This question gives you a lot of information, so break it down into smaller pieces. Both variables are negative numbers since the question states that both are less that 0. a must be a negative fraction, because it lies between 0 and –1, and b is a negative number smaller than –1. Pick numbers for both a and b that match these criteria; for example, $a = -\frac{1}{2}$ and $b = -2$. Plug these numbers into the answer choices to see which yields the greatest value:

$$\text{(A)}\quad a + b = -\frac{1}{2} + (-2) = -2\frac{1}{2}$$

$$\text{(B)}\quad a - b = -\frac{1}{2} - (-2) = -\frac{1}{2} + 2 = 1\frac{1}{2}$$

$$\text{(C)}\quad \frac{1}{2}ab = \frac{1}{2} \times (2) = 1$$

$$\text{(D)}\quad \frac{a}{b} = \frac{-\frac{1}{2}}{-2} = \frac{1}{4}$$

$$\text{(E)}\quad \frac{ab}{2} = \frac{-\frac{1}{2} \times (-2)}{2} = \frac{1}{2}$$

The greatest value is (B): $a - b = 1\frac{1}{2}$.

8. **(A)** Algebra: Solving Inequalities   *Moderate*

Keep in mind that this problem involves a restriction on the amount of money that Jeannine can spend. The equation that models this situation is $\$15.99c \leq \$250$, where c represents the total number of CDs that can be bought. To find c, divide 250 by 15.99: $\frac{250}{15.99} = 15.6347$ CDs. Since it is not possible to purchase a fractional number of CDs, the greatest number of CDs that can be bought is 15. If they are to be divided equally among three friends, then each will receive $\frac{15}{3} = 5$ CDs.

9. **(D)** Special Math: Logical Reasoning   *Difficult*
In a club with 8 members, each member can play 7 other people. If a member plays each of the other members 4 times, then that member plays a total of 7 × 4 = 28 games against other members. Since there are 8 members in the club, you need to multiply this number by 8: 8 × 28 = 224 games are played by all of the members. This number counts each game twice, since it counts when Player I plays Player II as one game and when Player II plays Player I as another game, even though these are the same game. To take into account that each separate game involves two players, the total games must be divided by 2. Therefore, 224 ÷ 2 = 112 total games played.

10. **(C)** Arithmetic: Exponents   *Moderate*
To answer this question, you must solve for x in the equation and then plug that value into the expression. The trick to solving for x is recognizing that $256 = 4^4$, so you can rewrite the equation as $4^{3x-2} = 4^4$. Since the exponents must be equal if the bases are equal, you know that $3x - 2 = 4$ and $x = 2$. Now, plug 2 into the expression 3^{1-x}: $3^{1-2} = 3^{-1} = \frac{1}{3^1} = \frac{1}{3}$.

11. **(A)** Geometry: Coordinate Geometry   *Difficult*
The question asks you to determine what *must* be true, not what could be true, given the stated conditions. Read each statement and decide whether it must be true. Drawing a picture of the lines l, m, and n will help you assess each option.

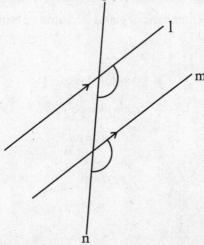

In option I, while n could be perpendicular to the two parallel lines, it is not necessarily perpendicular. You can draw n intersecting the two lines at any angle, such as the one in the picture above. So, statement I is not true.

Likewise, in option II, if l and m have positive slopes, it could be possible for n to have a positive or negative slope intersect the two lines. Line n could also have no slope (a horizontal line) or an undefined slope (a vertical line), and it would intersect the two lines. So, statement II is not true.

The question states that lines l and m are parallel, so statement III, which says that these lines intersect, cannot by definitionbe true.

Therefore, none of the three statements are true, and the correct answer is (A).

12. **(D)** Algebra: Simplifying Expressions   *Moderate*
The three terms in the numerator share a common factor, rst. If you factor this term out, you can simplify the expression by canceling rst from the numerator and denominator:

$$\frac{rst(r^2) + rst(s^2) + rst(t^2)}{rst} = \frac{rst(r^2 + s^2 + t^2)}{rst}$$

$$r^2 + s^2 + t^2$$

13. **(D)** Arithmetic: Rates   *Difficult*
This question requires the rate formula: Rate of Work Time = Part of Job Completed.

Let x represent the total amount of time that it will take Jerome and Denise to complete the job. Their rate of work is the reciprocal of the amount of time needed to complete the job if working alone. Jerome's rate is , and Denise's rate is $\frac{1}{q}$. The fractional part completed by Jerome is $\frac{1}{p} \cdot x = \frac{x}{p}$. The fractional part completed by Denise is $\frac{1}{q} \cdot x = \frac{x}{q}$. If they work together to complete the job, the sum of these fractional will equal 1: $\frac{x}{p} + \frac{x}{q} = 1$. Now, solve in terms of p and q by multiplying each term by the lowest common denominator, pq.

$$pq(\frac{x}{p}) + pq(\frac{x}{q}) = pq(1)$$

$$qx + px = pq$$

$$x(q + p) = pq$$

$$x = \frac{pq}{q + p}$$

14. **(C)** Geometry: Triangles   *Difficult*

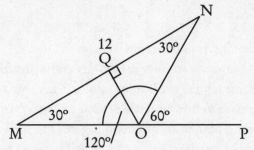

If ∠*NOP* measures 60°, then its supplementary angle ∠*MON* measures 120°. Since you now know two angles in the △*MON*, you can figure out the third: ∠*NMO* measures 30°. By drawing line $\overline{OQ}$ perpendicular to $\overline{MN}$, you can divide △*MON* in half and form two congruent triangles. The congruent triangles, △*MOQ* and △*NOQ*, are 30-60-90 special right triangles. Applying the properties of the special right triangle, if you let *x* represent the shorter leg $\overline{OQ}$, then the longer leg $\overline{MQ}$ can be represented by $x\sqrt{3}$, and the hypotenuse $\overline{MO}$ can be represented by 2*x*. Now you need to figure out the value of *x*: $\overline{MN} = 2(\overline{MQ}) = 2(x\sqrt{3}) = 12$. Solve for *x* by dividing both sides by 2.

$$x = \frac{12}{2\sqrt{3}} = \frac{6}{\sqrt{3}} \in \frac{\sqrt{3}}{\sqrt{3}} = \frac{6\sqrt{3}}{3} = 2\sqrt{3}$$

Therefore, $\overline{MO} = 2x = 2(2\sqrt{3}) = 4\sqrt{3}$.

15. **(A)** Algebra: Building Expressions and Equations   *Difficult*
The question asks you to find *a* in terms of *d*. The easiest way to approach this problem is to use substitution. You know that $a = 2b$ and $b = 5c$. Plug 5*c* for *b* into the equation for *a*. You end up with: $a = 2(5c)$, or $a = 10c$. Since you also know that $c = \frac{d}{10}$, plug in for *c* in the new equation for *a*. You can then find *a* in terms of *d*: $a = 10(\frac{d}{10})$, or $a = d$.

16. **(B)** Arithmetic: Odd and Even Numbers   *Easy*
The easiest way to solve this problem is to pick numbers to represent the variables *x* and *y*, keeping in mind that the numbers must satisfy the given criteria. Since *x* is even and *y* is odd, let $x = 2$ and $y = 1$. Now, plug these numbers into each of the options and see which produce even numbers.

   I. x + y = 2 + 1 = 3 = odd

   II. x − y = 2 − 1 = 1 = odd

   III. xy = 2 × 1 = 2 = even

Since any number multiplied by an even number will always be even, III is the only situation that works.

17. **(E)** Special Math: Charts and Graphs   *Moderate*

Remember to read the question carefully before attempting to answer it. You are asked for the number of students who chose blue as a color. There are two pie slices that have blue as an option: one with yellow and blue (32% of votes), and the other with blue and white (x% of votes). These must be added together to obtain the total number of votes. You need to find the missing percentage, x. All slices added together must equal 100%, so $18\% + 20\% + 15\% + 32\% + x\% = 100\%$, or $85\% + x\% = 100\%$, so $x\% = 15\%$. The total percentage of voters who chose blue as a school color was $32\% + 15\% = 47\%$. Since there were 1,200 votes cast, students who chose blue.

$47\% \times 1200 = 0.47 \times 1200 = 564$

18. **(E)** Arithmetic: Mean, Median, and Mode   *Moderate*

To find the average of a set of bowling scores, add all of the scores together and divide by the number of games bowled. This problem states the average of 5 scores, one of which is unknown. Let x represent the unknown score. The average of the bowling scores is $\frac{156 + 193 + 163 + 188 + x}{5} = 185$. $156 + 193 + 163 + 188 + x = 185 \times 5$.

$700 + x = 925$, so $x = 225$.

19. **(E)** Algebra: Multiplying Binomials   *Moderate*

Expand each binomial, using the distributive property. Then, add the results.

$$(w + z)^2 = (w + z)(w + z) = w^2 + wz + wz + z^2 = w^2 + 2wz + z^2$$

$$(w - z)^2 = (w - z)(w - z) = w^2 - wz - wz + z^2 = w^2 - 2wz + z^2$$

$$(w + z)^2 + (w - z)^2 = w^2 + 2wz + z^2 + w^2 - 2wz + z^2 = 2w^2 + 2z^2$$

20. **(C)** Geometry: Coordinate Geometry   *Easy*

It is easy to visualize the distance between *P* and *Q* if you first draw a diagram. On a coordinate system, plot and connect the points for *P* and *Q*.

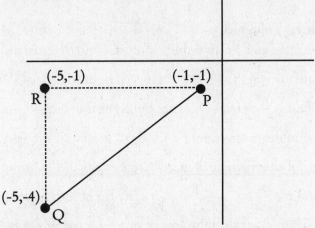

Since $\overline{PQ}$ is not parallel to either axis, to find its length, think of it as the hypotenuse of a right triangle. Draw a line through point *P* that is parallel to the *x*-axis and a line through point *Q* that is parallel to the *y*-axis. Draw and label the point *R* at the location where these points meet, (–5, –1). Find the distance of the legs of the newly formed right triangle by counting the distance of point *R* from points *P* and *Q*. $\overline{RP}$ is 4 units long and $\overline{RQ}$ is 3 units long. Apply the Pythagorean Theorem to find $\overline{PQ}$.

$$PQ^2 = RP^2 + RQ^2$$
$$PQ^2 = 4^2 + 3^2$$
$$PQ^2 = 16 + 9 = 25$$
$$PQ = \sqrt{25} = 5$$

21. **(C)** Geometry: Triangles   *Easy*

In this problem, you are given the following angle relationship: $\angle A > \angle B$ and $\angle B > \angle C$. So, $\angle A > \angle B > \angle C$. The lengths of the sides opposite these angles share the same relationship. $\angle A$ is opposite *BC*, $\angle B$ is opposite *AC*, and $\angle C$ is opposite *AB*. Therefore, $BC > AC > AB$.

22. **(E)** Arithmetic: Probability   *Moderate*

Probability is equal to $\dfrac{\text{expected outcome}}{\text{total possible outcomes}}$. You are asked to find the probability that an event will NOT occur. Make sure that you know what the question is asking before marking the answer. Since there are 60 minutes in an hour, 60 represents the total number of outcomes. The amount of time in which commercials are not shown is when the television show is on or when the credits are running; 44 + 4 = 48 minutes. Therefore, the probability that a commercial will not be on is $\frac{48}{60} = \frac{4}{5}$.

23. **(C)**   Geometry: Polygons   *Moderate*

Since *FGHI* is a square and $\overline{FG}$ is 5 units long, $\overline{GI}$ and $\overline{HF}$ must also be 5 units long. and are also hypotenuses of the 45-45°-90° special right triangles *GDI* and *HBF*. What you have left to find is the area of two special right triangles whose hypotenuses are both 5. According to the properties of a 45-45-90 special right triangle, if *x* represents the length of a leg of the triangle, then $x\sqrt{2}$ represents the length of the hypotenuse. Then, $x\sqrt{2} = 5$ and $x = \frac{5}{\sqrt{2}} = \frac{5}{\sqrt{2}} \cdot \frac{\sqrt{2}}{\sqrt{2}} = \frac{5\sqrt{2}}{2}$. The leg of the right triangle is $\frac{5\sqrt{2}}{2}$. The area of the shaded region is twice the area of one right triangle, which is calculated as (0.5)(base)(height). So, the area of the two triangles is $2[\frac{1}{2}(\frac{5\sqrt{2}}{2} \cdot \frac{5\sqrt{2}}{2})] = 2[\frac{1}{2}(\frac{50}{4})] = \frac{25}{2}$.

24. **(A)**   Algebra: Solving Linear Equations   *Easy*

Perpendicular lines are lines whose slopes are negative reciprocals of each other. For example, negative reciprocals are $\frac{1}{2}$ and $-\frac{2}{1}$. To solve this problem, rewrite the given equation in slope-intercept form, $y = mx + b$, where *m* is the slope. The perpendicular line will have a slope that is the negative reciprocal of the given slope.

$$3x - 2y = 5$$

$$-2y = 3x + 5$$

$$y = \frac{-3}{-2}x + \frac{5}{-2} = \frac{3}{2}x - \frac{5}{2}$$

The slope of the given line is , so the negative reciprocal is . The only answer choice with this slope is (A), $y = x + 4$.

25. **(C)**   Arithmetic: Divisibility and Remainders   *Difficult*

Pick a number that is evenly divisible by 6 to represent *n*. Then, plug that number into each of the answer choices to see which choice is evenly divisible by 8. Let *n* = 6, the smallest positive number that fits this situation.

(A) $\frac{2}{3}n = \frac{2}{3} \times 6 = 4$ $4 \div 8 = \frac{1}{2}$

(B) $\frac{3}{4}n = \frac{3}{4} \times 6 = 4\frac{1}{2}$ $4\frac{1}{2} \div 8 = \frac{9}{16}$

(C) $\frac{4}{3}n = \frac{4}{3} \times 6 = 8 \qquad 8 \div 8 = 1$

(D) $3n = 3 \times 6 = 18 \quad 18 \div 8 = 2\frac{1}{4}$

(E) $n^2 = 6^2 = 36 \qquad 36 \div 8 = 4\frac{1}{2}$

$\frac{4}{3}n$ is the only answer choice that results in a whole number when divided by 8, so (C) is the right answer to this question

Quantitative Comparison Explanations (15)

1. **(B)** Arithmetic: Mean, Median, and Mode   *Easy*
In Column A, to find the mean, add the numbers in the set and divide the result by the number of values in the set.

$$\frac{4.5 + 7.9 + 3.3 + 8.1 + 4.5 + 6.2 + 8.0 + 5.9 + 7.4 + 6.4}{10} = \frac{62.2}{10} = 6.22.$$

In Column B, to find the median, first order the items from least to greatest.

$$3.3, 4.5, 4.5, 5.9, 6.2, 6.4, 7.4, 7.9, 8.0, 8.1$$

The median is the middle value. Since there is an even number of values, the median is the average of the two middle values, 6.2 and 6.4. $\frac{6.2 + 6.4}{2} = 6.3$.

2. **(C)** Geometry: Circles   *Easy*
In Column A, you need to find the radius, r, given a circumference of 4π. The formula for the circumference of a circle is $2\pi r$. Set the formula for circumference equal to the given circumference and solve for r. $2\pi r = 4\pi$, so $r = \frac{4\pi}{2\pi} = 2$.

In Column B, you need to find the radius, r, given an area of 4π. The formula for the area of a circle is πr^2. Set the formula for area equal to the given area and solve for r. $\pi r^2 = 4\pi$, so $r^2 = \frac{4\pi}{\pi} = 4$ and $r = \sqrt{4} = 2$.

Since both columns are equal, the correct answer is (C).

3. **(A)** Arithmetic: Signed Numbers   *Easy*
Pick numbers for both m and n that match the given criteria, and then plug these numbers into each column. Both m and n are less then 0, and m is smaller than n. If you let $m = -2$ and $n = -1$, then the value in Column A is $-\frac{1}{2}$, and the value in Column B is $-\frac{1}{1}$, or -1, so Column A is greater than Column B.

4. **(D)**   Algebra: Solving Inequalities   *Easy*

Don't be tempted to think that r is smaller than t simply because of the inequality. It is easy enough to plug in a few possible values for r and t to show this isn't true. If you let both r and t equal 0, then $0 < 0 + 5$ results, and this is true. So both columns could be equal. If you let $r = 5$ and $t = 1$, then $5 < 1 + 5$ results, and this is also true. So, Column A could be greater than Column B. Since more than one outcome is possible, more information is needed in order to solve this problem, and the answer is (D).

5. **(B)**   Geometry: Coordinate Geometry   *Moderate*

Parallel lines have equal slopes, so the slope of a line parallel to MN would have the same slope as MN. Perpendicular lines have slopes equal to the negative reciprocal of a given line. So, if MN is positive, the perpendicular line is negative, and vice versa. Only the sign of the slope of MN needs to be found in order to determine which column has the greater value. Point M is in the second quadrant, so a must be negative and b must be positive. Point N is in the fourth quadrant, so c must be positive and d must be negative. The slope of $MN = \dfrac{d-b}{c-a} = \dfrac{(-)-(+)}{(+)-(-)} = \dfrac{(-)+(-)}{(+)+(+)} = \dfrac{-}{+} =$ negative slope. Since MN is negative, all lines parallel to it must be negative, so Column A is negative. Likewise, all lines perpendicular to MN must be positive, so Column B is positive. Since positive values are greater than negative values, Column B is greater than Column A.

6. **(D)**   Arithmetic: Primes   *Moderate*

You know that both q and 5 are prime numbers. However, you don't know what prime number q is. If $q = 5$, then $5q$ has only one distinct prime factor, 5, and Column B would be greater. However, if q equals any prime number except 5, then $5q$ has two distinct prime factors, and both columns would be equal. Since there is more than one possible solution, more information is needed in order to answer this question.

7. **(D)**   Algebra: Building Expressions   *Moderate*

Subtract x^2 from both columns. This leaves $+y^2$ in Column A and $-y^2$ in Column B. If $y = 0$, then the quantities in both columns are equal. If $y \neq 0$, then the quantities are not equal. The answer is (D) because there is not enough information to determine the answer.

8. **(B)** Geometry: Triangles   *Moderate*

Each of the three triangles is a special 45-45-90 right triangle whose sides are in the ratio $x\colon x\colon x\sqrt{2}$. The length of the hypotenuse of the smallest triangle is 10, which is equivalent to $x\sqrt{2}$. a is the leg in the smallest triangle. To find the length of a, solve for x. $x\sqrt{2} = 10$, so $x = \dfrac{10}{\sqrt{2}} = \dfrac{10}{\sqrt{2}} \cdot \dfrac{\sqrt{2}}{\sqrt{2}} = \dfrac{10\sqrt{2}}{2} = 5\sqrt{2} = a$. So, the value of Column A is

$$2a = 2 \cdot 5\sqrt{2} = 10\sqrt{2}$$

Next, the value of b must be found. Each leg of the middle triangle is 10 units long, so the hypotenuse must be equal to $10\sqrt{2}$. This is also equivalent to the length of each leg of the largest triangle. Since the hypotenuse of any right triangle is longer than any leg, b must be greater than $10\sqrt{2}$ and therefore, must be bigger than the value in Column A.

9. **(A)** Arithmetic: Probability   *Difficult*

Probability is equal to $\dfrac{\text{expected outcome}}{\text{total possible outcomes}}$. There are 6^2, or 36, possible outcomes when rolling two 6-sided dice. For Column A, the possible prime number outcomes are 2, 3, 5, 7, and 11. There is one way to roll 2, two ways to roll 3, four ways to roll 5, six ways to roll 7, and two ways to roll 11. So, there are $1 + 2 + 4 + 6 + 2 = 15$ expected outcomes, and the probability of rolling a prime number is $\dfrac{15}{36}$.

For Column B, the possible outcomes that are divisible by 3 are 3, 6, 9, and 12. There are two ways to roll 3, five ways to roll 6, four ways to roll 9, and one way to roll 12. So, there are $2 + 5 + 4 + 1 = 12$ expected outcomes, and the probability of rolling a number divisible by 3 is $\dfrac{12}{36}$.

10. **(A)** Algebra: Solving Systems of Equations   *Moderate*

The systems of equations must be solved for x and y. To do this, multiply the second equation by 2 and add the result to the first equation. Adding the two equations will eliminate the y term and allow you to determine the value of x.

$$x + 2y = 0$$
$$\underline{4x - 2y = 20}$$
$$5x = 20$$

$$x = \frac{20}{5} = 4$$

Now, plug 4 in for x in the first equation and solve for y.

$$4 + 2y = 0$$

$$2y = -4$$

$$y = \frac{-4}{2} = -2$$

Next, plug the values for x and y into each column.

In Column A, $4 - (-2) = 4 + 2 = 6$.

In Column B, $4 + (-2) = 4 - 2 = 2$.

11. **(B)** Arithmetic: Ratio and Proportions   *Moderate*

First, determine the cost of 1 can of soup and 1 box of crackers. If 3 cans of soup cost $5.00, then 1 can costs $\frac{\$5.00}{3}$, or $1.67. Likewise, if 2 boxes of crackers cost $3.50, then 1 box costs $\frac{3}{4}$, or $1.75. To find the values of each column, multiply the number of items by the cost per item. In Column A, $2 \times \$1.67 + 1 \times \$1.75 = \$5.09$. In Column B, $1 \times \$1.67 + 2 \times \$1.75 = \$5.17$.

You could also have solved this by recognizing that a box of crackers is slightly more expensive than a can of soup. Since in Column B, there are 2 of the more expensive items being purchased, Column B is greater.

12. **(C)** Special Math: Problems with Strange Symbols   *Easy*

You are given two sets of criteria for the values within the symbols, one for even numbers and another for odd. In order to determine the values of each column, substitute the numbers in the columns into the correct equation.

Since an odd number is in Column A, plug that number into the second equation given. $\Theta 1 \Theta = (-1)^3 + (-1)^2 = 1 + 1 = 0$. So, Column A has a value of 0.

Since an even number is in Column B, plug that number into the first equation given. $\Theta 2 \Theta = 2^2 - 2(2) = 4 - 4 = 0$. So, Column B has a value of 0, and both columns are equal.

13. **(C)** Algebra: Manipulating Expressions   *Difficult*

Since $ab = 0$, at least one of the variables must be equal to 0. Let's assume that $a = 0$ and b is any other number. In Column A, we have $(0 + b)^2 = b^2$. In Column B, we have $(0 - b)^2 = (-b)^2 = b^2$, and both columns are equal.

We must also test the possibility that $b = 0$ and a is any other number. In Column A, we have $(a + 0)^2 = a^2$. In Column B, we have $(a - 0)^2 = a^2$, and both columns are equal.

Since each possible situation results in both columns being equal, (C) is the correct answer.

14. **(A)**   Arithmetic: Divisibility and Remainders   *Difficult*
Pick a number for *n* that has a remainder of 2 when divided by 5. Let $n = 12$. Plug this number into each expression shown in the columns.

In Column A, $8n = 8 \times 12 = 96$. $96 \div 5 = 19$ with a remainder of 1. So, the value of Column A is 1.

In Column B, $n + 8 = 12 + 8 = 20$. $20 \div 5 = 4$ with a remainder of 0. So, the value of Column B is 0.

15. **(D)**   Geometry: Polygons   *Difficult*
Just by looking at the two perimeters, a careless test-taker may be tempted to pick Column B as the greater value simply because the given perimeter is greater. However, there are several ways to draw rectangles with each of the given perimeters. A few possibilities are shown below.

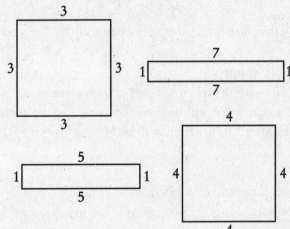

In the first row, the rectangle in Column A has an area of 9, while the rectangle in Column B has an area of 7. So, Column A is greater.

In the second row, the rectangle in Column A has an area of 5, while the rectangle in Column B has an area of 16. So, Column B is greater.

Since each situation produces different results, more information is needed. Thus (D) is the correct answer.

Grid-In Explanations (10)

16. **65** Geometry: Angles and Lines *Easy*

The angles measuring $x°$, 25°, and 90° must add to 180°, since they form a straight line. So you can write the equation: $x° + 90° + 25° = 180°$. Solve this equation for x.

$$x° + 90° + 25° = 180°$$

$$x° + 115° = 180°$$

$$x° = 180° - 115°$$

$$x° = 65°$$

17. **21** Algebra: Solving Linear Equations *Easy*

Start by factoring $(r + s)$ from the left side of the equation:

$$(8 - 3)(r + s) = 105$$

$$5(r + s) = 105$$

$r + s$ can be found by dividing both sides of the equation by 5. $r + s = = 21$.

18. **640** Arithmetic: Exponents *Moderate*

If the petri dish has 10 bacteria now, it will have twice as many, or $10 \times 2 = 20$, bacteria in a half hour. After 1 hour, there will be $10 \times 2 \times 2 = 10 \times 2^2 = 40$ bacteria. since there are 6 half-hours in 3 hours, after 3 hours there will be $10 \times 2^6 = 10 \times 64 = 640$ bacteria in the petri dish.

19. **90** Arithmetic: Ratios and Proportions *Moderate*

This problem can be solved using a proportion. Let m represent the number of minutes needed to travel 60 miles.

The trick here is to recognize that a unit conversion from hours to minutes is required. Converting $\frac{3}{4}$ of an hour to minutes yields $\frac{3}{4} \times 60 = 45$ minutes. Now insert the information you know into the proportion $\frac{\text{minutes}}{\text{miles}} . = \frac{\text{minutes}}{\text{miles}} : \frac{45}{30} = \frac{m}{60}$. Cross-multiply and solve for m.

$$45 \times 60 + 30m$$

$$2{,}700 = 30m$$

$$\frac{2{,}700}{30} = m$$

$$90 = m$$

20. **75** Geometry: Solids   *Difficult*

The volume of a cylinder is found using the equation $V = \pi r^2 h$, where r is the radius of the circular base and h is the height of the cylinder. The problem tells you that the height stays the same but the diameter is cut in half. The diameter of a circle is two times its radius, so if the diameter is cut in half, the value of the radius is also cut in half. The smaller cylinder will have a volume of $V = \pi(\frac{r}{2})^2 h = \pi \frac{r^2}{4} h = \frac{\pi r^2 h}{4}$. Thus, the smaller cylinder has a volume that is, or 25%, of the original cylinder.

The amount of change in volume is the difference between the original volume and the smaller volume. So, the volume of the cylinder decreases by $100\% - 25\% = 75\%$.

21. **33** Special Math: Logical Reasoning   *Difficult*

Of the 25 students on the soccer team, 9 are also on the football team, so $25 - 9$, or 16, students play soccer only. Likewise, of the 17 students on the football team, 9 are also on the soccer team, so $17 - 9$, or 8, students play football only. The total number of students who play these sports include those who play just soccer, those who play just football, and those who play both. Therefore, the total number of students is $16 + 8 + 9 = 33$.

22. **110** Geometry: Circles   *Moderate*

The measure of the arc formed by an inscribed angle's endpoints is twice the measure of the inscribed angle. To find the measure of arc AC, you first need to find the measure of $\angle ABC$ in $\triangle ABC$. Twice that value will be the measure of arc AC.

We know that AB is the diameter of circle O, so $\triangle ABC$ must be a right triangle and $\angle ACB = 90°$. Then, $\angle ABC = 180 - 90° - 35° = 55°$. Therefore, arc $AC = 2 \times 55° = 110°$.

23. **75** Special Math: Charts and Graphs   *Easy*

Saturday had the greatest sales with 100 cones sold, making $100 \times \$1.25 = \$125$. Monday had the least sales with 40 cones sold, making $40 \times \$1.25 = \$50$. The difference between these two amounts is $\$125 - \$50 = \$75$.

24. **32** Algebra: Solving Systems of Equations   *Moderate*

This problem is best solved by setting up a system of equations and solving them. Let c be the cost of each CD, and let d be the cost of each DVD. The two equations you can write are:

$$4c + 2d = 92$$

$$3c + 4d = 114$$

If you multiply the first equation by 2 and add the result to the second equation, you can eliminate the d term and solve for the value of c.

$$-8c\ 4d = -184$$

$$3c + 4d = 114$$

$$-5c = -70$$

$$c = \frac{-70}{-5} = 14$$

The CDs cost $14 each.

Plug the value for c into the original equation and solve for d.

$$4(14) + 2d = 92$$

$$56 + 2d = 92$$

$$2d = 36$$

$$d = \frac{36}{2} = 18$$

The DVDs cost $18 each. Now find the cost of 1 CD and 1 DVD: $14 + $18 = $32.

25. **80** Arithmetic: Fractions, Decimals, and Percents   *Difficult*
To find the amount saved, you first need to find the original price of the jacket. Let x represent the jacket's original price. With the first reduction of 25%, the sale price is 75% of the original price, or $0.75x$. With the second reduction of 20%, the new sale price is 80% of the first sale price, or $0.8(0.75x) = 0.6x$. Since the new sale price is $120, you can set up an equation to find x: $0.6x = \$120$, and $x = \frac{120}{0.6} = \$200$, the original price of the jacket. The amount saved is the original price minus the sale price. $200 - $120 = $80.

Multiple Choice Explanations (10)

1. **(D)** Arithmetic: Square Roots   *Easy*
Since p is greater than 0, it must be a positive number. If $p^2 = 8$, then $p = \sqrt{8}$, or 2. Therefore, $p^3 = (2\sqrt{2})^3 = 2^3 \cdot \sqrt{2}^3 = 8 \cdot 2\sqrt{2} = 16\sqrt{2}$.

2. **(E)** Special Math: Problems with Strange Symbols   *Easy*
Although this question appears tricky because of the strange symbol, it is not that difficult. To answer this question, all you need to do is substitute the numbers into the equation. Here, $x = 7$ and $y = 3$. Substitute these numbers to find the value of $y^x = 3^7 = 2{,}187$.

3.   **(E)**   Algebra: Solving Systems of Equations   *Difficult*

First, solve the system of equations. If you multiply the first equation by 2 and the second equation by 3, then add the two resulting equations, you can eliminate the variable d and solve for c.

$$2(2c + 3d = -6)$$

$$3(3c - 2d = 4)$$

$$4c + 6d = -12$$

$$\underline{9c - 6d = 12}$$

$$13c = 0$$

$$c = 0$$

Substitute $c = 0$ into either equation to find d.

$$2(0) + 3d = -6$$

$$3d = -6$$

$$d = -2$$

Now, plug $c = 0$ and $d = -2$ into the answer choices to see which one is NOT true.

   (A) $0 > -2$

   (B) $0 - (-2) > 0$

   (C) $0 + (-2) < 0$

   (D) $0 > 4(-2)$

   (E) $0(-2) < 0$

4.   **(B)**   Geometry: Circles   *Difficult*

The easiest way to solve this problem is to pick a value for the radius of the original circle. Let the original radius equal 1. The circumference of the circle is found using the formula $2\pi r$. So, the original circle's circumference is $2\pi(1)$, or 2π. If the radius is increased by 100%, it is doubled. The radius becomes 2 and the circumference becomes $2\pi(2)$, or 4π. The percent increase is equal to the amount of increase divided by the original circumference, multiplied by 100%. $\frac{4\pi - 2}{2\pi} + \frac{2\pi}{2\pi} = 1 \times 100\% = 100\%$ increase in the circumference.

5.   **(E)**   Arithmetic: Series   *Difficult*

In a geometric series, each term is multiplied by a common ratio, r, to produce the next term in the series. In this series, the second term, $\frac{1}{3}$, is multiplied by r to yield the third term, $\frac{1}{3}r$. The third term is multiplied by r to get the fourth term, $\frac{3}{4}$. Set up an equation for the fourth term and solve for r:

$$\frac{1}{3}r \times r = \frac{3}{4}$$

$$\frac{1}{3}r^2 =$$

$$r^2 = \frac{3}{4} \div \frac{1}{3} = \frac{3}{4} \times \frac{3}{1} = \frac{9}{4}$$

$$r = \sqrt{\frac{9}{4}} = \frac{3}{2}$$

The third term equals $\frac{1}{3}r$, or $\frac{1}{3} \times \frac{3}{2} = \frac{1}{2}$, and the fifth term equals $\frac{3}{4} \times \frac{3}{2} = \frac{9}{8}$.

6. **(B)**   Geometry: Solids   *Moderate*
The formula for the volume of a cylinder is $V = \pi r^2 h$, where r is the radius and h is the height of the cylinder. In this problem, you are given the values for the volume and height and are asked to find the diameter. First plug in the values for volume and height and solve for the radius. Remember that the diameter is twice the length of the radius, so you must multiply the radius by 2 to get the answer.

$$81\pi = \pi r^2(9)$$

$$81\pi = 9\pi r^2$$

$$\frac{81\pi}{9\pi} = 9 = r^2$$

$$r = \sqrt{9} = 3$$

The diameter is twice the radius: 3 x 2 or 6 inches.

7. **(B)**   Geometry: Geometric Visualizations   *Moderate*
Before finding the perimeter of the garden, you must determine the dimensions of the enlarged garden. This is done by first finding the area of the original garden. Area = 8 x 6 = 48 square feet. Since the area of the enlarged garden is twice as big, its area is 48 x 2 = 96 square feet. You know that the length stays the same in the enlarged garden, but the width changes. The new width is equal to $\frac{\text{enlarged area}}{\text{length}} = \frac{96}{8} = 12$ feet. So, the enlarged garden is 8 feet long and 12 feet wide. Therefore, its perimeter is 8 + 12 + 8 + 12 = 40 feet.

8. **(D)**   Arithmetic: Primes   *Easy*
The easiest way to solve this problem is by trial and error. Try multiplying some consecutive prime integers, such as 5 and 7, 7 and 11, 11 and 13, and see which one has a product of 221. 221 = 13 x 17. Therefore, $a = 13$ and $b = 17$, and $a + b = 13 + 17 = 30$.

9.   **(C)**   Algebra: Multiplying Binomials   *Difficult*

There is a lot of information in this problem. The easiest way to solve it is to take one piece at a time. First, expand the binomial.

$$(x + y)^2 = (x + y)(x + y) = x^2 + 2xy + y^2 = 50$$

You also know that $xy = 10$. Plug this value into the equation.

$$x^2 + 2(10) + y^2 = 50$$
$$x^2 + 20 + y^2 = 50$$

Subtract 20 from both sides of the equation to get the variables on one side of the equation.

$$x^2 + y^2 = 30$$

The problem asks for the value of $2x^2 + 2y^2$, which is the same as $2(x^2 + y^2)$. Since $x^2 + y^2 = 30$, $2(x^2 + y^2) = 2(30) = 60$.

10.   **(D)**   Arithmetic: Percents   *Difficult*

Although the price of the stereo decreased and increased by the same dollar amount, it did not decrease and increase by the same *percentage*. An easy way to solve this problem is to plug in a number for the original price. An easy number to work with is $100. With a 25% discount, the sale price will be $100 – $25, or $75. In order to get the price of the stereo back to $100, the price needs to be increased by $25. You need to find what percent of $75 is $25. Let p be the unknown percentage. Then, p x $7 = $255. $p = \frac{25}{75} = \frac{1}{3}$ and $\frac{1}{3}$ of 100% = 33%.

Practice Test 2

SAT PRACTICE TEST 2 ANSWER SHEET

MATH SECTION 1	MATH SECTION 2	MATH SECTION 3
1. Ⓐ Ⓑ Ⓒ Ⓓ Ⓔ	1. Ⓐ Ⓑ Ⓒ Ⓓ Ⓔ	1. Ⓐ Ⓑ Ⓒ Ⓓ Ⓔ
2. Ⓐ Ⓑ Ⓒ Ⓓ Ⓔ	2. Ⓐ Ⓑ Ⓒ Ⓓ Ⓔ	2. Ⓐ Ⓑ Ⓒ Ⓓ Ⓔ
3. Ⓐ Ⓑ Ⓒ Ⓓ Ⓔ	3. Ⓐ Ⓑ Ⓒ Ⓓ Ⓔ	3. Ⓐ Ⓑ Ⓒ Ⓓ Ⓔ
4. Ⓐ Ⓑ Ⓒ Ⓓ Ⓔ	4. Ⓐ Ⓑ Ⓒ Ⓓ Ⓔ	4. Ⓐ Ⓑ Ⓒ Ⓓ Ⓔ
5. Ⓐ Ⓑ Ⓒ Ⓓ Ⓔ	5. Ⓐ Ⓑ Ⓒ Ⓓ Ⓔ	5. Ⓐ Ⓑ Ⓒ Ⓓ Ⓔ
6. Ⓐ Ⓑ Ⓒ Ⓓ Ⓔ	6. Ⓐ Ⓑ Ⓒ Ⓓ Ⓔ	6. Ⓐ Ⓑ Ⓒ Ⓓ Ⓔ
7. Ⓐ Ⓑ Ⓒ Ⓓ Ⓔ	7. Ⓐ Ⓑ Ⓒ Ⓓ Ⓔ	7. Ⓐ Ⓑ Ⓒ Ⓓ Ⓔ
8. Ⓐ Ⓑ Ⓒ Ⓓ Ⓔ	8. Ⓐ Ⓑ Ⓒ Ⓓ Ⓔ	8. Ⓐ Ⓑ Ⓒ Ⓓ Ⓔ
9. Ⓐ Ⓑ Ⓒ Ⓓ Ⓔ	9. Ⓐ Ⓑ Ⓒ Ⓓ Ⓔ	9. Ⓐ Ⓑ Ⓒ Ⓓ Ⓔ
10. Ⓐ Ⓑ Ⓒ Ⓓ Ⓔ	10. Ⓐ Ⓑ Ⓒ Ⓓ Ⓔ	10. Ⓐ Ⓑ Ⓒ Ⓓ Ⓔ
11. Ⓐ Ⓑ Ⓒ Ⓓ Ⓔ	11. Ⓐ Ⓑ Ⓒ Ⓓ Ⓔ	
12. Ⓐ Ⓑ Ⓒ Ⓓ Ⓔ	12. Ⓐ Ⓑ Ⓒ Ⓓ Ⓔ	
13. Ⓐ Ⓑ Ⓒ Ⓓ Ⓔ	13. Ⓐ Ⓑ Ⓒ Ⓓ Ⓔ	
14. Ⓐ Ⓑ Ⓒ Ⓓ Ⓔ	14. Ⓐ Ⓑ Ⓒ Ⓓ Ⓔ	
15. Ⓐ Ⓑ Ⓒ Ⓓ Ⓔ	15. Ⓐ Ⓑ Ⓒ Ⓓ Ⓔ	
16. Ⓐ Ⓑ Ⓒ Ⓓ Ⓔ	16. Ⓐ Ⓑ Ⓒ Ⓓ Ⓔ	
17. Ⓐ Ⓑ Ⓒ Ⓓ Ⓔ	17. Ⓐ Ⓑ Ⓒ Ⓓ Ⓔ	
18. Ⓐ Ⓑ Ⓒ Ⓓ Ⓔ	18. Ⓐ Ⓑ Ⓒ Ⓓ Ⓔ	
19. Ⓐ Ⓑ Ⓒ Ⓓ Ⓔ	19. Ⓐ Ⓑ Ⓒ Ⓓ Ⓔ	
20. Ⓐ Ⓑ Ⓒ Ⓓ Ⓔ	20. Ⓐ Ⓑ Ⓒ Ⓓ Ⓔ	
21. Ⓐ Ⓑ Ⓒ Ⓓ Ⓔ	21. Ⓐ Ⓑ Ⓒ Ⓓ Ⓔ	
22. Ⓐ Ⓑ Ⓒ Ⓓ Ⓔ	22. Ⓐ Ⓑ Ⓒ Ⓓ Ⓔ	
23. Ⓐ Ⓑ Ⓒ Ⓓ Ⓔ	23. Ⓐ Ⓑ Ⓒ Ⓓ Ⓔ	
24. Ⓐ Ⓑ Ⓒ Ⓓ Ⓔ	24. Ⓐ Ⓑ Ⓒ Ⓓ Ⓔ	
25. Ⓐ Ⓑ Ⓒ Ⓓ Ⓔ	25. Ⓐ Ⓑ Ⓒ Ⓓ Ⓔ	
26. Ⓐ Ⓑ Ⓒ Ⓓ Ⓔ		
27. Ⓐ Ⓑ Ⓒ Ⓓ Ⓔ		
28. Ⓐ Ⓑ Ⓒ Ⓓ Ⓔ		
29. Ⓐ Ⓑ Ⓒ Ⓓ Ⓔ		
30. Ⓐ Ⓑ Ⓒ Ⓓ Ⓔ		

SAT TEST

Time—30 Minutes **25 Questions**	**In this section solve each problem, using any available space on the page for scratchwork. Then decide which is the best of the choices given and fill in the corresponding oval on the answer sheet.**

Notes:

1. The use of a calculator is permitted. All numbers used are real numbers.

2. Figures that accompany problems in this test are intended to provide information useful in solving the problems. They are drawn as accurately as possible EXCEPT when it is stated in a specific problem that the figure is not drawn to scale. All figures lie in a plane unless otherwise indicated.

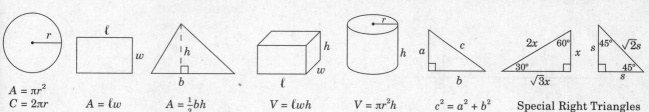

$A = \pi r^2$
$C = 2\pi r$ $A = \ell w$ $A = \frac{1}{2}bh$ $V = \ell wh$ $V = \pi r^2 h$ $c^2 = a^2 + b^2$ Special Right Triangles

The number of degrees of arc in a circle is 360.
The measure in degrees of a straight angle is 180.
The sum of the measures in degrees of the angles of a triangle is 180.

1.

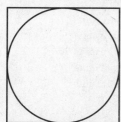

A circle is inscribed inside square *ABCD*. The area of the square is 49 square inches. What is the area of the circle?

(A) $\frac{7}{2}\pi$ in.^{2}

(B) 7π in.^{2}

(C) $\frac{49}{4}\pi$ in.^{2}

(D) $\frac{49}{2}\pi$ in.^{2}

(E) 49π in.^{2}

2. Jesse has five pennies, four nickels, six dimes, and seven quarters. If she chooses a coin at random, what is the probability that its value is less than ten cents?

(A) $\frac{5}{9}$

(B) $\frac{3}{11}$

(C) $\frac{5}{22}$

(D) $\frac{9}{22}$

(E) $\frac{15}{22}$

GO ON TO THE NEXT PAGE

3. If n is a positive integer and $n^3 \le 500$, how many possible values of n are there?

(A) 5
(B) 6
(C) 7
(D) 8
(E) 9

4. One U.S. dollar is equivalent to 1.83822 Australian dollars. How many U.S. dollars are equivalent to 25.00 Australian dollars?

(A) 0.46
(B) 0.74
(C) 13.60
(D) 45.00
(E) 45.96

5.

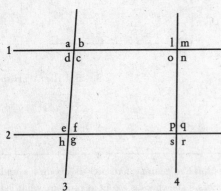

In the figure above, if line 1 is parallel to line 2, which of the following pairs of angles are congruent?

I. $\angle a$ and $\angle s$
II. $\angle c$ and $\angle p$
III. $\angle f$ and $\angle m$

(A) None
(B) I only
(C) III only
(D) II and III only
(E) I, II, and III

6. If $a = -1$ and $b = 2$, then $a^3 - a^2b + ab^2 - 2ab - b^3$ is equal to:

(A) −11
(B) −7
(C) −3
(D) −1
(E) 1

7. The product of seven numbers is negative. At most, how many of these numbers could be positive?

(A) 1
(B) 2
(C) 4
(D) 6
(E) 7

8. If $(z - 3)(5 + z) = z^2 + jz + k$, what is the value of $j + k$?

(A) −17
(B) −13
(C) −7
(D) 13
(E) 17

9. If y is a real number between 0 and 1, which of the following statements is NEVER true?

I. $y^2 > y$
II. $y^2 > 0$
III. $y^2 < 1$

(A) None
(B) I only
(C) II only
(D) III only
(E) II and III only

10. A rectangle has coordinates at (−4, −3), (3, −3), (3, 2), and (−4, 2). What is its area?

(A) 12 square units
(B) 30 square units
(C) 35 square units
(D) 42 square units
(E) 49 square units

GO ON TO THE NEXT PAGE

11.

Number of Minutes Studied

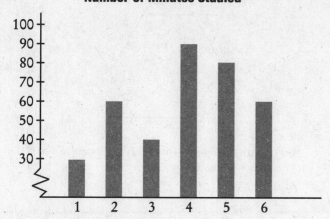

Between which two consecutive days was there the greatest percent change in the number of hours studied?

(A) Day 1 – Day 2
(B) Day 2 – Day 3
(C) Day 3 – Day 4
(D) Day 4 – Day 5
(E) Day 5 – Day 6

12. If x is a positive number less than 1, which of the following is a possible value for $\frac{1}{x^2}$?

(A) −1,000,000
(B) 0
(C) 0.001
(D) 1
(E) 1,000,000

13. Two buses left a bus station at the same time and traveled in the same direction. One bus traveled at a constant rate of 48 miles per hour. The other bus traveled at a constant rate of 55 miles per hour. After 90 minutes, how far apart were the two buses?

(A) 7 miles
(B) 10.5 miles
(C) 97 miles
(D) 103 miles
(E) 154.5 miles

14. If $m = \frac{x+y}{y}$ and $n = \frac{x}{x-y}$, what is the value of $\frac{m}{n}$?

(A) $\dfrac{xy}{x^2 - y^2}$
(B) $\dfrac{x^2 - y^2}{xy}$
(C) $\dfrac{x^2 + xy}{x - y^2}$
(D) $\dfrac{x - y^2}{x^2 + xy}$
(E) $\dfrac{x^2 + y^2}{x^2 - y^2}$

15. On a square-shaped baseball diamond, the distance from home plate to first base is 90 feet. What is the shortest distance from third base to first base?

(A) 90 feet
(B) $90\sqrt{2}$ feet
(C) 120 feet
(D) $120\sqrt{2}$ feet
(E) 180 feet

16. If a is a negative even integer and b and c are both negative odd integers, which of the following will result in an odd integer?

I. abc
II. $a + b + c$
III. $\dfrac{ab}{c}$

(A) None
(B) I only
(C) II only
(D) III only
(E) I and II only

17. The average of m and p is 50. The average of n and p is 53. What is the value of $n - m$?

(A) 0
(B) 1.5
(C) 2
(D) 3
(E) 6

GO ON TO THE NEXT PAGE

18. If $\frac{y}{2} + \frac{2}{y} = \frac{17}{4}$, then $4y$ could be

    (A) $\frac{1}{4}$

    (B) $\frac{1}{2}$

    (C) 2
    (D) 4
    (E) 8

19. Fifteen students are on the soccer team, and 11 students are on the basketball team. If 6 students play on both teams, how many students play on only one team?

    26

    (A) 5
    (B) 9
    (C) 10
    (D) 14
    (E) 20

20. Which set of ordered pairs forms perpendicular lines?

    (A) $(2, 8)$ and $(0, 5)(2, 0)$ and $(0, 6)$
    (B) $(3, 2)$ and $(4, 5)(2, 2)$ and $(1, 5)$
    (C) $(1, 5)$ and $(0, 3)(1, 7)$ and $(1, 10)$
    (D) $(3, 2)$ and $(0, 5)(1, 1)$ and $(2, 2)$
    (E) $(2, 4)$ and $(2, 3)(4, 0)$ and $(5, 4)$

21. If the altitude, a, of a triangle is decreased by $\frac{1}{3}$, and the base, b, is doubled, which of the following expressions could be used to determine the area of the resulting triangle?

    (A) $\frac{1}{3}ab$

    (B) $\frac{2}{3}ab$

    (C) $\frac{4}{3}ab$

    (D) $2ab$

    (E) $\frac{8}{3}ab$

22.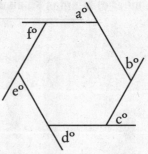

    The figure above represents a regular hexagon. What is the sum of $a + b + c + d + e + f$?

    (A) 240°
    (B) 360°
    (C) 432°
    (D) 720°
    (E) 1,080°

23. Tricia ate $\frac{1}{6}$ of a whole apple pie. Later, she ate $\frac{1}{5}$ of what remained. How much of the total pie is left?

    (A) $\frac{1}{30}$

    (B) $\frac{1}{3}$

    (C) $\frac{2}{3}$

    (D) $\frac{19}{30}$

    (E) $\frac{29}{30}$

24. If $\frac{6(x + 2)}{2x} + 3 = 0$, then $x =$

    (A) -2
    (B) -1
    (C) 1
    (D) 2
    (E) 3

25. If q is an odd integer greater than 1, what is the remainder when $(q + 2)^2$ is divided by 4?

    (A) 0
    (B) 1
    (C) 2
    (D) 3
    (E) 4

GO ON TO THE NEXT PAGE

SAT TEST

Time—30 Minutes 25 Questions	In this section solve each problem, using any available space on the page for scratchwork. Then decide which is the best of the choices given and fill in the corresponding oval on the answer sheet.

Notes:

1. The use of a calculator is permitted. All numbers used are real numbers.

2. Figures that accompany problems in this test are intended to provide information useful in solving the problems. They are drawn as accurately as possible EXCEPT when it is stated in a specific problem that the figure is not drawn to scale. All figures lie in a plane unless otherwise indicated.

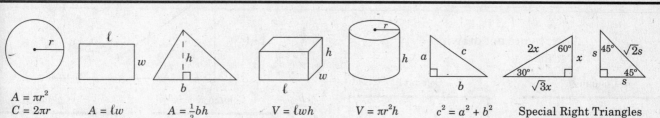
Directions for Quantitative Comparison Questions

Questions 1–15 each consist of two quantities in boxes, one in Column A and one in Column B.
You are to compare the two quantities and on the answer sheet fill in oval

A if the quantity in Column A is greater;
B if the quantity in Column B is greater;
C if the two quantities are equal;
D if the relationship cannot be determined from the information given.

AN E RESPONSE WILL NOT BE SCORED.

Notes:

1. In some questions, information is given about one or both of the quantities to be compared. In such cases, the given information is centered above the two columns and is not boxed.
2. In a given question, a symbol that appears in both columns represents the same thing in Column A as it does in Column B.
3. Letters such as x, n, and k stand for real numbers.

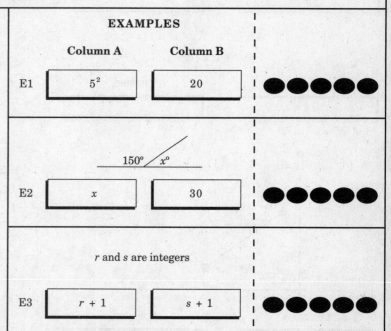

EXAMPLES

Column A	Column B

E1 | 5^2 | 20 | ●●●●●

E2 | x | 30 | ●●●●●
(150° $x°$)

r and s are integers

E3 | $r + 1$ | $s + 1$ | ●●●●●

1.

$$S = \{-2.5, -4.2, 2.1, 2.5, 3.2, -4.2, 2.5\}$$

Column A	Column B
The mean of S	The median of S

2.

Note: figure not drawn to scale

Column A	Column B
l	w

3.

$$25 < \frac{1}{n^2}$$

Column A	Column B
$\frac{1}{5}$	n

4.

$$r > 0 \text{ and } s < 0$$

Column A	Column B
$r + s$	$s - r$

5.

Column A	Column B
The length of AB	$a + b$

6.

k is a prime number less than 50.

q is a prime number less than 25.

Column A	Column B
kq	$\frac{k}{q}$

7.

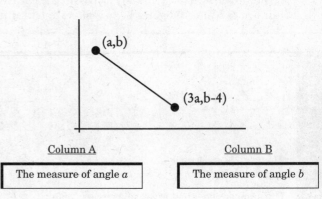

Column A	Column B
The measure of angle a	The measure of angle b

8.

The garden below contains a border on each side that is x units wide.

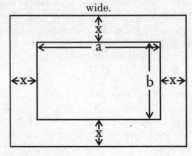

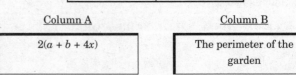

Column A	Column B
$2(a + b + 4x)$	The perimeter of the garden

GO ON TO THE NEXT PAGE

9.

It takes 4 hours for 6 painters to paint a house. Each painter works at the same rate.

Column A	Column B
The number of hours it takes 2 of the painters to paint 2 houses	The number of hours it takes 3 of the painters to paint 3 houses

10.

$$m \, \emptyset \, n = \frac{m^2 + n^2}{n - m}$$

$$m \, \# \, n = \frac{m^2 - n^2}{m - n}$$

Column A	Column B
$-1 \, \emptyset \, 1$	$1 \, \# \, -1$

11.

$G = \{2, 4, 5\}$ and $H = \{1, 2, 3\}$

g is picked at random from set G.

h is picked at random from set H.

Column A	Column B
The probability that $g + h$ is even	The probability that gh is even

12.

x is an integer less than 0.

Column A	Column B
$2x - x$	$-(x - 2^x)$

13.

$(a + b)^2 = 20$ and $a^2 + b^2 = 10$

Column A	Column B
ab	$a + b$

14.

y and z are integers

$4 < y < 8$ and $3 < z < 7$

Column A	Column B
The remainder when y^2 is divided by 3	The remainder when z^2 is divided by 3

15.

A pizza sells for $0.10 per square inch. A medium pizza's diameter is $\frac{5}{8}$ as long as a large pizza.

Column A	Column B
The cost of one large pizza	The cost of two medium pizzas

GO ON TO THE NEXT PAGE

SAT TEST

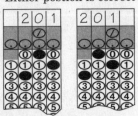
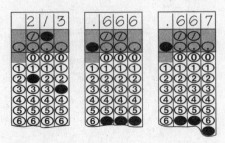
16. If $2^6 \times 4^6 = y^3$, then $y =$

17. If $m = \frac{3}{2}$ and $n = \frac{1}{2}$, then $mn + m^2 + n^2 + mn =$

18.

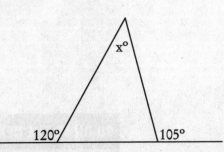

What is the measure of angle x?

19. In a senior class, the ratio of boys to girls 4 to 5. If 28 girls are out one day, the ratio of boys to girls becomes 1 to 1. How many students are in the senior class?

20. A soup manufacturer doubled the radius on a can of soup. If the height remains the same, by what percentage has the can's volume increased?

GO ON TO THE NEXT PAGE

21.

Number of Hours Watching TV	Number of Students
≥ 0 and < 1	6
≥ 1 and < 2	12
≥ 2 and < 3	8
≥ 3 and < 4	5
≥ 4 and < 5	2
≥ 5	3

The chart above shows the number of hours that students in a sociology class watch television on a typical day. What percentage of students watch at least 2 hours of TV a day?

22. Meg filled her 17-gallon gas tank to capacity. Her car averages 24 miles per gallon and she travels 147 miles per week. After how many whole days will Meg's gas tank be empty again?

23. A city's Little League is comprised of 10 different teams. This season, each team will play every other team in the league exactly 3 times. How many games will be played?

24.

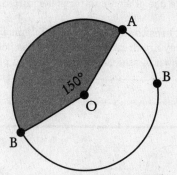

The area of the shaded region in circle O above is $\dfrac{15}{\pi}$. What is the circumference of circle O?

25. The fraction $\dfrac{333}{2222} = 0.149864986...$, or $0.1\overline{4986}$. The digits 4986 repeat endlessly. What digit is in the 100th place to the right of the decimal point?

GO ON TO THE NEXT PAGE

SAT TEST

Time—30 Minutes
10 Questions

In this section solve each problem, using any available space on the page for scratchwork. Then decide which is the best of the choices given and fill in the corresponding oval on the answer sheet.

Notes:
1.   The use of a calculator is permitted. All numbers used are real numbers.

2.   Figures that accompany problems in this test are intended to provide information useful in solvin gthe problems. They are drawn as accurately as possible EXCEPT when it is stated in a specific problem that the figure is not drawn to scale. All figures lie in a plane unless otherwise indicated.

1.   If $0 < x < y$, which statement below MUST be true?

        I. $\sqrt{x} < \sqrt{y}$
        II. $y\sqrt{x} = x\sqrt{y}$
        III. $x^2 < y^2$

    (A)   I only
    (B)   III only
    (C)   I and III only
    (D)   II and III only
    (E)   I, II, and III

2.   In the series $\frac{1}{r} \cdot \frac{2}{-2}, \frac{3}{-2}, \ldots$, the value of the 5th term is 15,625. What is the value of r in the 5th term?

    (A)   0.2
    (B)   0.5
    (C)   5
    (D)   6.9
    (E)   3,125

3.   The average of 3 consecutive prime numbers is $16\frac{1}{3}$. What is the value of the largest of these prime numbers?

    (A)   13
    (B)   17
    (C)   19
    (D)   23
    (E)   49

4.   If the diameter of a circle is doubled, by what percent does its area increase?

    (A)   50%
    (B)   100%
    (C)   200%
    (D)   300%
    (E)   400%

GO ON TO THE NEXT PAGE

5. Let $x\vartheta$ be defined by the equation $x\vartheta = x^2 + x$ for all positive values of x. If $x\vartheta = 156$, then a possible value of x could be

(A)   8
(B)   12
(C)   13
(D)   15
(E)   16

6.

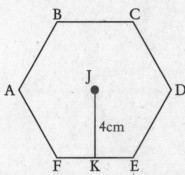

Figure *ABCDEF* is a regular hexagon with altitude *JK* equal to 4 centimeters. What is the perimeter of *ABCDEF*?

(A) $12\sqrt{3}$ cm
(B) $16\sqrt{3}$ cm
(C)   24 cm
(D)   48 cm
(E) $48\sqrt{3}$ cm

7. If the lateral surface area of a cylinder is doubled and the height remains constant, by how much does the radius of the enlarged cylinder increase?

(A) $\sqrt{2}$ times
(B)   2 times
(C) $2\sqrt{2}$ times
(D)   4 times
(E)   8 times

8. Dried fruit costs $3.80 a pound, and mixed nuts cost $4.60 a pound. What is the approximate price, per pound, of a trail mix consisting of two pounds dried fruit and one pound mixed nuts?

(A) $4.07
(B) $4.16
(C) $4.20
(D) $4.25
(E) $4.33

9. A sweater is on sale for 40% off the original price. For one extra day, there is an additional $\frac{1}{4}$ off the marked-down price. If the new sale price of the sweater is $36, what was its original price?

(A) $55
(B) $61
(C) $80
(D) $103
(E) $360

10. If s sprockets cost q times as much as w widgets, and t thingamajigs cost p times as much as s sprockets, how much do t thingamajigs cost?

(A) $\dfrac{w}{pq}$

(B) $\dfrac{pq}{w}$

(C) $\dfrac{wq}{p}$

(D) $\dfrac{p}{wq}$

(E) wpq

S T O P

IF YOU FINISH BEFORE TIME IS CALLED, YOU MAY CHECK YOUR WORK IN THIS SECTION ONLY.
DO NOT TURN TO ANY OTHER SECTION IN THE TEST.

SAT Math
Workbook
Practice Test II
Explanations

Answers to SAT Math Workbook Practice Test II

Question Number	Correct Answer	Right	Wrong	Question Number	Correct Answer	Right	Wrong	Question Number	Correct Answer	Right	Wrong

Section I: Multiple Choice Answers (25)

Question Number	Correct Answer	Right	Wrong	Question Number	Correct Answer	Right	Wrong	Question Number	Correct Answer	Right	Wrong
1.	C			10.	C			19.	D		
2.	D			11.	C			20.	E		
3.	C			12.	E			21.	B		
4.	C			13.	B			22.	B		
5.	A			14.	B			23.	C		
6.	A			15.	B			24.	B		
7.	D			16.	A			25.	B		
8.	B			17.	E						
9.	B			18.	C						

Section II: Quantitative Comparisons Answers (15)

Question Number	Correct Answer	Right	Wrong	Question Number	Correct Answer	Right	Wrong	Question Number	Correct Answer	Right	Wrong
1.	B			6.	A			11.	B		
2.	D			7.	A			12.	C		
3.	A			8.	C			13.	A		
4.	A			9.	C			14.	D		
5.	D			10.	A			15.	A		

Section II: Grid-In Answers (10)

Question Number	Correct Answer	Right	Wrong	Question Number	Correct Answer	Right	Wrong	Question Number	Correct Answer	Right	Wrong
1.	64			5.	300			9.	12		
2.	4			6.	50			10.	8		
3.	45			7.	20						
4.	252			8.	135						

Section III: Multiple Choice Answers (10)

Question Number	Correct Answer	Right	Wrong	Question Number	Correct Answer	Right	Wrong	Question Number	Correct Answer	Right	Wrong
1.	C			5.	B			9.	C		
2.	A			6.	B			10.	E		
3.	C			7.	A						
4.	D			8.	A						

Test II Explanations

Section I: Multiple Choice Explanations (25)

1.   **(C)**   Geometry: Circles   *Easy*

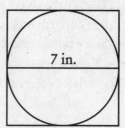

In the figure above, note that the length of the square's side is equal to the diameter of the circle. Since the area of the square is 49 in.^{2}, the square has a side equal to $\sqrt{49}$, or 7 in., so the diameter of the circle also equals 7 in. The radius is in., and thus the area of the circle $= \pi r^2 = \pi(\frac{7}{2})^2 = \frac{49}{4}\pi$.

2.   **(D)**   Arithmetic: Probability   *Easy*

Probability is equal to $\dfrac{\text{expected outcome}}{\text{total possible outcomes}}$. The total possible outcomes is the total number of coins. There are $5 + 4 + 6 + 7$, or 22 total coins, so the denominator is 22. The expected outcome is the number of coins with a value of less than 10 cents. There are 5 pennies and 4 nickels, so $5 + 4$, or 9 coins fewer than ten cents, so 9 is the numerator. The probability that the value is less than 10 is $\dfrac{9}{22}$.

3.   **(C)**   Algebra: Solving Inequalities   *Easy*

Solve for n by taking the cube root of each side of the inequality. $\sqrt[3]{n^3} \le \sqrt[3]{500}$, and $n \le 7.937$. The largest integer smaller than 7.937 is 7, so n can have 7 possible positive integer values: 1, 2, 3, 4, 5, 6, and 7.

4.   **(C)**   Arithmetic: Ratios and Proportions   *Easy*

The ratio can be used to solve this problem. Let x represent the unknown number of US dollars. Set up a proportion based on the given information: $\dfrac{1}{1.83822} = \dfrac{x}{25}$. Cross-multiplying, $1.83822x = 1 \times 25$ so $x = \dfrac{25}{1.83822} = 13.60$.

5.   **(A)**   Geometry: Angles and Lines   *Easy*

Take a look at each statement separately to see which, if any, are true.

Statement I deals with angles a and s. Since lines 1 and 2 are parallel, the angles congruent to $\angle a$ are c, e, and g. Because lines 3 and 4 are not necessarily parallel, $\angle a$ is not congruent to $\angle s$, so statement I is false. Statement II deals with angles c and p. Since lines 1 and 2 are parallel, the angles congruent to $\angle c$ are a, e, and g. Because lines 3 and 4 are not necessarily parallel, $\angle c$ is not congruent to $\angle p$, so statement II is false. Statement III deals with angles f and m. Since lines 1 and 2 are parallel, the angles congruent to $\angle f$ are h, b, and d. Because lines 3 and 4 are not necessarily parallel, $\angle f$ is not congruent to $\angle m$, so statement III is also false. None of the statements is true.

6. **(A)** Algebra: Substitution   *Easy*

Use substitution to solve this problem. Substitute -1 for a and 2 for b into the equation $a^3 - a^2b + ab^2 - 2ab - b^3$ and simplify.

$$(-1)^3 - (-1)^2(2) + (-1)(2)^2 - 2(-1)(2) - (2)^3 =$$

$$(-1) - (1)(2) - 4 - 2(-2) - 8 =$$

$$-1 - 2 - 4 + 4 - 8 =$$

$$-11$$

7. **(D)** Arithmetic: Signed Numbers   *Easy*

If the product of a set of numbers is negative, an odd number of factors must be negative. This problem asks you to find the greatest possible number of *positive* factors. Put another way, you must first find the fewest possible number of negative factors. Since 1 is the smallest odd number possible, 7 total factors minus 1 negative factor = 6 positive factors.

8. **(B)** Algebra: Multiplying Binomials   *Moderate*

First, multiply the two binomials and simplify the result.

$$(z - 3)(5 + z) = 5z + z^2 - 15 - 3z = z^2 + 2z - 15$$

Compare the result with $z^2 + jz + k$.

$$z^2 + jz + k = z^2 + 2z - 15$$

The letter j represents the number in front of the z term, so $j = 2$. The letter k represents the constant term at the end of the trinomial, so $k = -15$. Therefore, the value of $j + k = 2 + (-15) = -13$.

9. **(B)** Arithmetic: Exponents   *Moderate*

Since y is between 0 and 1, it must be a fraction. To solve this problem, choose a fraction for y and plug it into each statement shown to see which statements are NOT true.

Remember to read the question carefully to ensure that you solve for what is being asked. Let $y = \frac{1}{2}$.

In statement I, $(\frac{1}{2})^2 > \frac{1}{2}$, or $> \frac{1}{2}$, which is NOT true, so statement I is part of the solution.

In statement II, $(\frac{1}{2})^2 > 0$, or > 0, which is true, so statement II is not part of the solution.

In statement III, $(\frac{1}{2})^2 < 1$, or < 1, which is true, so statement III is not part of the solution. Statement I is the only solution, so the answer is B.

10. **(C)** Geometry: Coordinate Geometry   *Easy*

By drawing the points on a coordinate system, you can determine the dimensions of the resulting rectangle and then find its area.

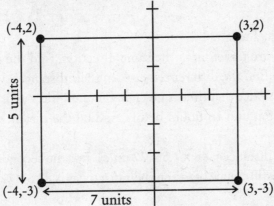

The length of the rectangle is 7 units and the width is 5 units. Therefore, its area is 7 x 5 or 35 square units.

11. **(C)** Special Math: Charts and Graphs   *Difficult*

To find the greatest percent change, use the formula $\frac{\text{change in minutes}}{\text{original minutes}}$ x 100. The result with the largest absolute value has the greatest change. The percent change for Day 2 is the change in minutes from Day 1 to Day 2. $60 - 30 = 30$, so the overall change is $\frac{30}{30} = 1$ x 100%.

From Day 2 to Day 3, $\frac{40-60}{60} = \frac{-20}{60} = -\frac{1}{3}$ x 100 $= -33\frac{1}{3}\%$

From Day 3 to Day 4, $\frac{90-40}{40} = \frac{50}{40} = \frac{5}{4(3)}$ x 100 $= 125\%$

From Day 4 to Day 5, $\frac{80-90}{90} = \frac{-10}{90} = -\frac{1}{9}$ x 100 $= -11.1\%$

From Day 5 to Day 6, $\frac{60-80}{80} = \frac{-20}{80} = -\frac{1}{4}$ x 100 $= -25\%$

Since 125% is the greatest amount, Day 3 to Day 4 has the greatest change.

12. **(E)** Algebra: Simplifying Expressions   *Easy*

Choose a value for x that fits the given criteria, and plug it into the expression $\frac{1}{x^2}$. Let $x = \frac{1}{2}$. Then, $= \frac{1}{\left(\frac{1}{2}\right)^2} = \frac{1}{\frac{1}{4}} = 4$. Now, look at the possible answer choices to see which might work. Since x is positive, it is not possible for a negative number to result, so A is not correct. The only way to get 0 as a solution is for 0 to be in the numerator, so B is not correct. When plugging a fraction in for x, a number greater than 1 results, so C is not correct. For the solution to equal 1, x must equal 1, so D is not correct. E is the only correct answer, for it is a positive number greater than 1.

13. **(B)** Arithmetic: Rates   *Moderate*

Since the two buses are traveling in the same direction, find the distance traveled by each and subtract to find the difference between their distances. Use the formula distance = rate x time. Notice that time is given in minutes, but rate is given in hours. You need to convert 90 minutes to hours before finding the distances. 90 minutes = 1.5 hours.

For the first bus, distance = 48 x 1.5 = 72 miles. For the second bus, distance = 55 x 1.5 = 82.5 miles. The difference between their distances is 82.5 − 72 = 10.5 miles.

14. **(B)** Algebra: Building Expressions and Equations   *Moderate*

Plug the given values for m and n into the expression $\frac{m}{n}$ and simplify.

$$\frac{m}{n} = \frac{\frac{x+y}{y}}{\frac{x}{x-y}} = \frac{x+y}{y} \div \frac{x}{x-y} = \frac{x+y}{y} \times \frac{x-y}{x} = \frac{(x+y)(x-y)}{xy} = \frac{x^2-y^2}{xy}$$

15. **(B)**   Geometry: Triangles   *Easy*

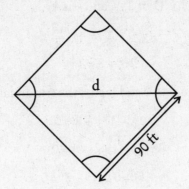

In the figure above, d represents the distance from first base to third base. Since the baseball diamond is a square figure, d is the hypotenuse of a 45°-45°-90° right triangle. If x represents the length of a leg in a 45°-45°-90° right triangle, $x\sqrt{2}$ represents the length of the hypotenuse. Since one leg of the triangle is 90 feet long, the hypotenuse must be $90\sqrt{2}$ feet long.

16. **(A)**   Arithmetic: Odd and Even Numbers   *Moderate*
Pick values for a, b, and c that fit the given criteria. Let $a = 2$, $b = 1$, and $c = 3$. Plug these values into each statement to see which results in an odd integer.

In statement I, $abc = (2)(1)(3) = 6$, which is not odd.

In statement II, $a + b + c = (2) + (1) + (3) = 6$, which is not odd.

In statement III, $\dfrac{ab}{c} = \dfrac{(-2)(-1)}{-3} = \dfrac{2}{-3}$, which is not an integer.

Therefore, none of the statements work, and the answer is A.

17. **(E)**   Arithmetic: Mean, Median, and Mode   *Moderate*
If the average of m and p is 50, then $\dfrac{m + p}{2} = 50$, and $m + p = 100$. If the average of n and p is 53, then $\dfrac{n + p}{2} = 53$, and $n + p = 106$. Solve the first equation for p and plug the result into the second equation.

$$p = 100 - m, \text{ so } n + (100 - m) = 106$$

$$n - m = 106 - 100 = 6$$

18. **(C)**   Algebra: Solving Linear Equations   *Moderate*
Be careful to note that this question asks for the value of $4y$, not y. Remember to read the question carefully and be sure to solve what is being asked. To find $4y$, first find the value of y. To do so, multiply the given equation by the least common denominator

(LCD) of all denominators shown. This will eliminate the fractions and make the problem easier to solve. The LCD of 2, y, and 4 is $4y$.

$$4y(\frac{y}{2} + \frac{2}{y}) = 4y(\frac{17}{4})$$
$$2y^2 + 8 = 17y$$

Set the resulting equation equal to 0 and factor the trinomial.

$$2y^2 - 17y + 8 = 0$$
$$(2y - 1)(y - 8) = 0$$
$$(2y - 1) = 0 \text{ or } (y - 8) = 0 \text{ so}$$
$$y = \text{ or } y = 8$$

Therefore, $4y = 4(\frac{1}{2}) = 2$ or $4y = 4(8) = 32$, so (C) is the only answer that works.

19. **(D)** Special Math: *Logical Reasoning Moderate*

Six students play on both sports teams. So, 15 6, or 9, students play only soccer, and 11 6, or 5, students play only basketball. Therefore, $9 + 5$, or 14, students play on only one team.

20. **(E)** Geometry: Coordinate Geometry *Difficult*

Perpendicular lines are lines whose slopes are negative reciprocals of each other. For example, negative reciprocals are $\frac{1}{2}$ and $-\frac{2}{1}$. To solve this problem, find the slopes of each set of ordered pairs and see which slopes are negative reciprocals of each other.

Slope $= \dfrac{y_2 - y_1}{x_2 - x_1}$.

In A, the slopes are and $\dfrac{6-0}{0-(-2)} = \dfrac{6}{2} = \dfrac{3}{1}$.

In B, the slopes are and $\dfrac{-5-(-2)}{-1-(-2)} = \dfrac{-3}{1}$.

In C, the slopes are and $\dfrac{10-7}{1-(-1)} = \dfrac{3}{2}$.

In D, the slopes are and $\dfrac{-2-1}{2-(-1)} = \dfrac{-3}{3} = \dfrac{-1}{1}$.

In E, the slopes are and $\dfrac{4-0}{5-4} = \dfrac{4}{1}$, which are perpendicular.

21. **(B)** Geometry: Triangles *Moderate*

The formula for the area of a triangle is $A = \frac{1}{2}ab$, where a is the altitude and b is the base. In this problem, both a and b change. Since a decreases by $\frac{1}{3}$, it becomes $\frac{2}{3}a$, and *b* doubles to become 2*b*. Plug these new values into the area formula and simplify: $A = \frac{1}{2}\left(\frac{2}{3}a\right)(2b) = \frac{4}{6}ab = \frac{2}{3}ab$.

22. **(B)**   Geometry: Polygons   *Difficult*

To find the sum of the exterior angles of a hexagon, it helps to draw triangles from one vertex inside the hexagon, as shown in the figure below.

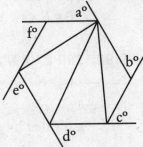

Four triangles can be formed from the hexagon. The sum of the angles in any triangle is 180°, so the sum of the angles in a hexagon is 4 × 180° = 720°. Therefore, a single angle inside the regular hexagon is $\frac{720°}{6} = 120°$. Each angle of a hexagon, plus its exterior angle, forms a straight line, so they add to 180°. The measure of each exterior angle is 180° − 120° = 60°. The exterior angles, *a*, *b*, *c*, *d*, *e*, and *f*, each equal 60°, and their sum = 6 ° × 60° = 360°. (You may know that the sum of the exterior angles of any polygon is 360°.)

23. **(C)**   Arithmetic: Fractions   *Difficult*

The problem asks for the amount of pie that is left. If Tricia first eats $\frac{1}{6}$ of the pie, then $\frac{5}{6}$ remains. If she later eats an additional $\frac{1}{5}$ of the pie, then $\frac{4}{5}$ remains. So, the total remaining amount is $\frac{5}{6} \times \frac{4}{5} = \frac{20}{30} = \frac{2}{3}$.

24. **(B)**   Algebra: Solving Linear Equations   *Difficult*

It is sometimes easier to solve an equation containing fractions if the fraction is eliminated. To do this, multiply both sides of the equation by the denominator, 2*x*, and then solve.

$$2x\left(\frac{6(x+2)}{2x}+3\right) = 2x \times 0$$
$$6(x+2) + 2x(3) = 0$$
$$6x + 12 + 6x = 0$$

$$12x + 12 = 0$$

$$12x = -12$$

$$x = -1$$

25. **(B)** Arithmetic: Divisibility and Remainders   *Difficult*

The easiest way to solve this problem is to pick a value for q that fits the given criteria. Then, plug that value into the given expression, divide by 4, and determine the remainder. Let $q = 3$. Then, $(3 + 2)^2 = 5^2 = 25$. $25 \div 4 = 6$ with remainder 1.

Section II: Quantitative Comparison Explanations (15)

1.   **(B)** Arithmetic: Mean, Median, and Mode   *Easy*

The mean is the sum of all items in a set, divided by the total number of items. The mean of S is $\dfrac{-2.5 - 4.2 + 2.1 + 2.5 + 3.2 - 4.2 + 2.5}{7} = \dfrac{-0.6}{7} \cong -0.085^{.}$.

The median is the middle value of a set of items. To find the median, arrange the numbers in the set in order from least to greatest or greatest to least, and then find the middle value. $S = \{-4.2, -4.2, -2.5, 2.1, 2.5, 2.5, 3.2\}$. The value in the middle is 2.1. Since $0.0857 < 2.1$, Column B is greater.

2.   **(D)** Geometry: Polygons   *Easy*

When you see a problem with a figure that is not drawn to scale, NEVER assume anything about the figure. In this problem, side l looks longer than side w, but because the figure is not drawn to scale, you cannot assume anything about the length of each side. More information is needed.

3.   **(A)** Algebra: Solving Inequalities   *Easy*

Solve for n by first multiplying each side of the inequality by n^2.

$$n^2 \cdot 25 < \frac{1}{n^2} \cdot n^2$$

$$25n^2 < 1$$

$$n^2 < \frac{1}{25} < \sqrt{\frac{1}{25}}$$

$$n < \frac{1}{5}$$

Therefore, Column A is greater.

4.   **(A)**   Arithmetic: Signed Numbers   *Easy*
Pick any positive number for r and any negative number for s. Plug these into each column to see which is bigger. Let $r = 1$ and $s = 1$.

In column A, $r + s = 1 + (1) = 0$.

In column B, $s - r = 1 - 1 = 2$.

Since $0 > 2$, Column A is greater.

5.   **(D)**   Geometry: Coordinate Geometry   *Moderate*
The distance formula, $\sqrt{(x_1 - x_2)^2 + (y_1 - y_2)^2}$, can be used to find the length of AB, where $(x_1, y_1) = (a, b)$ and $(x_2, y_2) = (3a, b - 4)$.

$$\sqrt{(a - 3a)^2 + (b - (b - 4))^2} = \sqrt{(-2a)^2 + (4)^2} = \sqrt{4a^2 + 4^2} = \sqrt{4(a^2 + 1)} = 2\sqrt{a^2 + 1}$$

Since there are no given values for either a or b, they cannot be compared to AB. More information is needed.

6.   **(A)**   Arithmetic: Primes   *Moderate*
Choose values for k and q that fit the given criteria. Then, plug the values into both columns. Let $k = 41$ and let $q = 3$. In column A, $kq = 41 \cdot 3 = 123$. In column B, $\dfrac{k}{q} = \dfrac{41}{3} = 13.6$. $123 > 13.6$, so column A is greater. However, because the values of q are a subset of k, it is a good practice to test different values for k and q. In our first trial, we chose $k > q$. Let's now try values such that $k < q$. Let $k = 2$ and $q = 5$. In column A, $kq = 2 \cdot 5 = 10$. In column B, $\dfrac{k}{q} = \dfrac{2}{5} = 0.4$. $10 > 0.4$, so Column A is still greater.

7.   **(A)**   Geometry: Triangles   *Moderate*
Notice that the figure is not drawn to scale. This means that you cannot assume that one angle is greater than the other just because it appears that way. To find out which angle is greater, find the lengths of the sides opposite the angles. The greater the side opposite the angle, the greater the angle. It is given that ΔABC is a right triangle, AC is 15 units, and AB is 39 units in length. $\angle a$ is opposite CB, which is unknown. $\angle b$ is opposite AC. To find CB, use the Pythagorean Theorem.

$$AB^2 = AC^2 + CB^2$$

$$39^2 = 15^2 + CB^2$$

$$1{,}521 = 225 + CB^2$$

$$1{,}296 = CB^2$$

$$CB = \sqrt{1,296}$$

Since $36 > 15$, $CB > AC$, so the angle opposite CB, $\angle a$, is greater.

8.   **(C)**   Algebra: Multiplying Binomials   *Easy*

With the border, the length of the garden is $a + 2x$, and its width is $b + 2x$. The perimeter is twice the length plus twice the width, or $2(a + 2x) + 2(b + 2x) = 2a + 4x + 2b + 4x = 2a + 2b + 8x = 2(a + b + 4x)$. Therefore, both columns are equal.

9.   **(C)**   Arithmetic: Ratio and Proportions   *Difficult*

It is given that 6 painters can paint one house in 4 hours.

In column A, only 2 painters are working, so it will take 3 times longer to paint one house. $4 \times 3 = 12$ hours for 2 painters to paint one house. Since there are 2 houses, $12 \times 2 = 24$ hours for 2 painters to paint 2 houses.

In column B, 3 painters are working, so it will take 2 times longer to paint one house $= 4 \times 2 = 8$ hours for 3 painters to paint one house. Since there are 3 houses, it will take $8 \times 3 = 24$ hours for 3 painters to paint 3 houses.

Therefore, both columns are equal, and the correct answer is (C).

10.   **(A)**   Special Math: Problems with Strange Symbols   *Moderate*

There are two symbols involved in this problem. Column A uses one symbol. To find the value of column A, substitute 1 for m and 1 for n in the first given expression.

$$-1 \oslash 1 = = \frac{(-1)^2 + 1^2}{1 - (-1)} = \frac{1 + 1}{1 + 1} = \frac{2}{2} = 1$$

Column B uses the arrow pointing left. To find the value of Column B, substitute 1 for m and 1 for n in the second given expression.

$$1 \oslash -1 = = \frac{1^2 - (-1)^2}{1 - (-1)} = \frac{1 - 1}{1 + 1} = \frac{0}{2} = 0$$

Since $1 > 0$, Column A is greater.

11.   **(B)**   Arithmetic: Probability   *Difficult*

In column A, the possible outcomes of $g + h$ are: $2 + 1 = 3$; $2 + 2 = 4$; $2 + 3 = 5$; $4 + 1 = 5$; $4 + 2 = 6$; $4 + 3 = 7$; $5 + 1 = 6$; $5 + 2 = 7$; $5 + 3 = 8$.

Of these, $\frac{4}{9}$ of them are even.

In Column B, the possible outcomes of gh are: $2 \cdot 1 = 2$; $2 \cdot 2 = 4$; $2 \cdot 3 = 6$; $4 \cdot 1 = 4$; $4 \cdot 2 = 8$; $4 \cdot 3 = 12$; $5 \cdot 1 = 5$; $5 \cdot 2 = 10$; $5 \cdot 3 = 15$.

Of these, $\frac{7}{9}$ of them are even. Therefore, Column B is greater.

12. **(C)** Algebra Manipulating Expressions   *Moderate*

Pick a negative integer for x and plug it into the given expressions to see which column is greater. Let $x = 2$. In column A, $2^x - x = 2^{-2} - (-2) = +\dfrac{1}{2^2} + 2 = \dfrac{1}{4} + 2 = 2\dfrac{1}{4}$.

In column B, $-(x - 2^x) = -x + 2^x = -(-2) + 2^{-2} = 2 + \dfrac{1}{2^2} = 2 + \dfrac{1}{4} = 2\dfrac{1}{4}$. Both columns are equal, so the correct answer is (C). Another way in which this problem can be solved is by rewriting the expression in Column B. $-(x - 2^x)$ is the same as $-x + 2^x$ or $2^x x$. This precisely matches the expression in Column A.

13. **(A)** Algebra: Solving Systems of Equations   *Difficult*

First, expand the binomial equation $(a + b)^2 = 20$ and see if it can be simplified.

$$(a + b)^2 = 20$$

$$(a + b)(a + b) = 20$$

$$a^2 + ab + ab + b^2 = 20$$

$$a^2 + 2ab + b^2 = 20$$

$$2ab + a^2 + b^2 = 20$$

You are also given that $a^2 + b^2 = 10$. Plugging 10 in for $a^2 + b^2$ results in $2ab + 10 = 20$ so $2ab = 10$ and $ab = 5$. Therefore, the value of column A is 5.

To find the value of column B, refer to the equation $(a + b)^2 = 20$. Take the square root of both sides. $\sqrt{(a + b)^2} = \sqrt{20}$, so $a + b = \sqrt{20} \cong \pm 4.47$. Since $5 \cong \pm 4.47$, column A is greater.

14. **(D)** Arithmetic: Divisibility and Remainders   *Difficult*

The only possible values for y are 5, 6, and 7. In Column A, the possible results are 0 and 1, since the remainder when $5^2 \div 3$ is 1, the remainder when $6^2 \div 3$ is 0, and the remainder when $7^2 \div 3$ is 1.

The only possible values for z are 4, 5, and 6. In Column B, the possible results are 0 and 1, since the remainder when $4^2 \div 3$ is 1, the remainder when $5^2 \div 3$ is 1, and the remainder when $6^2 \div 3$ is 0.

However, because we don't know the exact values of y and z, more information is needed to solve this problem.

15. **(A)** Geometry: Circles   *Difficult*

Since the medium pizza is of the width of a large pizza, let the diameter of the medium pizza be 5 inches, and let the diameter of the large pizza be 8 inches. Compare the areas of the 2 medium pizzas with the area of the large pizza. The greater of these will have the greater cost. The area of a circle is πr^2, where r is the radius.

In Column A, if a large pizza has a diameter of 8, its radius is half that, or 4. So the area of a large pizza is $\pi(4)^2 = 16\pi$ in.^{2}.

In Column B, if a medium pizza has a diameter of 5, its radius is half that, or 2.5. So, the area of two medium pizzas is $2 \cdot \pi(2.5)^2 = 2 \cdot \pi(6.25) = 12.5\pi$ in.^{2}.

Since 16π in.$^2 > 12.5\pi$ in.^{2}, Column A is greater.

Grid-In Explanations (10)

16. **64**   Arithmetic: Exponents   *Easy*

The equation in this problem has two different bases. To solve this, first rewrite the equation with like bases, and then simplify.

$$2^6 \times 4^6 = (2^2)^6 = 2^6 \times 2^{12} = 2^{6+12} = 2^{18}$$

To find y, 2^{18} must be rewritten with an exponent of 3. Since $18 \div 3 = 6$, $2^{18} = (2^6)^3 = y^3$. So, $y = 2^6 = 64$.

17. **4**   Algebra: Substitution   *Easy*

This is a direct substitution problem. Substitute $\frac{3}{2}$ and $\frac{1}{2}$ for m and n into the expression $mn + m^2 + n^2 + mn$.

$$(\tfrac{3}{2})(\tfrac{1}{2}) + (\tfrac{3}{2})2 + (\tfrac{1}{2})2 + (\tfrac{3}{2})(\tfrac{1}{2}) =$$

$$\frac{3}{4} + \frac{9}{4} + \frac{1}{4} + \frac{3}{4} =$$

$$\frac{16}{4} =$$

$$4$$

18. **45**   Geometry: Angles and Lines   *Moderate*

Recall that the sum of the angles in a triangle is 180°. The two supplementary angles to the given angles plus $x°$ equals 180°. The supplementary angle to 120° is 180° − 120° = 60°. The supplementary angle to 105° is 180° − 105° = 75°. Therefore, 60° + 75° + $x°$ = 180°. So, $x° = 180° − 60° − 75° = 45°$.

19. **252**   Arithmetic: Ratios and Proportions   *Moderate*

The ratio of boys to girls can be written as $4x:5x$. When the 28 girls are out, the new ratio becomes $1x:1x$. Since the number of boys did not change, their original ratio, $4x$, stays the same, so the new ratio can be written as $4x:4x$. The ratio of girls changes from

5x to 4x when the 28 girls are out, so 5x 28 = 4x. Solve for x. 5x 4x = 28, so x = 28. The problem asks for the number of students in the senior class. The number of boys is 4x = 4 × 28 = 112. The number of girls is 5x = 5 × 28 = 140. The total number of students is 112 + 140 = 252.

20. **300** Geometry: Solids   *Moderate*

To solve this, first find the original can's volume. A can of soup is a cylinder, and the volume of a cylinder is $\pi r^2 h$, where r is the radius and h is the height. For the original can, let r = 1 and h = 1. Then, its volume is $\pi(1^2)(1)$ or π. Next, find the volume of the new can, whose radius is doubled. Now, r = 2 and h = 1. The volume of the new can is $\pi(2)^2(1)$, or 4π. The percent change in volume is found by the formula $\frac{\text{change in volume}}{\text{original volume}} \times 100\%$.

21. **50** Special Math: Charts and Graphs   *Easy*

The solution to this problem is found by adding the number of students who watch more than 2 hours of television per day and dividing by the total number of students. The number watching more than 2 hours per day is 8 + 5 + 2 + 3 = 18. The total number of students is 6 + 12 + 8 + 5 + 2 + 3 = 36. So, $\frac{18}{36} = 0.5 = 50\%$ of the students watch more than 2 hours of television per day.

22. **20** Algebra: Solving Linear Equations   *Moderate*

To find out how many days she can wait before refilling her tank, divide the total number of miles that Meg's car is expected to travel on a full tank by the average number of miles that she travels per day. Meg's car can travel on 17 gallons × 24 miles per gallon, or 408 miles, before it will run out of gas. She travels 147 miles per week, so she must travel an average of 147 ÷ 7, or 21, miles per day. $\frac{408}{21} \approx 19.43$, or 20 whole days before her gas tank is empty.

23. **135** Special Math: Logical Reasoning   *Difficult*

In the 10-team Little League, each team plays against the other 9 teams for a total of 10 × 9 = 90 games. Since they play each team 3 times, 90 × 3 = 270 games are played. This counts each game twice, since it counts Team 1 against Team 2 as one game and Team 2 against Team 1 as another game. However, this is the same game. To take into account that each separate game involves two teams, the total number of games played must be divided by 2. Therefore, 270 ÷ 2 = 135 total games are played.

24. **12** Geometry: Circles   *Difficult*

You need to find the radius in order to solve this problem. Once the radius is known, the circumference of circle O, $2\pi r$, can be found. You know the area of the shaded region, which makes a 150° central angle within the circle. Therefore, the percentage of the circle that is shaded is $\dfrac{150°}{360°} = \dfrac{5}{12}$.

$\dfrac{5}{12}$ of the area of circle $O = \dfrac{15}{\pi}$. Area $= \pi r^2$, so $\dfrac{5}{12}\pi r^2 = \dfrac{15}{\pi}$. Solving for r yields

$$\frac{5}{12}\pi r2 = \frac{15}{\pi}$$

$$\frac{5}{12}\pi r^2 = \frac{15}{\pi} \times \frac{12}{5\pi}$$

$$r^2 = \frac{36}{\pi^2}$$

$$r = \sqrt{\frac{36}{\pi^2}} = \frac{6}{\pi}$$

Therefore, the circumference of circle $O = 2\pi r = 2\pi \cdot = 12$.

25. **8** Arithmetic: Fractions, Decimals, and Percents   *Difficult*

Instead of trying to count out 100 digits, recognize that one of the four repeating digits, 4986, will be in the hundredth place after the decimal. Because the first digit following the decimal doesn't repeat, ignore that digit and focus on the 4 repeating digits. Therefore, we need to locate the 100 – 1, or 99th, digit. Since the pattern repeats, we need to figure out the remainder when 99 is divided by 4. 99: $4.99 \div 4 = 24\,r^3$. Since 3 is the remainder and 8 is the 3rd repeated digit, 8 is the digit in the 100th place to the right of the decimal.

Multiple Choice Explanations (10)

1. **(C)** Arithmetic: Square Roots   *Easy*

Pick values for x and y that fit the given criteria, and then plug them into each statement to see which is true. Let $x = 1$ and $y = 2$.

In statement I, is the same as $\sqrt{1} < \sqrt{2}$, which implies that $1 < 1.414...$, which is true.

In statement II, is the same as $2\sqrt{1} = 1\sqrt{2}$, which implies that $2 = 1.414...$, which is false.

In statement III, $x^2 < y^2$ is the same as $1^2 < 2^2$, which implies that $1 < 4$, which is true. Since only statements I and III are true, (C) is the correct answer.

2. **(A)** Arithmetic: Series *Easy*

In the given pattern, the fifth term would be $\frac{5}{r^5}$. Set this equal to 15,625 and solve for r.

$$\frac{5}{r^5} = 15,625$$

$$5 = 15,625 r^5$$

$$\frac{5}{15,625} = \frac{1}{3125} = r^5$$

$$\sqrt[5]{\frac{1}{3,125}} = \sqrt[5]{r^5}$$

$$\frac{1}{5} = r$$

$$0.2 = r$$

3. **(C)** Arithmetic: Primes *Easy*

The easiest way to solve this problem is to use trial and error. Look at the average of the three prime numbers. Choose primes that are close to that value. Since the average is $16\frac{1}{3}$, try finding the average of the prime numbers 13, 17, and 19. The average is equal to the sum of the three numbers divided by 3. So $\frac{13 + 17 + 19}{3} = \frac{49}{3} = 16\frac{1}{3}$. This works.

The problem asks for the largest of these three prime numbers, 19.

4. **(D)** Geometry: Circles *Moderate*

To solve this, pick a value for the original circle's diameter and find its area. Then double the diameter and find the enlarged circle's area. Let $d = 2$ in the original circle. Then the radius $r = 1$ and the area $= \pi r^2 = \pi(1)^2 = \pi$. In the enlarged circle, $d = 4$. So the radius $r = 2$ and the area $= \pi r^2 = \pi(2)^2 = 4\pi$.

The percent change in area is found by the formula $\frac{\text{change in area}}{\text{original area}} \times 100\%$. So the percent change is $\frac{4\pi - \pi}{\pi} \times 100\% = \frac{3\pi}{\pi} \times 100\% = 3 \times 100\% = 300\%$.

5. **(B)** Special Math: Problems with Strange Symbols *Moderate*

Since $x\,\vartheta = 156$ and $x\,\vartheta = x^2 + x$, $x^2 + x = 156$. Set this equation equal to 0 and solve for x.

$$x^2 + x = 156$$

$$x^2 + x\ 156 = 0$$

$$(x + 13)(x - 12) = 0$$

$$(x + 13) = 0; x = 13$$

$$(x - 12) = 0; x = 12$$

Since x is positive, 12 is the only answer that fits.

6. **(B)** Geometry: Polygons   *Difficult*

To solve this, it helps to draw a line from the center of the hexagon to the vertex as shown in the figure below. This forms a 30°–60°–90° right triangle FJK.

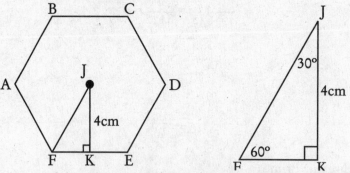

You know the ratio of the sides in a 30°–60°–90° right triangle. $FK = x$; $JK = x\sqrt{3}$; $FJ =$

$2x$. Therefore, 4cm $= x\sqrt{3}$ and $x = \dfrac{4}{\sqrt{3}} = \dfrac{4}{\sqrt{3}} \cdot \dfrac{\sqrt{3}}{\sqrt{3}} = \dfrac{4\sqrt{3}}{3} = FK$. $FE = 2FK = 2 \cdot$

$\dfrac{4\sqrt{3}}{3} = \dfrac{8\sqrt{3}}{3}$. Therefore, the perimeter of $ABCDEF = 6 \cdot \dfrac{8\sqrt{3}}{3} = \dfrac{48\sqrt{3}}{3} = 16\sqrt{3}$.

7. **(A)** Geometry: Geometric Visualizations   *Moderate*

The surface area of a cylinder is $SA = \pi r^2 h$, where r is the radius and h is the height of

the cylinder. Pick values for the surface area and height, and then find the radius. Then,

double the value of the surface area, keeping the height the same, and see how the

radius changes. Let $SA = 4\pi$ and $h = 1$. Then, $4\pi = \pi r^2(1)$, so $r^2 = \dfrac{4\pi}{\pi} = 4$ and $r = 2$. Now,

let $SA = 8\pi$ and $h = 1$. Then, $8\pi = \pi r^2(1)$, so $r^2 = \dfrac{8\pi}{\pi} = 8$ and $r = \sqrt{8} = \sqrt{4 \times 2} = 2\sqrt{2}$.

The radius changes from 2 to $2\sqrt{2}$, or becomes $\sqrt{2}$ times greater.

8. **(A)** Algebra: Solving Systems of Equations   *Difficult*

Two pounds of dried fruit cost 2 x $3.80, or $7.60. One pound of mixed nuts costs

$4.60. Together, the cost is $7.60 + $4.60 = $12.20 for 3 pounds of the mix, so it costs

$\dfrac{\$12.20}{3} = \$4.0\overline{6}$, or about $4.07 per pound.

9.   **(C)**   Arithmetic: Percents   *Difficult*

Let p represent the original price of the sweater. If it's on sale for 40% off, you are paying 60% of the original price. If the additional markdown is $\frac{1}{4}$, you are paying $\frac{3}{4}$ · (60%), or 45% of the original price, p. Since the final sale price after both markdowns is $36, 45%$(p) = \$36$. 45% is the same as 0.45, so $0.45p = \$36$, and $p = \frac{36}{0.45} = \$80$.

10.   **(E)**   Algebra: Building Expressions   *Difficult*

Translate each of the statements into a mathematical sentence. $s = qw$ and $t = ps$.

Since you are asked to find the cost of t thingamajigs, in terms of w, solve for t so that w is part of the answer. This can be done by substituting qw for s in the equation equaling t. So, $t = ps = p(qw) = wpq$.

Take
the
NEXT
STEP
in
TEST
PREP

SparkNotes™ interactive online test preparation system will raise your scores on the SAT, ACT, and SAT II subject tests in Biology, Physics, U.S. History, Math IC and IIC, and Writing.

testprep.sparknotes.com

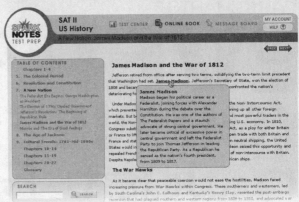

Our Entire Book Online Get a fully searchable, hyperlinked version of the SparkNotes book we sell in stores for each test.

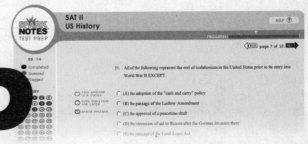

Practice Tests Make Perfect Up to 5 interactive practice tests with complete explanations for each question.

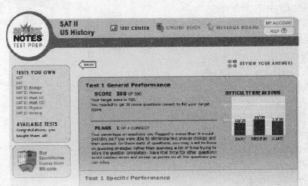

Instant Diagnostic Feedback Get instant results: overall score, strengths, weaknesses, progress. Then see a personalized study plan that links back to the book.

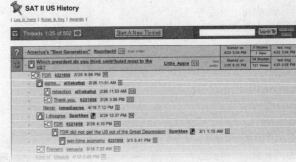

Don't Go It Alone Message boards connect you to other students taking the same test you are.

Awesome and Affordable We've made test prep dynamic, interactive, and affordable. At $14.95 it's the best deal online or off.

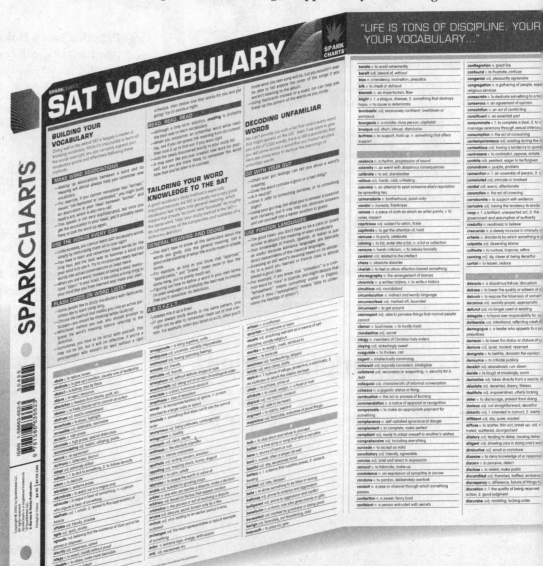

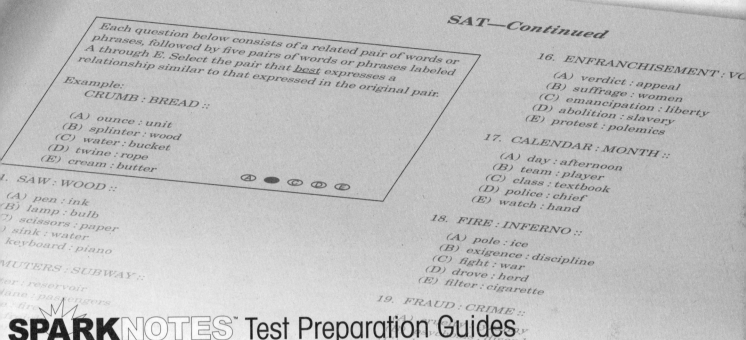